THE MAN WHO WAS GREENMANTLE

THE MAN WHO WAS GREENMANTLE

A Biography of Aubrey Herbert

<<<◆◇◆>>>

Margaret FitzHerbert

JOHN MURRAY

FIFTY ALBEMARLE STREET · LONDON

For my aunts,
Gabriel Dru
and Bridget Grant

First published 1983
by John Murray (Publishers) Ltd
50 Albemarle Street, London W1X 4BD

Typeset by Inforum Ltd, Portsmouth
Printed and bound in Great Britain by
Butler & Tanner, Frome

British Library Cataloguing in Publication Data
FitzHerbert, Margaret
The man who was Greenmantle
1. Herbert, Aubrey
I. Title
941.081'092'4   DA566.9.H/
ISBN 0–7195–4067–4

Contents

Illustrations

Foreword

In September 1923 John Buchan wrote in a letter to a friend: 'I am greatly saddened this week by Aubrey Herbert's death. The most delightful and brilliant survivor from the days of chivalry . . . he was the most extraordinary combination of tenderness and gentleness, with the most insane gallantry that I have ever known – a sort of survivor from crusading times. I drew Sandy in Greenmantle from him.' The fictional Sandy Arbuthnot, master of foreign tongues and exotic disguises, is first introduced in *Greenmantle* through the mouth of Sir Walter Bullivant of the Foreign Office, who says: 'Billy Arbuthnot's boy? . . . I know the fellow . . . I know his record too. There's a good deal about him in this office. He rode through Yemen, which no white man ever did before. The Arabs let him pass, for they thought him stark mad and argued that the hand of Allah was heavy enough on him without their efforts. He's blood-brother to every kind of Albanian bandit. Also he used to take a hand in Turkish politics, and got a huge reputation.'

Aubrey had indeed ridden through the Yemen, had made friends with many an Albanian bandit, and been deeply involved in Turkish politics. As to his reputation, it was huge but narrow, made among friends and contemporaries, among Turks and among Albanians, but not in the press or the public eye. Within that small company of friends and contemporaries the portrait of Sandy was instantly recognised when *Greenmantle* first appeared in 1916. Aubrey's wife, Mary, in a letter to her brother-in-law Mervyn Herbert, wrote: 'I must confess I prefer my Aubrey to his Sandy but I daresay it's like him.' She sent a copy to Aubrey, who was in Salonika. His only comment was 'He brings in my nerves all right doesn't he?'

Nerves, however, were not Aubrey's most obvious characteristic. Beside his spirit of adventure and deeds of daring he was best remembered for the delight of his conversation and his air of immense amiability. Ronald Storrs in *Orientations* found 'something of Shelley in his crystal unearthly goodness', while L.E. Jones in *An Edwardian Youth* wrote:

Aubrey lived in high romance. Every girl was a poem to him and to most of them he wrote one. He simmered and bubbled and boiled over with enthusiasm, for whatever Aubrey had in his head he made at least a phrase, sometimes an epigram, often some verses. He delighted in words as some women in jewels, but he did not keep them, as most jewels are kept, for great occasions. All his thoughts were open and at our service, he had no reserves with those he liked; and because his mind was singularly original and fertile, as well as romantic, there was no resisting the charm of his conversation. His activities were abreast of his knightly imagination.

Not only did Aubrey not hoard his words, he was sometimes guilty of using a choice phrase more than once. From this bad habit Maurice Baring coined the expression an 'Aubrey' which meant the repetition in a letter to one correspondent of a passage already used to another. However, the most celebrated 'Aubrey' was not perpetrated by Aubrey but by his friend, Raymond Asquith, who having paid two consecutive visits, one in the north of Scotland and one in Cornwall, to hostesses mutually unacquainted, wrote to each in his Collins that their respective chauffeurs who had transported him to the station, had driven 'with the passion of Shelley and the precision of Pope'. Each hostess had repeated the phrase, which then gained such currency that the 'Aubrey' was discovered, to the chagrin of both ladies, but probably not to the mortification of Raymond, who was made of sterner stuff.

In almost every published description of Aubrey the word 'chivalrous' appears with tedious regularity. Perhaps because knightly virtues were so particularly admired in this period, his contemporaries in praising Aubrey singled out this facet of his character. Edward Cadogan, his exact contemporary at Eton and Balliol, wrote: 'Aubrey was cast in a mould different from the normal individual. He was the embodiment of chivalry and was therefore, I suppose, born out of due time and place, although it is difficult to determine to what age in history in all the world his soul belonged.'

To Cadogan it was not obvious, as it is now, that Aubrey was entirely a man of his times. Cadogan belonged to the same generation as Aubrey, and could not discern, as later generations can, the true lineaments of his age. These sons and grandsons of the men who built the Empire were themselves neither builders nor destroyers. They were marked neither by the purpose and energy of their predecessors nor by the guilt and hesitation of their successors. Their inheritance was an ease around the world, and an infinite self-confidence. Following their knightly imaginations, wandering across the face of the earth, they had no axe to grind. Theirs was, briefly, an age of chivalry, soon to be laid at rest in the trenches of the Great War, an age in which Aubrey Herbert had a natural place.

* * *

It may seem strange that a man so extravagantly admired in his own times should so long have escaped the biographer's pen. He flits in and out, a shadowy figure, in books about T. E. Lawrence, Raymond Asquith, Hilaire Belloc, Mark Sykes, George Lloyd, Oswald Mosley, Gertrude Bell and many others. No earlier attempt at his life was made because his widow, Mary Herbert, regarded biography as a vulgar breach of privacy. On her death in 1970 her son Auberon deposited Aubrey's papers with Lord Kinross, whose knowledge of the Ottoman Empire had already whetted his interest in Aubrey Herbert. He had scarcely started work on a biography when he died, a few indecipherable notes the only legacy of his labours. The papers then passed to Mr Christopher Sykes, another skilful biographer with a deep knowledge of the Middle East, whose father, Mark, had been a close friend of Aubrey. Mr Sykes kept the papers for some time. By chance I happened to be dining with an aunt of mine – a daughter of Aubrey's – when he telephoned to say that reluctantly he was abandoning the project. At the time I was in search of a task to while away hours hanging heavily on my hands in Aubrey's old stamping ground, the Middle East. I asked if I might make the attempt. Recklessly my aunts, the two surviving daughters of Aubrey Herbert, entrusted the papers to my unscholarly care. The result does little justice to the subject but I like to think that perhaps Aubrey, who was himself above all an amateur, would not have minded that his life should eventually be written by an amateur grand-daughter, born long after the events here recounted.

1

Beloved Son
and Blind Schoolboy

Aubrey Herbert was born on 3rd April 1880, two months before the fiftieth birthday of his father, Henry Howard Molyneux Herbert, fourth Earl of Carnarvon.

Circumstances had been kind to Lord Carnarvon. Born to great riches and endowed with a fine intellect, he had no need to struggle for the prizes of life. Hampered only by a conscience of exceptional delicacy, he had progressed from youth to late middle age in a predictable and distinguished fashion. At the age of eighteen, while an undergraduate at Oxford, Carnarvon succeeded to his title and possessions. The possessions were extensive. The first Earl of Carnarvon, a grandson of the eighth Earl of Pembroke, had established a useful tradition of marrying heiresses, so that by the time the fourth Earl came into his own there was much to inherit, despite the profligacy of his father, the third Earl.

The third Earl (1800–49) had been an eccentric and a romantic. A keen observer of revolutions, he travelled from one European disturbance to another. At Nice he harangued a revolutionary mob in French. In Genoa he was nearly killed in a political brawl; in Spain he was captured by Catalan guerillas; in Paris he fought a duel. As to romance, he bought a rock in Switzerland on which he inscribed lines commemorating his romantic travels with Lady Guildford and Lady Harrowby. Marriage to Henrietta Howard of Greystoke Castle, Cumberland, heiress of Teversal in Nottinghamshire, did not bring his travels to an end. In 1838 he set off for Constantinople, taking with him his wife, his seven-year-old heir Henry and his five-year-old daughter Eveline. He left behind his younger sons Alan and Auberon. The journey began badly. At Terni the children's nurse died. In Rome their governess died. More were engaged. In Constantinople Henry fell victim to Asiatic plague. After his son's recovery the third Earl was persuaded to return to England where he devoted his considerable energies to the rebuilding of his principal seat, Highclere Castle, and the education of his precociously clever son and heir.

He took the matter seriously, writing to his sister that he was making 'an attempt to solve arithmetical problems on a new system. I have been doing this partly for my own instruction but principally for my dear Boy's eventual use, by making him a better man of figures than his Papa has been and on principles clearer than those generally adopted.' Eventually surrendering the scholastic tutelage of the boy to more conventional ministrations, he continued to take an active interest in his education. At the age of ten Henry was receiving almost daily letters of encouragement. 'I hope you are a dear good boy, and that *optime* comes as thick upon the lists as blackberries upon the branches, not a mediocrity I implore for the sake of all the toads upon the terrace, but optime, optime, optime.'

The third Earl's exhortations fell upon fertile ground. Henry prospered in his studies. Before he went to Eton he was reading Homer, Virgil, Horace and Herodotus for pleasure and wrote to his father, 'I do four different kinds of verse, Elegiacs, Sapphics, Alcaics and Iambics, of which Sapphics are my favourite.' At Oxford he took a first in Greats and after spending a few years in travel, settled down to marriage and politics. He chose, in the Carnarvon tradition, an heiress as his wife, Lady Evelyn Stanhope, only daughter of the sixth Earl of Chesterfield. In politics, he nearly shone, but his sensitive conscience proved a barrier to advancement. Before the birth of Aubrey he had already twice been a cabinet minister, as Colonial Secretary under Derby in 1866 and again under Disraeli in 1874. On both occasions he had felt impelled to resign office on matters of principle. In 1875 his wife died after the birth of their fourth child, Victoria. Three years later Carnarvon married again. Departing from family custom, he chose a girl of no fortune, less than half his age and his first cousin.

Elsie Howard, daughter of Carnarvon's uncle, Henry Howard of Greystoke Castle, was twenty-two years old when her distinguished middle-aged cousin came to stay at Greystoke in the autumn of 1878. She was an earnest young woman, clever, clear-complexioned and wilful. With large grey eyes and a grave yet girlish demeanour she captivated Carnarvon, who saw in her a perfect stepmother for his children and an invigorating companion for himself. On leaving Greystoke he wrote to his aunt: 'I think you have probably observed the great charm that Elsie has for and over me. In her and her most beautiful character I see all that I could entirely love and all that would be the happiness of my life . . .' His aunt's reply was not wholly encouraging. She thought the difference in age, twenty-five years, a little excessive. A few days later Carnarvon wrote again: 'I am quite conscious of all that you say as against what I desire. I know the risks and in a certain sense the sacrifices which I ask dear Elsie to incur – still I hope that they are not, looking at everything, more than marriage often involves. But with this feeling not only would I not have you urge her in any way, but I should think myself miserably selfish if I were to do so. Nothing would induce me to put the slightest pressure on her; and if after hearing all I have to say she feels that it cannot be, the past so far as she is concerned shall be as if it never had been and she will be absolutely free.'

Elsie, when finally consulted, decided to accept Carnarvon. He left her little time for regrets. Less than a month after his initial declaration he and Elsie were quietly married on 26th December 1878 at the church at Greystoke. Although the discrepancy in age had caused some anxiety, no one seems to have given a thought to the close consanguinity of the protagonists.

After the marriage Lord Carnarvon took his bride to Pixton, his sporting estate in the West Country, and thence to Italy. There they chanced on a little fishing village called Portofino. Elsie was enchanted by it so Carnarvon bought for her a great stretch of the peninsula. Together they planned a house to be built on the top of the hill, looking over the port on one side and out to sea on the other. The house was constructed of Portland stone, shipped out from England. It was named Alta Chiara (Highclere in Italian) although the Portofinesi to this day call it Villa Carnarvon.

On their return to England Lord Carnarvon brought Elsie back to Highclere where she found her young cousins to whom she had become stepmother. The eldest, Winifred, was already fourteen and quite grown up. Only eight years younger than her stepmother, she accepted Elsie immediately. Her sister Margaret, aged eight, had only fading memories of her own mother and soon found a second mother in Elsie; while Victoria, the little four-year-old god-daughter of the Queen, who had never known her mother, grew to look on Elsie as her own. Only the twelve-year-old Lord Porchester, known as Porchy, hung back. Although always polite and dutiful, he remained aloof. Elsie never really captured his affections, then or later, as she did those of his sisters.

On 3rd April 1880, in the midst of the General Election that swept Gladstone into power for the second time, Elsie gave birth to a son. Carnarvon noted with pleasure that the baby's birthday was the same as that of his 17th-century kinsman, George Herbert, the poet. The baby was christened Aubrey Nigel Henry Molyneux, but was always called Hereward by his adoring parents, who fondly believed that they were both directly descended, through the Howards, from Hereward the Wake.

Nearly three years later Aubrey was joined in the nursery by his brother Mervyn. The two brothers were to be particularly close in affection, though very different in character, all their lives. Although both boys had in their blood a double strain from the great family of Howard, those 'Ducal and illustrious Howards' who, in the words of Burke's Peerage, 'stand next to the Blood Royal, at the head of the Peerage of England', neither boy was particularly Howard in temperament. Aubrey was a clear throwback to his grandfather, the third Earl, possessing the same thirst for travel, eccentricity of manner and romanticism. These characteristics were also to be found in Aubrey's uncle Auberon Herbert, youngest brother of the fourth Earl, a vegetarian, agnostic, republican and pacifist. Mervyn, on the other hand, took after his father both physically and temperamentally.

It was on Aubrey, however, that Carnarvon doted. The four children of his first family had been brought up formally and distantly. Carnarvon had seen them at appointed times and taken only a passing interest. Elsie, however, though employing the usual large number of nursery retainers, had a more modern approach to motherhood and busied herself in the minutiae of nursery life. And Carnarvon, no longer encumbered with affairs of state, busied himself also. Aubrey was constantly in his father's company. His early infancy and first birthday were passed in Madeira where Carnarvon spent his days learning Portuguese, improving his German and translating the *Odyssey*. Aubrey's childhood continued to be unsettled. He was seldom left behind at Highclere but moved seasonally in his parents' wake between Highclere, London (43 Portman Square), Pixton and Portofino.

In the summer of 1885, soon after Aubrey's fifth birthday, Carnarvon reluctantly agreed to return to office in the first Salisbury administration. He accepted a seat in the cabinet and became Viceroy of Ireland on the understanding that a policy of conciliation towards Ireland should be employed and that he himself should be allowed to retire after six months. The family moved to Viceregal Lodge, Dublin.

Carnarvon succeeded Lord Spencer as Viceroy. Spencer had been, undeservedly, the object of envenomed hate in Ireland and had been unable to stir without an armed escort. Carnarvon decided to govern without the Crimes Act and refused a military escort for his public entry on horseback into Dublin. He made friends with the Catholic hierarchy, met Parnell in London in secret, visited every corner of the country and won the hearts of the people. He wrote to Lord Cranbrook, then Lord Chancellor: 'my whole mind seems to be divided with deep pity for what I see on every side and anxiety for the future. It is a most unhappy country, dowered – as in a fairy tale – with great gifts and great misfortunes.' The Conservative cabinet in England, however, rejected Carnarvon's policy of conciliation. True to form, Carnarvon resigned.

Thus, after only seven months as Viceroy, he left Ireland on 30th January 1886, two days after the final defeat of the Conservative government in the House of Commons, as the result of Parnell's switching of Irish Nationalist support from the Conservatives to the Liberals.

In April the same year Aubrey passed his sixth birthday at Portofino. Carnarvon, freed from office, was again able to give his full attention to his son. For some time he had been worried about Aubrey's eyesight. Now a visit to a leading oculist, Dr Leibnek, confirmed his fears. Dr Leibnek diagnosed a congenital malformation of the eyes which he blamed on the consanguinity of the boy's parents. He ordered that the eyes could only be used for lessons four times a day for five minutes at a time, a total therefore of twenty minutes a day. For Carnarvon the news was a bitter blow. He had delighted in the boy's brightness and had hoped to make a scholar of him in his own likeness. A typewriter, then a comparatively new invention, was bought and Aubrey was taught, not very successfully, to type by touch. Dr Leibnek's advice was strictly observed. Aubrey used his eyes for only twenty minutes a day and his education was thus almost exclusively by ear.

The next year, 1887, the Carnarvons departed on a nine-month sea voyage to Australia and South Africa. Aubrey and Mervyn were left behind. They went to stay, accompanied only by their nanny, Mrs Osmond, and their German governess, Fraulein Berger, with their aunt Eveline Portsmouth. Lady Portsmouth, Carnarvon's sister, was a woman of unquenchable maternal instincts (she was herself the mother of six boys and six girls) and made an excellent surrogate mother for the boys.

On his return Carnarvon again devoted much of his time to Aubrey, reading aloud to him and coaching him in Latin. Meanwhile he sought other professional opinions on the boy's eyesight. For the child was to all intents and purposes, blind. He saw only a few yards and saw nothing distinctly.

In this period the leading oculist in Europe was Dr Pagenstecker of Wiesbaden in Germany. Aubrey was first sent to see him aged eight, accompanied by Fraulein Berger. Pagenstecker, while agreeing with the limitations on the use of Aubrey's eyes imposed by Leibnek, held out some hope for the future. He saw little likelihood of deterioration and recommended an operation when the boy was older. On Aubrey's next visit Carnarvon decided to accompany his son. He had a formidable list of questions he wished to put to Pagenstecker, covering every possible eventuality, such as: 'When bathing in the sea, ought he to dive?' or more bizarrely, 'May he, and if so for how long at a time, sit on the floor, with his back bent doing basket-work?'

Father and son left Portofino in late April 1890, soon after Aubrey's tenth birthday, to visit the great oculist. The consultation was a success and Carnarvon was reassured. In a new spirit of optimism about Aubrey's future he put his name down for Eton. However Carnarvon's own health was now giving cause for concern. He had been back in England less than two weeks when he suffered a fainting fit. A month later on 28th June 1890, four days after his fifty-ninth birthday, he died in Portman Square.

For Aubrey it was a desolation. He had adored his father. Ten years old was old enough to understand his loss but scarcely old enough to bear it. Moreover his whole life was turned upside down. His home, Highclere, now belonged to his twenty-four year old half-brother Porchy. Elsie Carnarvon also was heartbroken. Her marriage had been wholly successful and under the fond regard of her husband she had blossomed and grown into a formidable woman. Now, widowed at thirty-four, she had to begin life anew. She had been left comfortably off. She had lost Highclere but Portofino and Teversal were hers. In leaving Teversal to Elsie, Carnarvon was only returning to a Howard what the Howards themselves had bestowed. There was a charming Elizabethan manor house, many prosperous farms, and a few coal mines on the estate. Elsie, however, did not at once settle there. First she went to Greystoke and then to Paris for six months before finally settling at Pixton.

Elsie still had in her charge her two younger step-children, Margaret and Vera, besides Aubrey and Mervyn. It was at her stepson Porchy Carnarvon's suggestion that she moved to Pixton. It was a favourite haunt of all the children. After two years, however, she grew tired of the isolation of Pixton and moved to Teversal. Of his three main childhood homes Highclere, Pixton and Teversal, Aubrey loved Pixton best. The years he spent at Teversal were interrupted. Margaret and Vera were of an age to be brought out in society and Elsie had to be in London to chaperone them to balls. She did not inflict this London life on her two boys but sent them for long visits to their aunt Eveline Portsmouth, who lived close to Highclere at Over Wallop.

Eveline Portsmouth was devoted to her nephews. Mervyn presented few problems, but Aubrey with his blindness was a constant cause of concern. Lady Portsmouth considered that Elsie was over protective. She was anxious that Aubrey should lead as ordinary a life as possible. Up to the age of thirteen Aubrey's schooling had been entirely in the hands of private tutors. His aunt was determined that when the time came he should go to public school. She wrote to Elsie: 'I am very anxious he should see no prospect of a home education but feel Eton is everything to gain.'

Elsie reluctantly agreed. The decision was made to send Aubrey to

Eton. For Aubrey it must have been a daunting prospect. He had no experience of school and no experience of companions of his own age. His sheltered life had led to a singularity of manner, very untypical of the average schoolboy.

In April 1893, soon after his thirteenth birthday, Aubrey arrived at Eton. The stately headmaster, Dr Warre, was at the peak of his power. Eton then was the cradle of the cult of physical bravery combined with intellectual achievement. This spirit had a determining influence on Aubrey as much as on his contemporaries, but the particular peculiarities of his situation set him apart from his companions at school. Almost blind, closeted for long hours with his private tutor, unable to excel at either games or work because of his eyesight, his career at Eton was inevitably unusual. His contemporaries and the brilliant set that succeeded them – the Grenfells, Ronald Knox, Patrick Shaw Stewart and company – were almost too attached to their school. For them it was the real world, whose triumphs, prizes and pleasures represented all that was most desired, and the things that came after, Oxford, London and finally the war, never quite matched up to those glorious years. The few survivors looked back to Eton as the golden time of their lives. Not so Aubrey.

Arthur Benson, his housemaster, was then in his early thirties. He ruled his house with an authority beyond question. Two gifts stood him in good stead. He was, first, an unequalled story teller. On Sunday evenings the younger boys would gather in his study while he sat in an armchair before the fire and held them spellbound for an hour, after which they were dismissed until the next week. His other gift was an ability to enter his boys' minds, gaining the confidence of even the most intractable and diffident.

Yet he never entirely gained Aubrey's confidence. And Aubrey was right to withhold his trust. Every month Benson wrote to Elsie reporting on Aubrey's physical and moral welfare. These letters, though showing an edifying conscientiousness, display a want of sympathy and a disproportionate disposition to find fault in a boy whose main offence was that he did not fit easily into the Eton mould.

Benson's early letters are mostly taken up with complaints about Aubrey's untidyness:

> He never puts a book back in its place and he throws everything about his room in fearful confusion, it takes up the time of the boys' maid to an extent which is not quite fair on the others, e.g. he never finds a book for himself but calls upon her before every school to get his books together: if he would put them in their place in the shelves all this would be unnecessary. The way too

in which he flings his food about is rather trying . . . He is very unbusinesslike about his work. I think Mr Little does his very best to keep this straight and annotates every piece of work with the day and hour it is to be shown up – but he contrives to lose work between Mr Little's room and the house in a bewildering way.

Mr Little, a protégé of Benson's, was Aubrey's private tutor. He was engaged by Elsie and lodged at her expense in the town. He remained with Aubrey throughout his years at Eton. His duties were light, part nurse, part coach. His main task was to read aloud Aubrey's preparation. This meant that Aubrey was with him during the periods set aside for study. They also took tea together. Though these arrangements may have been necessary they were unfortunate for they isolated Aubrey from the other boys. This isolation was aggravated by the fact that Aubrey played neither cricket nor football. His early days at Eton were solitary and forlorn. He wrote daily to his mother. The letters were uniformly cheerful. Elsie also wrote daily, and hoarded Aubrey's letters. The first letter, lovingly inscribed by Elsie 'the dear boy's first letter from Eton', begins with the unwelcome news that he has failed to get into the Remove; 'I have got into Upper IV. I am utterly savage with myself for having not got higher,' he wrote.

Almost immediately he became the target for 'ragging', a euphemism for bullying. Aubrey did not hide from his mother the persecution he underwent but the tone of his letters remained cheerful. His top hat was bashed in regularly. Aubrey's main concern was the extravagance. He wrote to his mother in October 1893, 'I am afraid I must be ruining you with all my expenses but the next topper that I have is going to come out of my own money. They got hold of it last night in chapel and I was not able to get hold of it till an hour afterwards but I washed it and inked it a little and now it looks awfly nice.'

Quite why Aubrey was singled out for this continual ragging, and how much he minded it, is hard to say. His brother, Mervyn, who joined him at Eton two years later, had no such difficulties. Obviously the isolation caused by his eyesight was a contributory factor, as was his lack of school experience. Another cause for derision may have been his country accent. But it was probably his general oddness which singled him out as a target. Aubrey was noticeably different. Later the boys came to appreciate Aubrey and enjoy him. He had one disarming gift – he was very funny. But his first few terms were hard going.

Benson was aware of Aubrey's difficulties but not sympathetic about them. He wrote to Elsie:

I have had to find fault with his being concerned too much in what they call 'ragging' – at first I thought the boys had been in fault and had been making Aubrey uncomfortable – but I came to the conclusion that as often as not it was A who began it. He wanders about, strays into his friends' rooms – and of course he has rather a sharp tongue. It is all good natured but I have told Aubrey that I do not intend there should be a noisy set in the house, and that he at least must not be responsible for any more.

Excuses were worse than useless; in another letter to Elsie, Benson writes: 'There is also, I think, a slight tendency in the boy to justify himself when he is really to blame. I hope he will not develop this – it is characteristic of an ingenious mind; but the faculty of bearing deserved blame is one that is worth cultivating.' Benson had also noted Aubrey's solitariness and lack of friends. He commented: 'I don't think it is exactly shyness which keeps him back from making more friends, because he is fearless enough when he chooses, and very indifferent I think to general opinion. I think it is that he really doesn't desire them; and I should like to see him a little more interested in other people.'
However, if Benson was critical, Aubrey was fortunate that he had another more powerful patron. Dr Warre was a neighbour at Pixton, and consequently took a great interest in Aubrey. He was often asked to tea or breakfast, a considerable privilege, though not always with happy consequences, 'I met Mrs Warre buying groceries yesterday. She appeared to be afraid that I would think they were for herself, she impressed me thoroughly that they were for a bazaar next week, to which she invited me and for which I shall have to pay eighteen pence. She invited me to breakfast this morning . . . Benson was greatly appeased when I asked for leave to go to the head for breakfast . . .'
And in a letter the next week comes the sequel:

I have been to the bazaar that Mrs Warre asked me to. Quite the most frightful experience which it has for ages been my pleasure to undergo. I took all my money up in my purse. Directly I came in I was assailed by I don't know how many girls and ladies at once. I was sold a roar sausage roll and a bouquet at once and at once commenced to nibble the bouquet. I got away from one stall only to be passed on to worse. Mrs Warre showed me where to put my hat at least it was seized away. I was passed about among these people till I had one penny left, when I was passed into Princess Christina's stall, I was perfectly helpless. She kept on saying this is only five and six and that's half a crown, please do buy this one, look about you I am sure you would like to buy a lot of things, and I had one penny. At last thank goodness she sighted another victim. She rushed off after him and I got away. Then a niece of Mrs Warre's, to whom she introduced me, came up with a lot of other ladies gaugiously dressed and asked me to come to tea and pay for it and sixpence too. I thanked her very much and said I must get my hat, I got it wondering what would

happen next when to my intense relief I found she had gone. I then sneaked
away. Never again will I go to a bazaar . . .

Like many schoolboys before and since, Aubrey often found himself in
financial difficulties. He was regularly rebuked by Elsie for borrowing
money from his older sisters and still worse, from the family servants. 'It
is better *never* to be lent money by servants,' Elsie wrote. Aubrey was
seldom at a loss to explain his impecuniousness: 'That purse Mer[vyn]
gave me has a wretchedly big mouth and all one's money goes racing out
of it. It does not fasten properly.'

While Aubrey ingenuously blamed purses, Elsie was hearing a different tale from the indefatigable Benson. 'I almost think Aubrey has too
much money to spend; I think he spent about twelve pounds last half
mostly in "sock". It is this latter thing that I regret, as he is well supplied
with food, but has I think too much in the way of sweet things at
irregular hours; he is never without a bag or box of something . . .'

Food, indeed, was a permanent preoccupation. Aubrey's relations
were good to him. Regular hampers came from Porchy, his mother, Aunt
Eveline, Aunt Gwendolyn (a spinster sister of his father's) and Winifred.
The Highclere hampers were particularly good, 'When you see Porchy
will you thank him so much for me. I ate $\frac{1}{2}$ the partridge and the
pheasant Friday night', but Elsie still worried that he wasn't getting
enough, 'Would you like to have an order for 6d. a day for meat on the
sock shop for your tea?' He did. 'I like my teas very much indeed. Tonight
I am to have sausages and tomorrow kippers' and, 'I really get excellent
teas at Mr Little's. I am going to have haddock tonight. I suppose I may
buy muffins and ask Mrs Harrison to butter them.' These teas were in
addition to a perfectly good school supper, though sometimes he complained, 'I have never eaten rat before. I always wondered what it was
like. They sent it in under the heading of rabbit pie. I know that two rats
have been killed by my dame's dog. Of course I can't be positif that it was
rat but it sertainly was not rabbit. It was rather nasty.'

Besides food, pets were Aubrey's main preoccupation. He had always
loved animals, and parting from his dog Duke at the beginning of each
term caused him agony. Some pets, however, were permitted at Eton
and during Aubrey's first year pets of various sorts were his chief joy. His
first term he acquired a jackdaw, a squirrel and a white mouse, which
apparently cost 2d. a week to feed. His fondness for animals and the
limitations of his means were in constant conflict: 'There are some larks
in a dreadfully small cage and I and two other chaps decided to buy them
and let them go but there are always others. I am not shure that it is
quite a good plan. They cost a good deal.' In another letter he ingenuously

asks, 'Do you think my squirrel would like a companion? If so will you
send me down the money.' Another term he writes, 'I want not to buy a
squirrel but a much nicer thing. A charming, delightful thing, it is called
a mongoose . . . I cannot get one down here . . . they only cost 15/– or a
little more.'

A less enduring enthusiasm was autograph hunting. He not only
pestered his mother but also his Aunt Eveline:

> Do you think it would be possible to get me any autographs of people like R. L.
> Stevenson. I want him terrifficly for somebody else. I am sure you must know
> many clever men, Mr Gladstone, Lord Salisbury or Henry James, Anthony
> Hope, R. Kipling and I believe you knew Dickens . . . I have just finished
> writing a poem to a windmill. It is a dreadful labour. If it would not incon-
> venience you might I have a cake on Thursday if you don't mind.

Aubrey's letters, despite the deplorable spelling, are often well
expressed for a boy of his age. It is surprising, therefore, that during this
time he was usually bottom or nearly bottom of his division. On the
other hand by now he spoke good Italian and French and moderate
German. Italian was his favourite language and he not only talked
correct Tuscan but could also prattle away to the Portofinesi in Ligurian
dialect. School holidays were often spent at Portofino. One winter was
spent in Rome, where he took his groom and rode and hunted in the
Campagna. Another winter Elsie and the two boys went camping in
Tangier with her brother Esmé Howard under the guidance of Walter
Harris.

After Aubrey had been at Eton two years and become resigned to
school life, Elsie perversely began to think that he might profit from a
term's absence. Ignoring Benson's protests, Elsie removed Aubrey from
Eton for the Easter half of 1895, which he spent in Italy with his mother
and tutor. He was joined on his return to Eton by his brother Mervyn
who, unlike Aubrey, passed straight into the Remove.

Aubrey more and more participated in the various activities of the
school. He rowed, skated, ran with the beagles, and academically his
work steadily improved, 'I would, if you liked, go in for the English essay
prize though of course there isn't the remotest possible chance of my
getting anything but the last place by a hundred marks.' In fact he came
second.

However, these improvements failed to impress Benson. He wrote to
Elsie:

> I still consider that he makes a mistake in being so ready to argue with boys,
> and that he parts with his dignity too easily: he turns everything too much

into a joke, and his spirits certainly seem quite irrepressible. You will not misunderstand me to say that I want boys to cultivate dignity: but I think some intermingling of seriousness is good, and it is not good to get in the way of regarding anything and everything as material for laughter and nothing else.

Aubrey was by this time sixteen years old and the question of whether to operate on his eyes became pressing. Dr Pagenstecker of Wiesbaden was insistent that the operation was now advisable. But Elsie was fearful. She needed much reassurance. Dr Pagenstecker painstakingly explained, 'The operation is the same which we perform in cases of cataract in young people. The capsule of the lens is divided by a needle and in consequence of that the lens gets by and by absorbed (operation of Division of the Lens).'

He proposed to operate only on the right eye, which was the healthier of the two, and to leave the left for near sighted work, like reading. Lady Carnarvon first decided to seek other professional opinions all over the Continent. She took Aubrey to see Dr Pfluger in Berne, Dr Fuchs in Vienna and Mr Baldwin in Florence. Dr Fuchs and Dr Pfluger both emphatically advised the operation, Dr Pfluger adding: 'If I had a child with this myopia, without doubt it would be operated.' He explained that the operation was discovered in the last century but had been rarely used until recent times when anti-septic treatment came in; since 1890 it had been performed with increasing frequency; in 1893 at a congress in Heidelberg only three oculists were in favour of it, but since then numbers had declared for it. Finally, after a visit to Pagenstecker in Wiesbaden in April, it was settled that the operation should take place the following autumn.

Thus on 27th September 1897, when Aubrey was seventeen, he entered Dr Pagenstecker's clinic in Wiesbaden. Elsie kept a fat file labelled 'Aubrey's eyesight' and the last item is an account of the operation:

The next morning, Tuesday 28th, Dr Pagenstecker operated. A. had cocaine dropped in the eye for some time before but no anaesthetic. It was very quickly over tho' it seemed long. I suppose about $\frac{1}{2}$ a minute – and though very uncomfortable it did not actually pain him. The pain came afterwards and lasted some hours. He stayed in bed two days, the Dr very pleased and satisfied with the look of his eye and by the end of the week he said he thought the second operation might be unnecessary . . . About the 21st (Oct) however they began to talk again of a second operation. The cataract had formed and did not seem to be absorbing of its own accord as they hoped it would. He was quite blind with that eye. On Saturday 23rd suddenly Dr Pagenstecker said he would return and operate in $\frac{1}{2}$ an hour's time. It was perfectly successful and Aubrey showed the greatest courage on both occasions.

The success of this operation fundamentally changed Aubrey's life. The boon was immeasurable. With the operated eye Aubrey could see distances, albeit indistinctly. He could shoot, and distinguish figures across a room, though not well enough to recognise them. He was no longer blind. From then on, until the day twenty-six years later, only five months before his death, when the retina of his eye detached itself, rendering him once more nearly blind, he was able to lead a normal life.

First, however, there had to be a considerable period of recuperation. Aubrey, Elsie and Vera stayed on in Wiesbaden for a few months. A tutor was found. News from Eton came regularly in letters from Benson, who still asserted a long-distance authority. Aubrey wrote poetry and short stories, one a haunting tale set in Sumatra, full of weird supernatural happenings, but marred by an abrupt ending. It was Benson (himself a minor poet) who had originally encouraged Aubrey in his poetry writing and he continued to do so. Aubrey missed Eton and was missed. Benson wrote, 'I have at last and about a week ago broken myself of the habit of trying the handle of your door when I go round in the evening.'

Gradually it became clear that if Aubrey wished to prepare to go up to Oxford the following autumn he would have to forfeit returning to Eton. The tutorial system there was not consistent with the limitations set by Dr Pagenstecker on the use of his eyes. In April 1898, Aubrey wrote to Benson explaining that he would not be coming back. Benson replied:

> We are all sorry that you should have to leave, but I don't see under the circumstances, what else could have been done . . .
>
> I wonder if you will take it favourably if I make up three maxims for you . . . They are very simple, (1) to always have *some* work going that does not interest you, (2) never to say unamiable things of people, however funny – I don't mean that talking about people is bad – but you may tell amusing things about people without being at all ill-natured, (3) in conversation to follow other people's lead rather than to pursue your own. These are old-fashioned advices and though they are not the weightier matters of the law, they are the point of the ram.
>
> This is a heavy letter, written on a rainy morning while the thrushes outside the window are scooping up worms by the score out on the lawn. Even the beech trunks are stained with wet.
>
> Well, my dear Aubrey, forgive me for prosing, and believe me ever affectionately yours, Arthur C Benson.

This letter does not impress. Benson seems in the end to have missed the point of Aubrey. His well-meant maxims not only start off with a split infinitive but seem positively designed, if taken seriously, to quench just those sparkling springs in Aubrey's character which were to delight and divert his friends in the years to come. Luckily Aubrey did not take them seriously. Indeed he seems entirely to have disregarded Benson's unsolicited advice.

2

The Parapets of Balliol

Aubrey went up to Oxford in October 1898 to read history at Balliol College. He hugely enjoyed Balliol where the petty vexations of Eton had no echo, and athletic achievement was not the passport to success. There were of course college regulations but these scarcely impinged: 'I have got the college rules, anyone I believe killing a proctor is immediately sent down' he informed his mother in one of his first letters home.

Lord Carnarvon had been to Christ Church and it is surprising that Aubrey did not follow him there. There had been Herberts at Balliol before, most notably the ill-fated Edward Herbert (a first cousin of Carnarvon) who was captured by Greek brigands in 1870 and murdered by them when he could no longer keep up with his captors in their flight from the forces of the law. Aubrey's choice of college was probably more influenced by his cousin Bron Herbert, now in his last year at Balliol. Whatever the reason for his choice, it was a happy circumstance that led Aubrey there. Balliol, more than any other Oxford college, had a life and spirit of its own. The great Dr Jowett had been dead five years and succeeded as Master by the less considerable Dr Caird, but the college had not lost its intellectual pre-eminence with the death of the old Master.

When Aubrey first arrived at Oxford he was eighteen and a half years old. Tall, over six foot, and slight, he presented an overwhelming impression of untidiness. Undergraduates of his day were not noted for sartorial fastidiousness; Aubrey, however, was manifestly badly dressed. Though the cast of his face was English and aristocratic with clear blue eyes and a long straight nose, his cropped hair and wildly gesticulating hands lent him a foreign air. His gait was unathletic and his movements uncoordinated. He arrived at Oxford sunburnt after a long summer spent in France perfecting his French.

His abandonment to the delights of Oxford was gradual. First letters home to his mother were critical, 'People come and sit and talk about nothing, especially the dons, and smile broadly and idiotically over everything'; but within a week he was writing, 'This is not half a bad place when one gets into it' and, 'There are any number of awfully nice people up here.' Many of the 'awfully nice people' he knew already from Eton. Of his old friends Gerard Collier, Edward Cadogan and Charlie Meade were at Balliol, but it was by his new friends that he was most exhilarated. Of these, two stand out: Raymond Asquith and Reginald Farrer.

Raymond Asquith, the eldest son of the future Prime Minister, had gone up to Balliol from Winchester the year before and had already started to reap that harvest of prizes and honours which made him a legend among his contemporaries. He had already got a first in Classical Moderations. This was to be followed by a first in Greats and a first in Jurisprudence. He effortlessly carried off the Craven, Ireland, Derby and Eldon prizes. He became President of the Union, and later was elected a Fellow of All Souls. He wore his brilliance with an apparent carelessness and a biting wit, an irresistible charm and a gift for friendship. Aubrey became a boon companion and a fast friend.

Reginald Farrer won no honours at the university. He was ugly, pygmy-bodied, and his mouth had no roof, which made his voice singularly unattractive, high and harsh. Yet he too had a brilliance, of a dark and tortured kind. Later he was to win fame as a botanical explorer and some small acclaim as a novelist and man of letters. Aubrey was fond of Reginald, but Reginald for his part loved Aubrey painfully and obsessively. Their relationship was complicated by Reginald's extreme touchiness on the one hand and Aubrey's affectionate casualness on the other. Aubrey was analytical neither of himself nor of others. Reginald was both. Aubrey was always on the crest of an enthusiasm, carrying others in his buoyant wake. Reginald stumped behind, painstakingly examining the state of his soul and the state of Aubrey's and the state of their friendship.

In a letter to Aubrey, after they had both gone down from Oxford, Reginald tried typically to explain his feelings, prompted by a casual accusation:

> I have been thinking a lot over what you said about my unfolding my soul to women and not to you . . . It is not that you are really too busy or too self-centred to attend. It is simply that you are so busy that one shrinks from bothering you about one's own affairs, unless they happen to be desperate. Another thing, you don't need my soul unfolding to you for you possess it as no-one else does or will . . . you are a very busy man, crowded up with friends and interests, living in a perpetual whirl of hurry. I, though a fiercer worker than you, am a far lazier soul, loving quiet and long days of self possession that would bore you to death in a week. Finally your incessant hurryings never seem to me to be about anything that really matters or brings contentment . . . If I ever see you, you are in a hurry between one woman and another

– looking forward to meeting A or wondering how you can shelve off B thus in a whirling interview I haven't time, for my affairs: yours take precedence in my interest, even as I like you a good deal better than I like myself.

Reginald was seldom happy, but in those Balliol days even he, snorting often in disgust and disagreement, was carried along by the general high spirits of his companions.

It was not only among the undergraduates that Aubrey made deep and lasting friendships. Hilaire Belloc was by then married and living at 36 Holywell, earning a living writing, lecturing and coaching. Aubrey's cousin Bron was a habitué of the house and early introduced Aubrey. Belloc's cosmopolitan rumbustiousness had immediate appeal. When, a year later, the Bellocs moved to London he and Aubrey continued to see much of each other. Belloc coached Aubrey in the vacations and was an admirable and conscientious teacher. His comments on the first essay that Aubrey wrote for him are longer than the essay itself. He began with two paragraphs of general encouragement, 'I see that you write essays well enough to make it worth your while to be very steady and keen about it . . .' He then gave six general principles for essay writing for schools:

You have committed an error of the commonest with men who are beginning and who are rapid in their work viz: *you have read the question to be more general than it was*. Beware of this. In History work it is so easy to write generalities that examiners since the beginning of the world have been on the lookout for this kind of thing, which they think, in their cunning, is done on purpose. The question here was . . .

Secondly. You don't quote nearly enough nor allude to enough facts as you go along. Therein schools differ from good or entertaining style. An honest man takes all knowledge for granted and writes a book to amuse you. In schools you must combine that with pride in knowledge and its expression, i.e. you have to aim at the detestable vices of the pedant.

Thirdly. Your arrangement suffers from the lack of a definite plan . . . A logical sequence is always something like this 'I assert A; just look at B & C how the facts bear me out. A also explains D. E is no rejoinder for I can rebutt it with F and G and I could talk (but will not) of H & I. So it is A and what a fine thing A is. Oh (peroration) K L M !' . . . It is never a logical sequence to say 'A was a man of such and such a type. By the way what a curious idea is the idea that B was made out of C!' The first words of an essay must state the whole in little.

Fourthly. A tendency to speak too strongly without enough facts showing through the texture of what you write.

Fifthly. You have a power of exact expression. Cling to that as to a sheet anchor.

Sixthly. Especially as you use a typewriter be as *neat and accurate as you can* in using exact letters and punctuation, make a 'clean unit' of your work on the physical side. It impresses men much more. Remember that it takes the place of voice and manner in written work.

These six general points were followed by seventeen particular points – for instance Aubrey had used the phrase 'the truth of the dictum'; Belloc comments, 'Avoid that type of word and phrase. I mean the dull and common type which base men use to be rid of ordinary English . . .'

Elsie paid Belloc £10 a week for coaching Aubrey in the vacations but Belloc though in severe financial straits was always reluctant to accept this. He wrote to Aubrey from Cheyne Walk in August 1900, 'I am very keen on getting in some final work with you before term begins and *I do not think it should be paid for*, which is what is called frank and clear. Come and stay here if you do not mind disorder and dirt. In every other thing except noise and distance the house is all right. Or if you don't I will come and see you so many hours at Charles St. Do manage it somehow, preferably here. I must not leave London I fear.' If, as she generally did, Elsie insisted on payment Belloc would return it to Aubrey in the form of magnificent presents. In February 1902, Aubrey reported to his mother: 'Belloc has just given me a new book. It smells delicious and must have been most expensive. He has had his initials and mine put on it with the date.'

Aubrey learnt more from Belloc than how to write history essays. He relished his company and the overflowing bounteousness of his mind, whether travelling with him to Portofino, when 'Belloc sang songs on the stern of the ship and harangued the stationmaster on the futility of French trains and what would happen if they had to mobilise', or exploring his gigantic prejudices over innumerable bottles of wine, or profiting from his knowledge of vineyards, 'Belloc knows of some champagne straight from the country at 3/– a bottle which I have drunk and know to be good. Shall I wire him to get some?'

One of Belloc's ambitions had been to be the first Catholic don at Oxford since the Reformation. It was one of the great disappointments of his life that this honour was denied him and fell instead to 'Sligger' Urquhart. Belloc despised Sligger and jeered at him for being a 'tame' Catholic. Certainly he was tamer than Belloc. He, too, used sometimes to coach Aubrey in the vacations. Aubrey had an affectionate contempt for him. 'He is not a bad sort of fellow but his underhand Jesuitical way of doing things has a way of irritating people extremely.' However Aubrey chose him as a coach for his last working vacation before schools. 'He knows his work thoroughly. He cannot give me the picturesqueness that Smug (A L Smith) or Belloc would, but I can to a certain inferior extent fill that in for myself. I must get hold of a man who knows it thoroughly. Sligger is absolutely indefatigable. He will coach me all the morning and write notes all evening and take his exercise at night.'

For his principal tutor, A. L. Smith, Aubrey had nothing but admiration. In a letter to his mother in February 1901, he writes, 'There is absolutely no-one like him. He is quite wonderful I think.' He too encouraged Aubrey. 'Smith told me yesterday, which rather pleased me,' Aubrey wrote to his mother, 'that my writing might get me a good first but he more than implied that it was the only thing that would.' Elsie wrote back, 'It is most encouraging that Mr Smith thinks so well of your writing – and it means that your great endeavour must be to get a clear knowledge of facts. Have you mapped out your work as I suggested?'

In fact, fortunately for Aubrey, whose grasp of facts was capricious and whose aptitude depended on a rich imagination and a gift of written expression, Smith, like Belloc, did not belong to the pedantic school of history writing. He maintained, 'A good historical mind ought not to be all precise detail, like a Pre-Raphaelite picture; there should be a haze in the middle distance, as in a good landscape painting . . .'

Aubrey's other history tutor was H. W. C. (Fluffy) Davis. As Sligger had thwarted Belloc of one ambition Fluffy Davis had of another, by beating Belloc for a fellowship of All Souls. All his life Belloc harped on this disappointment. In fact Davis was more suited to academic life than Belloc and was an excellent tutor. Aubrey liked and respected him.

The college servants as much as the dons were figures of importance in the Balliol scene. Hancock, the head porter, was a favourite of Aubrey's. He and Mrs Hancock once stayed at Pixton and were a great success at the servants' ball. So deeply ingrained became Aubrey's habit of consulting Hancock about trains that on one occasion he travelled from Pixton to Oxford to ask Hancock how to get to Aldershot.

Turner, the scout on staircase XIV where Aubrey lived, was another stock Balliol character. An eternal grumbler, he was often heard muttering, 'If that there 'onerable 'Erbert thinks 'e can turn this 'ere staircase into 'is play-'ole 'e'll find 'e's mistook.'* Nevertheless he was displeased when Aubrey moved to other quarters: 'Turner has heard that I am going to change my rooms, and goes about like a sphynx bereaved of its young, although I have promised him Mer[vyn] as a sop,' Aubrey wrote to his mother.

Aubrey's letters to his mother constitute the chief source of information about his time at Oxford. But, not surprisingly, these make no mention of the climbing and other exploits for which he was famed. L. E. Jones writing many years later claimed, 'There are some tall houses in

King Edward Street at which I still look up with trembling at the knees when I remember how Aubrey traversed the face of them, forty feet up, with finger holds alone, with a swing from ledge to ledge', and John Buchan, in his autobiography, wrote, 'To go tandem driving with him at Oxford required fortitude for he was very blind; to mountaineer with him deserved a Victoria Cross for he was both blind and desperate'. The legend of his misdeeds was still alive in 1920 when T. E. Lawrence, writing to Aubrey from All Souls, urged him to come and stay, 'It's quite a nice place now that it's entirely empty. And it's nearly opposite the bank you burgled one night, and that will remind you of several things.' This was an allusion to an occasion when Aubrey, traversing the roof-tops in his usual fashion, singing Italian love songs as he went, had the misfortune to fall through the roof of the bank. The bank manager held him up at gun point. Such stories, however, are not to be found in Aubrey's letters to his mother.

At Oxford Aubrey was able to keep his dogs. At Eton he had always missed them dreadfully. Throughout his years at Oxford he never had less than two dogs in residence, while at Teversal he kept a mixed pack. At one stage the dog population at Teversal had grown to the extent that Elsie insisted he sell or part with some. In his answering letter Aubrey listed sixteen dogs by name with whom he was prepared to part. How many more he retained is not mentioned. During his last year at Oxford Aubrey also kept a horse.

Animals, however, had always been a source of solace and pleasure to Aubrey. At Oxford he discovered new pleasures, one of which was undoubtedly drink. He and his friends drank copiously. Aubrey acquired a taste for champagne and then and later always drank it for preference. He also began to smoke. These social habits were serenely countenanced by Elsie although she took exception to less obvious vices such as travelling on Sundays.

Elsie's influence on Aubrey did not disappear at Oxford, or indeed ever, but it did diminish. Aubrey still wrote to his mother often, if not daily. The letters are short, commonly broken off with an excuse like, 'There is a most appalling person who has just come in. I forsee he will stay for at least an hour. Goodbye yr most affec Hereward.' Several times he dissuades her from coming up to hear him speak at the Union, 'it would agitate me rather'. And once he shows indignation, 'I do not understand your letter of today. Whatever else it may be, it is not, I think, wrong to miss a train, which even the College authorities endorse. It is the first time it has happened to me since going to Oxford and I do not understand why it is that you think it is an every day occurrence or that I am like Uncle Auberon.'

His uncle Auberon was often in Oxford in these days in pursuit of his campaign to abolish examinations, which he considered harmful to education. Whether Auberon Herbert missed trains or not, Aubrey certainly often did. And a few months later, obviously having forgotten about their brush on the subject he sent Elsie a detailed account of a massive missing of trains. 'I went up on Friday for the night meaning to see Bron on the way but being agitated got into the express and passed Taplow, coming back I missed two trains because I could not get a hansom and then got into another express, although the porter swore it was not, and again passed Taplow. But I returned to see him.' Elsie wisely forbore to comment.

Bron Herbert (later Lord Lucas) was Aubrey's cousin, the only son of his Uncle Auberon. To Aubrey he was like an elder brother. They only overlapped at Oxford for one year but during that year were constant companions. Bron introduced Aubrey to his set, which included Maurice Baring, John Buchan, Cubby Medd and also many of Aubrey's nearer contemporaries like Raymond Asquith. Bron was not an intellectual although he had a passionate love for music and poetry. He was a child of nature with a great knowledge of birds and beasts and all wild things. Now he was at Taplow, being nursed by his cousin Lady Desborough. He had gone out to the Boer War as a correspondent for *The Times* and *Manchester Guardian*. In deference to the strong pacifist views of his father he had refrained from enlisting. In South Africa he had been wounded in the foot, and on his return to England it was found that the leg had to be amputated below the knee. A man of splended physique, he had at Oxford been an all-round athlete and rowing blue. Raymond Asquith, in a letter to Aubrey, wrote: 'He has the face and figure of a god, and such charm and distinction as I never saw in any other man.' The amputation appalled his friends but Bron with courage and cheerfulness overcame the catastrophe and was soon stalking, playing tennis and even riding in steeplechases. Nevertheless it was a sobering shock to Aubrey and his circle.

The South African war hung over the Oxford of Aubrey's day not as a gloomy shadow, but as a beckoning beacon. It was not a war, one would have thought, to appeal to romantic youth, but appeal it did. Dedicated as Aubrey and his companions were to the spirit of adventure, war seemed the ultimate adventure. All the daredevil scaling of walls and rooftops and reckless tandem driving were tame compared to an actual battlefield. The justice or injustice of the cause was of little interest.

When war broke out on 11th October 1899, Aubrey was beginning his second year at Oxford. He was among the first to fall victim to war fever. Many from Balliol volunteered. 'Nothing else is talked about all day,'

Aubrey wrote to his mother. Alarm bells should have rung for Elsie but she remained complacent. Even when Aubrey joined the volunteers, the implications seem to have escaped her. 'I am glad you have joined the volunteers and I hope you will be most diligent in drill and rifle practice', she wrote from Portofino in January 1900, although she was less indulgent about her brother Esmé Howard who had joined the Duke of Cambridge's Own, a regiment of gentleman troopers, and was likely to be sent out to South Africa in the near future: 'It is a great pity when people can't realise what their real duty is. His certainly does not lie in South Africa.' Aubrey's telegram two weeks later came as an appalling shock. In it he informed his mother that he had taken the Queen's shilling and enlisted in the same regiment as his Uncle Esmé.

Elsie hurried back from Portofino. She met Aubrey in Paris for a few hours. He had to rush back for his drill. Elsie was despairing. She could not move Aubrey. She knew, but he would not accept, that South Africa would ruin his eyes. Every month since the operation his right eye had improved and grown stronger. To subject it now to the dust storms of South Africa was to throw away everything that had been gained. Finally, after interminable arguments, Aubrey agreed that she should telegraph Pagenstecker in Wiesbaden. Pagenstecker was horrified. His verdict was conclusive; Aubrey yielded to maternal pressure.

For Aubrey it was a bitter blow. It was not just the forfeiture of an adventure; it was, he felt, a loss of honour. Even the contrary assurances of Lord Lansdowne, then Secretary of State for War, to whom Elsie took him, or of Lord Wolseley the Commander-in-Chief, to whom his Aunt Eveline took him, failed to console. Aubrey returned to Oxford, but obstinately continued with his soldiering. He joined the Oxford Yeomanry and later the Sherwood Rangers who were based near Teversal. He had obtained leave of absence from the university for the Hilary term of 1900 when he enlisted. Now his vacations also were exclusively taken up with military training. Easter, which was usually spent at Portofino, was instead passed drilling at Worksop. His army fever persisted all through 1900 and into the next year when Aubrey missed another term, on manoeuvres with his regiment. One pleasant side effect of these absences was that he was able to stay up at Oxford for four years instead of the three which would have been customary for someone reading history.

By 1901 much of the war frenzy had subsided and although Aubrey still fulfilled his territorial obligations with the Sherwood Rangers, the passion had abated. His sense of shame at being prevented from going out to South Africa nevertheless remained and of this Elsie was aware. In January 1901 she wrote to him from Portofino: 'In the case of any

serious decision on your part, as for instance engaging yourself or volunteering I rely on your affection and duty towards me to communicate
with me on the subject *before* committing yourself. You have great
capabilities, and with a life brimfull of pleasant things. Certain well-
defined duties – to your family, your property, your country . . .'

Aubrey, for his part, shamed as he was at not going, had lost all real
desire to go. Bron's pro-Boer sentiments may have weighed with him,
but probably more telling were the accounts of other Balliol men who
were trickling back to Oxford from South Africa. He wrote to his mother
about one such man, who had been one of four survivors out of eleven in
an outpost, 'He said that they had orders to bayonet the wounded Boers;
many of course refused but on several occasions he saw it done.' That
was not the sort of war Aubrey had had in mind when he enlisted.

Aubrey's coming of age was not celebrated until the summer of 1901.
His actual birthday in April was passed at Portofino. Elsie gave him a
horse. However she had already given him a more handsome gift. Elsie
bought from her stepson Porchy, Aubrey's favourite Herbert house,
Pixton, and with it five thousand rolling acres on Exmoor. That summer
Aubrey took possession of Pixton. It was a large 18th-century house,
with Victorian additions, of great charm but no architectural distinction. Set high on a hill amidst magnificent trees in a deer-filled park, it
soon became a magnet for Aubrey's friends. There were many house
parties. Edward Cadogan wrote of them years later, 'I look back to these
bachelor house parties as among the happiest experiences of my existence. They included our elect Balliol circle . . .'

Sometimes members of the elect stayed in other country houses
amidst alien people. Then they would write disparaging letters to each
other about their hosts and fellow guests. Thus Raymond Asquith wrote
to Aubrey from Malmesbury, 'Here I follow the hounds at a respectful
distance and hobnob with the gentry of Wiltshire, who are as dull a lot
as one can find. My host is mad and doesn't shoe his horses but his butler
is quite a gentleman.' Or from Clovelly, where he wrote, 'This place is so
charming that I can't see my way to leaving it at present. On the human
side it leaves a good deal to be desired – though there is one woman here
with a really beautiful soul – but most of the men are simply affable
lunatics, nothing more – real $\frac{1}{2}$ bits. It is not often one finds oneself in
company of which one can truly say one is as much above it as Sligger is
above the monkeys, but so it is with me . . .'

Tainted with youthful conceit, rejoicing in their exclusiveness, this
Balliol band brought zest and wit to the houses where they stayed and
were forgiven and welcomed by their hosts. Aubrey stayed away less
than most. He entertained at Portofino, Teversal and Pixton but his

yeomanry commitments left little time for visiting. Perhaps his soldiering was part of an unconscious desire to maintain a separate life. Always, Aubrey shunned sets. At Oxford, for the only time in his life, he could have been said to be a member of one, that Balliol group led by Raymond Asquith. Later, Raymond was the leading spirit in another set, the Coterie, to which many of Aubrey's friends and his wife belonged; but Aubrey remained outside. He was with them but not of them. He disliked the inbred self-absorption of such groups. At Balliol this lifelong reluctance to be labelled and grouped was temporarily overcome. Aubrey rejoiced with them in their exclusiveness, looked for no better companions, gave himself up, heart, soul and sinew to his Balliol friends and their junketings.

Most of his friends, being men of words rather than action, gave vent to their feelings about the South African war at the Union. There were many debates and in most Aubrey participated. He spoke both for and against the South African war but was only roused to passion on personal issues, as when he spoke in defence of Lord Lansdowne. The motion was 'That in the opinion of this House the Secretary of State for War [Lord Lansdowne] is unworthy of a place in the Cabinet.' Aubrey's performance earned him praise from *The Oxford Magazine*: 'Hon A M Herbert made very much the best speech we have heard from him. By chastening his wit and amplifying his periods he has advanced from the epigrammatic incoherence of his earlier efforts to a happy combination of dignity and impudence. His sentences were excellently framed, his arguments were full of pith and relevance, his turns of phrase were always vigorous and often felicitous. Also he is brief.' The motion was defeated 27 to 32.

Aubrey was, however, on the losing side in a debate about which he had much stronger feelings. In November 1901 the Union debated the motion, 'That this House applauds the action of the War Office in dismissing Sir Redvers Buller.' Sir Redvers Buller had been given the command of the First Army Corps in South Africa and it was under his generalship that the English had suffered the reverses which made them the laughing stock of the world. On his return to England he made an indiscreet speech which led to his dismissal. At the time there was much feeling in the country that he had been unjustly treated, particularly in his native Devon where there were large 'indignation meetings' on his behalf. He was a holder of the Victoria Cross and, before the Boer War, had been a national hero.

Aubrey felt strongly the injustice of Buller's dismissal. His feelings were not in any way objective. Sir Redvers was a close cousin. His mother, Charlotte Howard, had been a sister of Lord Carnarvon's mother and of

Elsie's father. He was therefore doubly a first cousin to Aubrey at one remove. Aubrey had known and revered him throughout his boyhood. The Union was packed for the debate. Aubrey led against the motion. *The Oxford Magazine* described his speech as 'occasionally somewhat incoherent' but said 'he succeeded in amusing as well as interesting the House', but not in convincing them. The motion was carried 136 votes to 57.

Prompted by his interest in South Africa, Aubrey's involvement with the Union grew. He became in turn secretary, Junior Treasurer, Librarian and Vice President. His days as secretary are easily picked out in the Union records. The minutes, usually neatly penned, lapse into chaotic disorder; huge black words fall across the page in blind or drunken disorder. Apart from the Union, Aubrey belonged to many University clubs, political (in the Conservative interest), poetic (the Horace club), dining (the Gridiron) and of course the Annandale club at Balliol of which he was a famously riotous member.

Meanwhile, though his contributions at the Union were gaining him reputation and approval, Aubrey's antics elsewhere were less pleasing to the authorities. His roof-climbing feats were becoming notorious. He was in continuous trouble with the proctors. Also, among the serious, staid Scottish undergraduates who were always a strong element at Balliol, his endless practical jokes were taken in increasingly bad part. A tea party, given by one such undergraduate for his parents under a plum tree in the quad was disrupted by Aubrey, who having earlier climbed the plum tree and hidden there, dropped out of it, scattering china and food, explaining to the outraged Scots that he had fallen from the tree because he was 'ripe'. This sort of behaviour, combined with repeated raids on the college laboratory and the preserves of neighbouring colleges, and other incursions, led the authorities to conclude that his activities should be curtailed. By the end of May 1901 their patience was exhausted. The Master of Balliol wrote to Aubrey who was away training with the Sherwood Rangers and rusticated him for the rest of the term. Aubrey was indignant. He sent off a barrage of letters – to the Master, to Slligger Urquhart and to his friends at Balliol. The Master replied:

There was no thought of punishing you for what you have done before this term, though a repetition of what you are known to have done before does not make the offence less grave. But we have evidence that you were over the walls before you went down, and, unintentionally or not, damage was done. Among other things telegraph wires were broken in Trinity and a cornice in St John's College was thrown down. You are quite aware that going over the walls is a serious offence against College rules, and in this case it has led to a demand being made upon us by the other colleges to put up additional barriers. Such acts are apt to lead to reprisals and since you went down they have actually led to windows in Balliol being broken by men coming over the walls from Trinity . . .

But I think we have a right to look to one of your standing as having got beyond the school boy feeling of wishing to evade rules, which are quite reasonable, simply because they are rules. A soldier above all ought to make it a point of honour to support discipline.

There was a postscript: 'Perhaps I should add, in reference to your complaint of our condemning you unheard, that in this case no defence was possible; you and not Bonham-Carter were seen upon the roof by Mr Urquhart.' Maurice Bonham-Carter, known as Bongie and later to marry Raymond Asquith's sister Violet, was not rusticated like Aubrey but merely fined.

The next term Aubrey no longer had rooms in College but lodged at Tackley House. Mervyn had by now left Eton in a blaze of cricketing glory and was also up at Balliol. On Aubrey's advice he did not try for the Brackenbury History scholarship (Aubrey had tried and failed). Aubrey, worldly-wise, explained to his mother, 'what they like is strings of paradoxes fathered on good old platitudes that they can understand,' he did not think that Mervyn had 'yet got the trick of writing meaningless nonsense in good periods'. Mervyn, however, had inherited Elsie's command of, and love for, facts and her zest for work. He, too, decided to try for a first and in due course was rewarded. Meanwhile the brothers rejoiced in their reunion. Mervyn had some of Aubrey's natural ebullience but was without his marked singularity. Their strong affection for each other was noted by all. Aubrey's friends adopted Mervyn immediately. Aubrey wrote to Elsie in the first week of the new term, 'Mer has settled down and is I needn't say very much liked. He is beginning to talk more.'

While Mervyn was embarking on his Oxford career, Aubrey was now in his last year, entering what Reginald Farrer called 'the valley of the shadow of schools'. Aubrey spent the Easter vacation of 1902 with friends at Portofino. It was his last working vacation and he had Sligger in attendance. Reginald Farrer, at home in Lancashire, longing to be at Portofino, wrote, in his arch and flowery way:

I hope (but without conviction) that your party has as yet done nothing too extreme – that peace and propriety reign together, that sobriety and work have kissed one another. Tell somebody to write me a candid and convincing account of all your words and ways and works – of the perils by sea and rock and balcony – of the country inns, of revelry and the lovely maidens left lamenting – lest Sligger be forced by the dictates of honesty and manhood to bring back with him to Balliol some wizened Anna as his timeworn bride. My prophetic eye goes ranging far ahead, and I seem to see a Balliol strain in the Portofinesi of another generation for which your united studies can alone account. Do you, by the day, entertain the local royalties at lunch; and is it probable that Beb and Raymond [Asquith] will each make prize of a many quateringed Princess?

Excuse all these insinuendoes, but really when one is so retired and quiet as here, if one comes to write a letter one can only fall to imagining evil of one's correspondents, in default of any startling wickedness of one's own to write about . . .

Reginald's 'insinuendoes' were, for once, not entirely wide of the mark. Raymond Asquith, while not paying court to many a quateringed princess was at least playing ping pong with them. At Castello Brown, a neighbouring crusader castle owned by the British Consul, there was a house party which included a few minor German royalties. Raymond in a letter to Harold (Bluetooth) Baker described his ping-pong opponent as 'a German princess (Taxis I think) dirty-minded and an enormous eater'. And in the same letter 'perils by sea and rock' are given colour: 'Aubrey missed his footing today and fell off, into the sea luckily, whence he was recovered by a retainer who follows us in a boat.'

Aubrey was scornful of Princess Taxis's ping pong. 'I could beat her left-handed and blindfolded,' he wrote to his mother. However the Princess's habit of always addressing Aubrey in Italian (a language she reserved for servants) while addressing his servant Vergil in English as 'my dear' rather nettled him.

Also staying at Castello Brown was a young girl from Ireland, Augusta Bellingham. Aubrey tumbled headlong in love with her. Raymond describing her to Bluetooth wrote that she was, 'lively and quite pretty but too small to attract me – certainly not of the *Megethos* for a tragedy. Aubrey lifts her about the rocks, takes her about in boats to see caves and talks a good deal of nonsense about her intermediately.'

Despite the heady Mediterranean atmosphere and the dawn of new love, Aubrey managed to get in a fair amount of work with Sligger. It was a serious reading party and four of the eight Balliol men present ultimately got firsts.

All through his time at Oxford Aubrey employed a secretary, sometimes male, sometimes female. His eyesight had improved considerably and he no longer needed a personal tutor to read aloud all his books. He read a certain amount himself, extremely rapidly using the unoperated eye, holding the book so close that it often touched his nose. His handwriting remained huge and abominable but he seldom wrote by hand.

However, despite long practice, his mastery of the typewriter remained weak and so he always dictated his essays. For Schools he obtained special permission to dictate his papers to a newspaper reporter but it is uncertain whether he availed himself of the privilege when he sat his exams in the summer of 1902.

After Schools were over, in a great letting off of steam, Aubrey went on the rampage. This time the College authorities were unforgiving. He was sent down.

Aubrey was dejected. He felt his fortunes were at a low ebb. The only place he wanted to be was at Oxford, and from there he was banned. He felt also (wrongly) that he acquitted himself badly in Schools. Like Reginald Farrer who wrote, 'How I loathe coming to the end of a chapter', he found it hard to close his Balliol chapter. Raymond Asquith also wrote complaining of depression. Aubrey replied 'I'm also d . . . d depressed', but added, 'chiefly from constipation' and then described the inadequate lavatory facilities of the house in which he had been staying. 'I used to retire every day to a marsh some miles from the house, with a magazine, but the last two days it rained . . .' However, his depression had graver roots than constipation. In the same letter to Raymond Asquith he wrote, 'I think society's bloody – the women look like ant eaters and talk like the sea serpent.' He was definitely out of sorts.

Predictably Elsie had the answer. She had for some time been plotting the next stage in Aubrey's career. She had long thought that the diplomatic service would suit him. For the past year every time she met an ambassador she would explore the possibilities of an honorary attaché-ship. Thus in July 1901 she wrote that she had made friends with Sir Claude Macdonald, 'another string to our diplomatic bow', and in February 1902 she wrote, 'You will be glad to hear that I have this morning heard from Sir A Nicholson. He says: "If I am at Tangier next year I should be much pleased to have your son as hon attache".'

The Tangier plan fell through but meanwhile Elsie's first fish was landed. His Majesty's Ambassador in Tokyo, Sir Claude Macdonald, late of Peking where he had masterminded the resistance of the legations at the time of the Boxer revolt, was persuaded that he needed an honorary attaché. Aubrey was pleased by the prospect. His friends were not. Raymond Asquith dismissed the plan as 'mad folly'. He wrote to Reginald Farrer:

Going to Japan at 10 days' notice as an honorary attache! Can you imagine anything more feverishly absurd? To put oneself 12,000 miles away from anybody fit to speak to, in a country where the men have no faces and the women have no feet, and the houses are made of paper, and the books begin at the end and end in the middle, and the scenery is imported every year from the Savoy theatre and retained on the hire system until Gilbert and Sullivan want it again in London! The proctors ought to forbid him to go; but they always do their duty at the wrong moment – like anyone else who does it at all.

Aubrey, meanwhile, wrote to Raymond a letter of passionate though rather incoherent justification:

My dear Raymond,

I thought you would have approved of the Japanese plan. I think I should be a fool or a cynic if I did not. I think it is splendid . . .

What you say about Balliol is *nonsense*. When you have known the best (Balliol) the second best (London) does not attract. As well or better be 12,000 miles away as 12. The result is the same. In the first case you are free, in the second you are encumbered with tantalising possibilities. If I stay in England I shall see you and the other fellows once in the most unsatisfactory of blue moons. It'll be a damned life that is neither cheese nor herring and I hate milk and water middlemen among people or institutions . . .

At present I am feeling blasé without justification, I mean experiences. We've had our time at Oxford and a damned good past it's been but to try and live in it again is to misrepresent it. It's the present that compensates (or fails to compensate) for the present and therefore as I can't get Balliol I prefer Japan. As for the Diplomatic side I quite admit that is the worst feature of the case. It has not dazzled me, it has not even startled me, in fact it has left me almost unmoved but my people want me to do something and that is the simplest thing. I don't take my view of life or diplomacy from Anthony Hope any more than you get your theology from *Lamentations*. Goodbye, dear Raymond, come and see me in Japan . . .

I have got a second in schools with which I'm fairly pleased. I leave next Wednesday. If you are in London that night I'll come and see you though I can't till late, about 12 p.m. Mind you write.

Aubrey had not got a second. He had got a first, to the great delight of Elsie and of Raymond, who wrote to Bluetooth Baker: 'Aubrey's first pleased me a good deal. He must have got it entirely on his imagination, which really does assimilate and illumine the things that interest him – such as the mediaeval Empire – the examiners must have agreed with me rather than you in this matter, as he was certainly quite ignorant of many of his subjects – political science, political economy and constitutional history eg!'

When Aubrey left England at the end of July, he left in ignorance of this signal success and in a mood, if not of despondency, of little cheer.

3

Lotus Eating and Turkish Delight

The work of an honorary attaché was not arduous. Aubrey spent the next few years at two different Embassies, first in Tokyo and then Constantinople. His labours in Chancery were seldom interesting, important or useful but the post provided a respectable excuse for foreign travel and living abroad and was therefore congenial.

Aubrey had never visited America and so chose the western route to Japan. He was critical of New York: 'There is no privacy anywhere and the lower classes hate the English.' He left New York hastily having lent and lost all his money to a confidence trickster and made his way to Canada, which he liked as much as he had disliked the United States.

In Vancouver he found an Oxford friend and together they went to a gambling den where Aubrey lost all his money for the second time. Next they went to a bar. Aubrey wrote an account to his Balliol friend Tuppy Headlam:

> We were invited to 'go upstairs' with two Chinese women who looked like diseased telegraph poles. I said in pidgin English that we intended to be platonic and did not wish to go upstairs whereupon a gigantic negress said she would have us thrown out. Like a fool I showed the butt of my revolver and told her to call up her men. They turned on us like tigers, the old negress foamed at the mouth. I never saw such a sight, and the haste with which I departed was almost undignified.

On his way to Vancouver Aubrey had passed through Toronto where a cable was awaiting him with news of his first. In Vancouver he found letters of congratulation from his mother. He replied: 'the result was chiefly luck but I certainly owe that part of it which was not due to chance to you entirely.'

Aubrey believed in his luck. He had no great faith in his own abilities and attributed entirely to good fortune the relatively few worldly successes which came his way. He was not humble but he was without conceit. He never noticed or understood his hold on the hearts of his friends. He was unaware of his charm, which may well have been a main part of it. His comical manner and lightness of touch combined with his zestful enjoyment of all manner of people and places won him affection and devotion; but he always remained oblivious to the effect he had on people. Raymond Asquith at about this time summed up his character in a pithy phrase, 'You have the wine of life; others the headache.'

Japan proved an aberration in Aubrey's life. His sojourn there lasted less than a year and, but for a discreet tattoo on his arm in the form of an exotic bird, left no permanent mark. While there, he was temporarily entranced, but neither the country nor the people proved to have lasting appeal for him. He never revisited the islands. Raymond Asquith wrote: 'Your letters have been getting shorter and less coherent from which I fear I must infer that the East has laid her shining hand upon you and is leading you down the flowery pathways to the abyss of indolent sensuality.' He need not have worried. The East, indeed, did eventually lay its 'shining hand' on Aubrey, but the Near East not the Far East. Aubrey himself, many years later, looking back over his time in Japan, wrote: 'There was no permanent attraction for an Englishman in that enchanting land, unless, wearying of his own country he were to become first a Japanese scholar and then a Japanese.'*

Aubrey never became a Japanese scholar although he passed the lowest grade of Foreign Office exam and had what is termed 'a working knowledge' of the language.

The first weeks were taken up with finding a house, engaging servants and learning the routine of his work in Chancery. The afternoons were free; Aubrey's were spent learning the Japanese language or Japanese wrestling or working for All Souls. He had decided, after his surprising success in schools, to sit the All Souls examination the next autumn. 'I am thinking', he wrote to Raymond Asquith, 'of having a shot at it next year, since schools proved such a farce.' In another letter to Raymond he reported his Japanese as improving, 'I have an American accent now and an undercurrent of Japanese idiom', but it remained an undercurrent. He found that his habit of reading reproaches to his servants out of the dictionary had to be abandoned. Japanese was such a polite language that the mildest rebuke in English when translated became an offensive insult. His wrestling, also, did not progress with the speed he hoped. He wrote to his mother at the end of December telling her of his two resolutions for the New Year: 'to grasp this side of the Eastern question and to learn wrestling. I don't know which is harder but in both cases a little knowledge seems a dangerous thing.'

In his first months in Japan Aubrey pined a little for his old friends. He wrote to Raymond, 'It is damned lonely here. There is only one Balliol man and he a Jap.' And in another letter to Raymond he wrote, 'it seems so long since I met anyone of the old calibre that I have no longer the same criterion and do not know when I am talking nonsense.' He found it difficult being with a 'multitude of beings of your own species with whom you have nothing in common . . . their highest flights of fancy carry them back to Piccadilly at 11 p.m. or perhaps in the case of the more refined, to the Carlton.' However, in December 1902, the situation was remedied by the arrival of Reginald Farrer, who came to Japan to collect plants.

The two friends soon decided to live separately. When alone together, they quarrelled fiercely. Reginald held an image of Aubrey in his mind. He cared passionately when the original failed to live up to this image. Light disagreements escalated to heated arguments. They would attack each other with strong words. Aubrey neither remembered their rows nor bore rancour. Reginald forgot nothing. Every unkind word was cherished in his heart. He brooded over all slights, treasured them as a woman might treasure jewels, brought them out from time to time and polished them. 'You don't have (thank heaven)', Reginald wrote to Aubrey, 'my ineffaceable memory and my sense of the indelible permanence of things done or said once in a fit of some kind or another.'

With the arrival of Reginald, Aubrey saw less of both the diplomatic and expatriate community. The latter he had eschewed from the beginning, but the European diplomats, with their 'eyes like the more expensive kind of oysters' he mostly enjoyed, in particular the Italian Minister, who was always playing cards but always being beaten, 'owing', as he explained, 'to the ungentlemanly "'abit of the bloff"'.

Every member of the diplomatic corps was presented to the Mikado. Aubrey's turn came on New Year's Day 1903. He wrote to his mother, 'His clothes look like sacks, he is too holy to be touched so the tailor has to crawl in on all fours and after a few furtive glances to crawl out again.'

It was not, however, the life that interested Aubrey in Japan; it was the country itself and the 'topsy-turvy element' as he called it. Always Aubrey had delighted in things foreign and strange and Japan provided both in abundance. In a letter to Raymond Asquith written in early September he gave his first impression:

This is not a bad country. It is a land of clear colours and stories, a region of shadowless hours where earth has a garment of glories and a murmur of musical flowers, etc, the rest is as true but not as respectable. There is certainly not much to do, but it's not bad fun being sung to by a geisha while one girl rolls your cigarettes and another fans you. It's a curious blend of Omar and Kipling. One sees the most picturesque oriental sights, the dance of the five fans by electric light, or a Venus of Milo, only still more decolleté, quoting a guide book. I never struck a place where the necessity of readjusting one's ideas was so strongly brought home to one. One feels like an intelligent child looking through a telescope for the first time, or a savage in a balloon. In Europe one would insist upon explanations, here one is content to accept every contradiction from the water that has barely consistency to let you swim in it to the air that has not enough ozone to make it worth while breathing.

Aubrey's feelings about Japan were not consistent. His letters show a fluctuation between admiration, amusement and disgust. In one disparaging letter to Raymond he proved singularly unprophetic in his judgment: 'I don't believe this people will ever do anything. There is no initiative and nothing genuine in this country, not even its art, everything is borrowed, forged, plagiarized. They live on a kind of island in the rubicon between east and west.'

In another letter to Raymond, Aubrey tells how, dining with Farrer and two Japanese friends ('both Oxford men, they were English at the beginning of the evening and Japanese at the end') and finding himself a long way from home without a rickshaw, he went to a nearby tea house:

The lady of the house, escorting me to the bath was very apologetic, but I was tired and did not bother about what she said. In the morning when I woke up I found a figure kneeling at the head of my bed on the floor, and discovered it was a geisha who had been waiting, goodness knows how long, until I should awake when she proposed etc. It was annoying as it was very early, and I had to get up, as my explanation to the effect that no Englishman would be guilty of such an act before ten at night was not considered satisfactory. The mistress had apologised the night before because she had no supply for the demand she endowed me with.

Aubrey was far from unsusceptible to women. His fastidiousness may have in part derived from the romantic view he had of them and in part from his disgust at the behaviour of other Europeans in Japan, who were, by his account, all afflicted with venereal diseases from their excesses (although there is a hint in one or two letters that he may not himself have totally escaped contamination). He was, moreover, at this time still romantically attached to Miss Bellingham, the belle of Castello Brown. After their Easter meeting at Portofino Aubrey had pursued her with letters and poems.

Augusta Bellingham was the daughter of Sir Alan Bellingham, of

Castle Bellingham, Co. Louth, a convert to Rome. Miss Bellingham was also a fervent Catholic and she had made plain to Aubrey that if he wished to succeed in his suit he must embrace her faith. This Aubrey was prepared to do, but he was nervous about his mother's reaction to such a step. Before he left England he had failed to broach the subject, except in the most general terms by presenting the problem as a friend's rather than his own. He did however confide in his uncle Esmé Howard.

Esmé Howard, later Lord Howard of Penrith and British Ambassador in Madrid and Washington, was the youngest of Elsie's brothers and the uncle nearest in age and sympathy to Aubrey. By Howard standards he had been a little wild in youth, sporting a red tie and, as a last act of folly, enlisting in the Boer War. He was a man of intelligence, charm and humour and Aubrey was much attached to him. Moreover, Esmé had been converted to Catholicism a few years before when he married an Italian Catholic, Lady Isabella Giustiniani Bandini, whose father enjoyed the various and disparate titles of eighth Earl of Newburgh, Prince Giustiniani Bandini and Duke of Mondragono. Uncle Esmé might therefore have been thought likely to be sympathetic to Aubrey's predicament. But he was not. Esmé was devoted to his sister Elsie and would not encourage Aubrey in a course which might cause her distress. All concerned had learnt their lesson from the fiasco of Aubrey's attempted enlistment. There were other grounds for discouragement. Aubrey was only twenty-two years old at the time and manifestly unsuited to domesticity.

It was not, however, until Elsie came out to Japan that Aubrey brought himself to discuss the matter with his mother. And even then he left it to the last night of her visit. Aubrey accompanied her to Peking from where she was taking a train through China and Russia back to England. In Peking, in April, Aubrey told his mother about Miss Bellingham. Elsie managed to prevent the match. What tactics she used remain unclear, but she never regretted her interference. Her task may not have been difficult; she had received a written undertaking from Aubrey that he would never marry without her consent. Two years later Miss Bellingham married the fourth Marquis of Bute, a Catholic.

Elsie's visit to Japan was a great success. She arrived by boat in February 1903, accompanied by Mervyn, John Kennaway and a dog, which Aubrey had requested, and a lot of books for the All Souls exam, for which he had not asked. Aubrey had warned his mother that 'the petit monde of missionaries and merchants' were determined to meet her, but there were few opportunities because Aubrey whisked her away from Tokyo almost as soon as she arrived. They travelled round the remoter islands, staying in some discomfort and bitterly cold temperatures in Buddhist monasteries, and then took ship to Korea where they arrived in March.

Aubrey was both fascinated and repelled by Korea. To Raymond Asquith he wrote a prose description from Chemulpo:

I have never felt that any place was quite as tragic. It has a sort of distracted beauty, but it is barren beyond words. The wind feels like the inspiration of the Preacher, it is the very country of Ecclesiastes. They have never done with their dead. The whole population wear white clothes. Mourning is kept up for two years during which time they wear huge straw hats, big enough for a child to sleep in, cover their faces with a kind of fan, and never speak. It is unimaginable that round this blank desolation, and a people too tired even to lament, the politics of the Far East revolve.

He then recounts a 'faux pas' of the Japanese, who about four years before, had murdered the Queen, whose influence was anti-Japanese, 'by stamping on her with tailor-made swords' and afterwards, having already chucked all her women out of high windows, burning her. The Korean King 'has never felt quite the same towards Japan since'. Mervyn and John Kennaway, who accompanied Aubrey and Elsie to Korea, 'do not set a good example to the Koreans, becoming flushed with fizz before a late breakfast and hiccupping'.

After Korea Aubrey accompanied his mother and Mervyn to Peking and then went on with them to Tientsin where they embarked on the long railway journey across Siberia. Elsie wrote every day from the train, prettily illustrating her letters with sketches of the countryside, and gently complaining of frozen lavatories. Aubrey stayed on a little longer in China, mainly in order to be able to accept various invitations to shoot. He returned to Tokyo to find the Balliol group, Gerard and Eric Collier, John Kennaway and Reginald Farrer, well established but impoverished. Charlie Goschen and his brother also passed through and another Eton friend, Walter Guinness. There were endless comings and goings. April and May were the months for foreign visitors in Japan. Gertrude Bell came with her brother, an acquaintance of Aubrey's from Eton and Oxford. Aubrey liked Gertrude. Their paths were to cross many times again and this meeting in Japan was the beginning of a friendship. Gertrude wrote in her diary: 'Aubrey Herbert came to tea with us – he is a delightful creature. I am looking forward to seeing more of him', while Aubrey, equally enthusiastic, wrote to his mother, 'She is really a rather wonderful person, gives you information quicker than you can digest.'

Soon after Aubrey returned to Tokyo, he left again to go on manoeuvres with the Japanese Army. He found them very strange. The Japanese Generals found him very strange. They had never before had a foreigner on manoeuvres. On the whole Aubrey was critical of their war games. 'They are slipshod where we are automatic and automatic where we are intelligent', but 'the Generals have the opportunity of learning much more than ours because they stop the thing when they choose like a cinematograph.'

Aubrey galloped about between Generals, reciting Swinburne, 'which they understood as well as anything else I said', and exchanging cards. 'The other day I saw the infantry charge ½ a mile across a plain towards a well-defended wood. 150 yards away they knelt down in perfect line, fired ten volleys and retired – in good order. C'est magnifique mais ce n'est pas la guerre, as I remarked to the General with whom I happened to be exchanging a card at the moment the fight was hottest and who only knows Japanese.'

The manoeuvres over, Aubrey returned to Tokyo and tried to settle down to work for the All Souls exam. He found the study of the eighteenth century most uncongenial and yielded easily to the many distractions.

In July 1903, Reginald Farrer left for home. Reginald, who completed a novel on his journey (*The House of Shadows*), wrote to Aubrey on his arrival in England: 'all the claws of the old life closed on me. The east dropped away from me so suddenly it was almost tragic; at a blow it faded and the house and the place were just as they always had been till I felt in an hour that I had never been away at all. Japan is nothing but a ghost', and then typically he added, 'the only memories that really live are the self-reproachful.' His novel finished, he was already immersed in a new venture: 'I am trying to translate the Iphigenia at Aulis into vivid and violent prose. Do you think this is a waste of time? I wish you cared more for such things and then I should talk to you about them and should not be accused of having no interests because I decline to bore you with those I have! (Was ever such a memory – I believe my remembrances will survive my ghost by a thousand years . . .)'

In July Aubrey too began preparing to leave. There was a round of farewell parties. Aubrey wrote to Raymond:

> I am almost homeward bound. A series of misfortunes have attended me lately, beginning with my taking a heavy sleeping draught instead of a diarrhoea powder and omitting to wear braces when I went to a palace tiffin. They thought my skin was my handkerchief (no joke) . . . I have unfortunately gambled above my means. Can you Raymond lend me £15 when I return to England? . . . Now I am reformed, I feel like Algy Cecil when he had seen Balliol men extra drunk: a man of the world, tired, but still tolerant of vice.

The misfortunes multiplied. Two days before sailing Aubrey was bitten by a particularly venomous insect, which laid eggs under his skin;

these gradually erupted into a series of colossal boils. He made his way slowly and painfully down to the ship, 'a Chinese woman would have given me points in a steeple chase'. He was seen by the ship's doctor who immediately sent him to hospital. He spent the next fortnight in St Luke's Hospital, Tokyo, covered from ankle to thigh with poisonous eruptions. He could neither stand nor walk. When he recovered, he had to endure another round of farewell parties. Then the ship on which he had booked to leave, the *Tonkin*, burnt. 'It is too vexatious for anything,' Aubrey wrote to his mother. By the time he finally left at the end of August he had to hurry home for the All Souls examination and his plans for a long journey with stops in Malaya, Ceylon and India, where he had Oxford friends, were perforce curtailed. He had not done enough work for All Souls and in his last letter before leaving, he wrote to his mother, 'I hope you won't mind if I don't get this thing . . .' Elsie met Aubrey on his homeward journey in Paris and they went to Portofino together. From there they went to Pixton and Aubrey belatedly started swotting. He failed to get elected to All Souls. He was not cast down by the result; he had entertained little expectation of success.

The new year of 1904 found Aubrey, with his mother, in Egypt. Before he left England he had attended a number of balls, become enamoured of a number of girls and seen most of his old friends. The old, easy, male comradeship of Oxford had already begun to disintegrate as the members of his Balliol set were scattered in pursuit of their various careers. But neither geography nor careers weakened the bonds of the old fellowship as much as the impact of women in all their lives. Only Bron Herbert stood out against this general trend. He continued to hold all male parties at Pickets Post; he cursed women and all their ways; he would brook no defence; he forbade the topic. The rest of the group, however, succumbed to the delights of female society. They still met and caroused and went out shooting together, but their talk now was dominated by the subject of girls. When they stayed up all night, drinking, their discussions were no longer concentrated on philosophy, poetry, adventure, politics or war. Instead they dilated upon the feminine ideal, the role of beauty and intelligence, and the problems of female society.

Aubrey, away from England, carried on the discussion by correspondence, exchanging many letters with Raymond Asquith exclusively on the subject of women. Aubrey's views were often juvenile and always muddled. 'You have a rapid and contorted mind like the poet Pindar', was Raymond's kindly comment on one particularly convoluted missive. Raymond himself was more mature, both in outlook and expression. Their letters discuss the general questions of love and women, not the particular. 'I don't want confidences from you,' Aubrey wrote to Raymond. 'It's only drunkards or the bourgeoisie who mistake them for friendship.' On the other hand, he confided a good deal in Raymond: 'I tell you things because I have the average human desire for comprehension, because I know what I tell you is safe and also because you will not come in contact with those matters that have been close to me.'

While Aubrey was abroad, Raymond was tasting the delights of London Society. He described his new life to Aubrey:

> I have conceived a passion for the society of young women and am one of the common objects of the London ballroom. I make light of 5 parties on a single night and the smartest rout is dowdy without me. It is a dissipating and unholy life but not without interest and perhaps not without value: after all one's chief business is to find out what all kinds of people are like, and constantly seeing new ones for brief and feverish moments teaches one to do that and to do it quickly. I feel sure you will revel in it when you come back: you have the faculties for it – the joy of life, the joy of learning, the passion for noise and novelty and nonsense – all of which I need hardly tell you, I reckon among good qualities, and am pleasantly surprised to find how easily I can assume some shadow of them myself. All the same it is a wicked life: it saps the springs of one's earnestness and melts high purposes like butter: it is a life of sipping and chasing, and spares little room for brooding and building . . . Even with women I adore I find it hard not to be restless and self-conscious and superficial in the glare and rattle of these great suffocating brilliant parties – a dizzy pandemonium of piercing voices and prying eyes; really to enjoy the things ultimately worth enjoying one must have the leisure of the country with sunny spaces of forest and the ease of quiet stars . . .

In spite of Aubrey's passion for 'noise, novelty and nonsense' he never really enjoyed society life. However, in these early days he liked to think that he, too, would enjoy the glittering scene. He replied to Raymond's letter:

> I know I should have a very good time in London if I went there for the season, I love the talk and noise and the beauty of the people not to mention more material things in the way of fizz and caviar etc. But the trouble with me is that I like people too much. I don't want to be the fickle gay Lothario of the society novel, but if I meet a pretty girl it is as hard for me not to tell her how pretty I think her as it is for me to refrain from shouting when I see a beautiful view and am feeling well. Of course the personal idea is a weed of such fearful growth in every body, and the sexual spell so interwoven in our lives, that they don't always take this as it is meant. A girl I find refuses to be looked upon as a picture in a gallery . . . I dislike the precipice one always seems to be living upon when one goes into society.

Aubrey, also, was not altogether happy about Raymond's abandonment to society's pleasures. He wrote, 'I hope you are not going in too
much for society. You are sure to be spoilt ultimately if you do. Take the
advice which dear old Raper [Master of Trinity] gave me with regard to
stealing kitchen clocks, and leave that to meaner men.'

However, it was not society as such that concerned Aubrey and
Raymond but more the perplexities of fitting women into their lives. In
a more serious letter Raymond explained to Aubrey his views on the
matter:

There are several differences which make life with women a more difficult
and anxious task than life with men: it is partly that their minds work quicker
than ours and on different lines, and there is the effort of accommodating
oneself to their methods and their pace which causes a kind of intellectual
stitch: and partly the sexual impetus which makes one want to please a
woman more than one normally wants to please a man so that one's desire
outruns one's ability (which is an unfamiliar situation for some of us): and
partly also that the opportunities of pleasing are fewer owing to the conditions of social life: and therefore the effort is less diffused and more intense in
the slender moments into which it has usually to be condensed . . . Men see
enough of one another to take a good deal on trust; quite as we have all seen
enough of the world to believe that a chair goes on existing in the empty room
after we have left . . . but women see men so little and at such long intervals
that their faith in the existence of the non apparent is necessarily a weak one
. . . In the hectic communion of the dining table, in the scanty and precarious
solitudes of a house party one must express the pith of a month's speculation,
the heat of a month's emotions; and if it so happens that one's brain is torpid
or one's sensibility for the moment blunt, the fleeting crisis has come and gone
and left one discomforted and discredited like a runner whose ear has missed
the pistol, with one opportunity irrevocably gone and a heavy mortgage upon
the next . . . And it is this effort always to sparkle and always to glow which
brings home to one the latent inadequacy of one's vital and mental furniture.

The letter is twelve pages long and ends with an unnecessary apology.
'Poor Aubrey! I have written you a great dull essay.' Aubrey himself was
far too confused to write anything comparable; also his life and circumstances were different; but all Englishmen of his age and class, after an
exclusively male education, found themselves facing the same difficulties. The society girls to whom they addressed themselves were sheltered
behind the social conventions of the time, which promoted a great
formality, a veneration for beauty, a respect for purity and an exaggerated emphasis on wit and verbal repartee. Girls were goddesses, placed
on pedestals, to whom homage was paid in poetry and elaborate compliments. These compliments, or 'dewdrops', were cherished, collected and

exchanged by the recipients. Married women were less constrained; many had courts of young admirers whom they encouraged and petted. Aubrey, however, at this stage in his life, did not like married women. He wrote to Raymond, 'I never want to see any married women again, except those that are virgins in heart', and 'I don't like women, only girls.' Months later he was still of the same mind; he wrote, 'I wish it was a world of boys and girls . . . It seems rather futile to waste so much time learning the tricks that make up the thing we call a gentleman, only to learn that they are tricks in the end, though much finer of course than those of a performing poodle.'

Aubrey was ill-equipped to play society's complicated games. He was impulsive and easily carried away. 'Very often', he wrote to Raymond,

> I don't see girls for a considerable period, and then when I do, in a ball room perhaps, after champagne, with the chandeliers and the light above, it goes to my head and catches me by the throat. Excuse mixed metaphors. All the poetry I have ever known comes to me, and I feel all the music I have ever liked in my heart or veins or brain, I am not analyst enough to know or care, only I know what thinking faculties I have seem to produce a fountain, simply something rises up and beyond me. It's nonsense, it's incoherent but there it is. I want to kiss the particular pretty girl with whom I am . . .

Needless to say, Aubrey's attentions were often misinterpreted. 'Girls are always saying to me why are you in love with me or why were you? And I generally answer it is not with you at all, only a little bit of myself that I see reflected in you, or which you possess in a more developed degree than I do.' Such explanations can hardly have been well received. Nor would the objects of his admiration have been flattered by his plaintive cry, 'I don't see why you can't treat them as a sacrament and an amusement at one and the same time.'

However, to Aubrey, girls were only a minor preoccupation. His life was full. He stayed about two months in Africa with Elsie. While they were there the long-expected Russo-Japanese war broke out. Aubrey wanted to go to Tokyo as a war correspondent or as military attaché to the Japanese Army but neither hope was fulfilled. Raymond wrote, 'If you had gone it is quite certain that you would have been shot; no one I like ever goes to war without being either killed or wounded; and for you even peace is quite dangerous enough.'

After Egypt, Elsie and Aubrey moved on to visit Esmé Howard, who was now Consul-General in Crete. Aubrey, after the disappointment of his Japanese hopes, had applied for the post of honorary attaché in Constantinople. Sir Thomas Sanderson of the Foreign Office wrote to Sir Nicholas O'Conor, the Ambassador in Turkey, recommending Aubrey:

'The MacDonalds liked him very much. He is extremely original, and very clever . . . He was a feather-brained creature as a boy, but has now steadied down, though he is still to me a constant source of amusement, as I think he would be to you.' Sir Nicholas evidently liked this description and agreed to have Aubrey, but stipulated no date for his arrival. Aubrey decided to take advantage of this imprecision by travelling in the Balkans. His mother came with him as far as Athens, where she took ship for Italy.

Athens did not impress Aubrey. Raymond Asquith rebuked him in a letter, 'I'm afraid you will never make a Phil-Hellene, Aubrey. If only you had been taught Greek how you would have loved it: it was just what you needed to make you a great poet, to steady the oscillations of your vagrant fancy and limit the licence of your intemperate vocabulary.'

From Athens Aubrey made his way to Salonika, in Turkish-ruled Macedonia. Macedonia in those days, and indeed for many years to come, was a centre of unrest in the Ottoman Empire. There were Greeks, Armenians, Turks, Bulgars, Albanians, Slavs, Vlachs, Kurds, Serbs and Jews, all seething in various discontents; race fought against race, Christians fought against Moslems, and the Turks spasmodically suppressed the tumults with great harshness. The year before Aubrey's arrival, there had been an unusually fierce rising which had been crushed with such cruelty that the conscience of the European powers was aroused. They set up an international gendarmerie to keep the peace and protect the minorities.

Salonika itself was a peaceful, prosperous city that had grown fat and sleek on the tribulations of others. The majority of the inhabitants were Jews, who had always enjoyed a greater liberty under the Ottomans than any other subject race. A great number of them were nominal Moslems, known as Dunmes (converts). Many of them were also freemasons. These last were the real parents of the coming revolution of the Young Turks and Salonika was the cradle of the movement. But in March 1904 only the mutterings of unrest could be heard.

In Salonika Aubrey met a man who was to share many of his adventures and have no little influence on his life. This was a wild Albanian highlander named Kiazim.* Aubrey engaged him as his bodyguard and servant. Kiazim came of good family and was a 'bey' in Albania, but because he had killed a man in a blood feud he had been forced to leave his native land by unsympathetic Turkish authorities. He spoke only Turkish and Albanian and as Aubrey as yet spoke neither they had to converse through interpreters or by sign language. Kiazim had never been in service before. When Aubrey asked him to enter his employ

Kiazim neither hesitated before accepting nor enquired about his wages, but, in the manner of a disciple in the New Testament, forsook all and followed. Back at his hotel Aubrey found a waiter to interpret and to explain to Kiazim his duties. Kiazim watched the waiter with brilliant, restless eyes and then spoke in his deep rumbling voice. 'He asks you,' said the waiter, 'if he forgets anything or fails in his duty to stab him.' Kiazim meant what he said. Physical retribution was part of his creed. Kiazim was continually beating, and sometimes nearly killing, strangers whose only fault had been to jostle his master in the street. He was a man of great loyalty and presence but also of rough manners and natural violence. That night, little knowing how important a part Kiazim was to play in his life, Aubrey wrote to his mother: 'I've got a servant. I can't remember his name; most attractive, though he is dressed like a gamekeeper now. He is a good farmer too and so might come in useful at Pixton.' Kiazim did not remain dressed like a game-keeper for long. Instead he donned national dress, a spotless fustanella with jewelled pistol and dagger in his scarlet sash. He viewed Aubrey's evening attire first with bewilderment and then with contempt when he realised that Aubrey's revolver had no place in it.

With Kiazim, Aubrey explored Macedonia on horseback, staying first at Monastir and then Perlape. The country was most unsafe; they travelled with a mounted Turkish escort. Aubrey wrote to his mother, 'no country that I have been has interested me so much.' From Perlape they went on to Uskub where Aubrey managed to give his escort the slip. He was almost immediately arrested by a Turkish patrol and only escaped after some difficulty.

Back in Salonika a message was waiting, with instructions to report to Constantinople. Aubrey was reluctant to abandon his travels. He took a very indirect route by way of Koniah, deep in Anatolia. There Aubrey lingered, making friends with a group of distinguished Turkish exiles who lived quietly in banishment. Among them was Riza Tewfik Bey, poet and philosopher, who talked, wild-eyed, of Stuart Mill and Spencer; after the revolution in 1908 he was to come to Constantinople as a deputy.

On the journey from Koniah, Aubrey fell in with a troupe of Armenian actors and acrobats. One of them, on finding out that Aubrey was bound for the British Embassy, asked him to persuade the Ambassador to take up his case. The Armenian had fallen in love with a cousin within the prohibited degrees of consanguinity. Aubrey explained that it was impossible for the Ambassador to intervene and that there was nothing he could do. 'Let him write to the Patriarch', answered the Armenian, 'let him write constantly.' Some months later an anonymous gift of a Damascus sword arrived for Aubrey at the Embassy. With difficulty he traced it to the Armenian, now living happily married to his cousin. Aubrey explained that he could not claim responsibility for this satisfactory consummation. The Armenian's answer was to present him with another Damascus sword.

Aubrey arrived in Constantinople in mid-April. He had lost some weight. In some places the only available food had been yoghurt and dried bread. Politically, Aubrey's journey had nourished his anti-Turkish prejudices. In Crete he had embraced the nationalist cause. In Macedonia he had met the intimidated Christian minorities and heard ghastly tales of massacre and atrocity. At the same time he found that his personal inclination was towards the Turk. In a letter to his mother he compared unfavourably 'the cringing, unattractive Christians' with 'the genial, polished Turk', but he was disgusted with the evidence on every side of the cruelty and injustice of Ottoman rule and he felt a kinship with the despised Christians.

The Great Powers of the day had brought considerable pressure on the Sultan to improve the lot of the Christians and in Macedonia the European-officered gendarmerie performed a commendable task in protecting the subject races. The Powers, however, had to deal with a Sultan of great cunning, obstinacy and deviousness. Abdul Hamid II, better known as Abdul Hamid the Damned, had succeeded to the Ottoman throne in 1876. Two years later, at the Congress of Berlin, the consequence of Turkey's defeat at the hands of Russia, he had watched the Powers scrambling for his territories. Turkey lost nominal suzerainty over Rumania, Serbia and Montenegro. Bulgaria was created a principality and Eastern Roumelia an autonomous Turkish province. Bosnia and Herzegovina were handed over to Austrian administration. Greece gained some territory in Thessaly and Epirus. Russia took Kars and Batum, and the administration of Cyprus was given to England. Abdul Hamid deeply resented these provisions and resolved that the remaining Ottoman Empire should be preserved intact; with the single exception of Crete, he succeeded. Abdul Hamid revoked the constitution and thereafter ruled mainly by terror. The Sultan's great personal cowardice promoted, and fed upon, an effective and ruthless spy system. Abdul Hamid feared his own shadow. Secret reports of assassination plots stoked his fear. He dreaded poisoning and all his food was tasted in front of him before he would eat. His counsellors were virtual prisoners. The Sultan, feared and hated, sat in the centre of this poisonous web of intrigue and terror, reading over and over again the books of Conan Doyle (perhaps Abdul Hamid's only endearing quality was his passion for Sherlock Holmes, all of whose adventures were translated into

Turkish on his express order) or working at intricate marquetry in his carpentry work room.

Hatred for the Sultan was the only unifying factor in Constantinople in 1904; otherwise it was a splintered and decadent world. The Christian communities were divided amongst themselves and all were divided from the Turks. It was dangerous for Turks to be seen talking to a foreigner and so they mostly kept to themselves. The Greeks, Armenians and other Levantines mixed little outside their own communities, with the exception of the very rich merchants and bankers. The English colony was large and flourishing and less touched by the insidious decay of the capital than other groups.

The corps diplomatique, too, was much divided. National jealousies and intrigues made the Embassies deeply suspicious of one another. Yet despite – indeed perhaps because of – the general atmosphere of rot and corruption, plot and counter-plot, treachery and terror, Aubrey enjoyed himself. He was fortunate in his Ambassador. Sir Nicholas O'Conor was an enlightened Irish landlord, with a deep knowledge of the Ottoman Empire. His gifts were never fully appreciated by the English government and his advice was often foolishly disregarded. He had been Ambassador in Constantinople for six years when Aubrey joined the Embassy in 1904, and died in office four years later, just four months before the collapse of the despotism with which he had struggled for ten years. Sir Nicholas spoke no Eastern languages but he encouraged his staff to acquire as many as possible. The standard at the Embassy was high. Aubrey took lessons in Turkish, Arabic and Greek. Sir Nicholas was indulgent to youthful high spirits and was more amused than cross about Aubrey's misadventures. On one occasion Aubrey, wishing to be first to greet a beautiful girl arriving for dinner, jumped out of a first floor window in Therapia. A passing taxi was partly demolished. Aubrey broke his ankle and was unable to attend Chancery for some days but Sir Nicholas delighted in the incident. A brawl in a hashish den in Galata involving Aubrey and several other young members of the Embassy also met with his sympathetic interest. He tried to give his honorary attachés interesting tasks. Aubrey's first job was to keep the chronicle known as the Butcher's Book of Macedonia. In general, however, Aubrey found that the work in Chancery, as in Japan, was boring and mechanical. Because of his supposed proficiency with the typewriter he was sometimes asked to type despatches. One of his efforts was returned to Constantinople by the Foreign Office as a model of everything a despatch ought not to be. It was written to Lord Lansdowne and began 'My Dorl'.

The first months in Constantinople were made jollier for Aubrey by the arrival of his sister Margaret. She came out at the end of April and stayed until the end of June. Margaret had been from nursery days Aubrey's favourite among his half-sisters. She had neither Winifred's intellectual gifts nor Vera's wayward charm, but she was stalwart, loyal, loving, kind and sensible. She thoroughly enjoyed her stay. She went sight-seeing with Aubrey and Sir Edwin Pears and was conducted through the bazaars by Kiazim, who walked two paces ahead to clear her progress. She went to parties and picnics with Aubrey and seemed heart-whole and fancy-free. Aubrey was therefore more than a little surprised when she wrote to him on the day following her return to England with the news that she had become engaged to George Duckworth.

George Duckworth was no stranger to the family circle. First introduced to the family by Esmé Howard, he had soon become a favourite of Elsie's. He was a man of few brains but of a happy disposition, good-looking and well intentioned. Aubrey had never shared Elsie's predilection for his company. George Duckworth's main misfortune in life was that he was the half-brother of Virginia Stephen (Woolf) whose brilliant and venomous pen has ridiculed him for posterity. He himself was devoted to his two half-sisters Virginia Woolf and Vanessa Bell. The feeling was not reciprocated. Virginia claimed many times, in print and conversation, that George's clumsy sexual fondling in her early womanhood had led to her subsequent frigidity and that George's bungling social ambitions had led to her dislike of fashionable society.

Margaret also was aware of George's faults. She hoped that her marriage would not weaken her ties with Aubrey. But inevitably it did. Aubrey gradually saw less of Margaret and drew closer to his sister Vera, with whom he had squabbled in childhood. Vera, fey, child-like, always governed by a series of charitable enthusiasms, was younger and prettier than Margaret. She was popular with Aubrey's friends and in his absence entertained them in her house in London. She wrote to Aubrey, 'the old Oxford lot seem to be living in the house.' The most assiduous caller was Reginald Farrer, who fancied himself a little in love with her. Vera preferred Raymond Asquith and fancied herself a little in love with him. Of Reginald she wrote, 'You know my opinion of Reginald – he is a cad, but an amusing one', but added 'I can't have him here every day.'

Margaret's wedding was fixed for September and Aubrey was bidden to return. The summons came as a blow because he had planned to travel that month in Macedonia with his cousin Bron and Raymond Asquith. Raymond wrote, 'It is thoughtless of your sister to be married on the eighth of September – a most unsuitable date. Tell them they must be married earlier or later or not at all. Bron is very much annoyed about it and so am I.'

After the wedding Aubrey returned to Constantinople. However, he had hardly arrived before he set off again. The genial Persian Ambassador, Mirza Riza Khan, who was famous for having written a poem to peace in thirty-two different languages at the Hague Conference, had become a friend. He invited Aubrey to stay at Borjum in the Russian Caucasus, where he had a magnificent house. After lingering a few days in Tiflis, Aubrey arrived at Borjum to find that the Ambassador had rented a beautiful jewelled house nearby for Aubrey's exclusive use. But his enjoyment of these comfortable arrangements had to be cut short. Politically, the visit proved ill-timed. The Russo-Japanese war, still raging, caused the Russian authorities to be deeply suspicious of British travellers. England was in formal alliance with Japan and there were rumours that she was about to enter the war on the Japanese side. The governor of the Caucasus, Prince Woronzoff-Dashkoff, instituted enquiries about the English visitor and his magnificent servant. Kiazim, now dressed in his best national finery (a great red flat fez with a mane of black silk, tight black and white Gheg breeches and leggings, a coat and waistcoat made almost entirely of gold thread, the whole decked out with numerous revolvers and daggers), attracted a great deal of attention.

Aubrey's host sent for him and, with much wringing of hands about the sacred duties of hospitality, explained that it was beyond his power to protect him; the Russians believed him to be a military attaché and proposed to incarcerate him for the duration of the war; he suggested Aubrey leave for Batoum where there was a British consul. After lunch Aubrey returned to his separate house, followed by a troop of Cossack soldiers. He found Kiazim in a rage. In Aubrey's absence two men had entered the house and searched it, and Kiazim, catching them red-handed, had used violence on them. All day the Cossack troop remained outside the house. That night Aubrey went to the station accompanied by the Persian military attaché. At the station the Persian said, 'Do you see those two officers with their Cossacks?' 'I have seen very little else all day,' Aubrey replied. 'Well', said the Persian 'they are going to arrest you. Pray accept it calmly. Ils sont tellement brutaux.'

Aubrey called Kiazim, gave him some money and told him to make his way to the British Consul at Batoum and explain what had happened. Kiazim flatly refused, 'I have eaten your salt. I am not going to return and be asked "Where is your master?" This matter touches my honour. My life is yours.'

However, the sacrifice was not necessary. They boarded the train unmolested. Next morning Aubrey discovered his luggage had been searched, but only his revolver taken. At Batoum they took ship for Constantinople.

By Christmas Aubrey and Kiazim were back in England. Kiazim caused a sensation, and not only in the servants' hall at Pixton where he made many friends. On the first shooting day at Pixton after their arrival, Aubrey, who had omitted to explain to his servant how shoots worked, sent Kiazim to escort a late arrival to his stand. While they were on their way the first drive began. There was a volley of fire. Kiazim, suspecting an ambush, threw the bewildered guest to the ground and lay protectively on top of him, with a drawn revolver in one hand and a dagger in his teeth. On the next shooting day Aubrey, more cautiously, kept Kiazim by his side, loading, but was discomforted then to find him decapitating the fallen birds with a huge dagger. Kiazim, after a lifetime of danger and turbulence, regarded his sojourn in safe, tame England as the greatest adventure of all. On his return to Turkey he saw himself as a man of importance and expected great respect, 'I, who have been to England', he used to bellow at the less privileged.

Before Aubrey left England again in January 1905 he was approached by a Colonel to join him on a projected journey to the Hejaz in Arabia to make strategic notes on the railway. Aubrey was disappointed at having to refuse but he felt he must return to Constantinople as Sir Nicholas O'Conor was growing impatient of his long absences. Aubrey was, however, comforted by the thought of a journey to Sana'a in the Yemen in the autumn, which he had arranged with Leland Buxton whom he had met by chance in the lobby of the House of Commons.

Travelling out by the Orient Express, Aubrey found his journey interrupted at Budapest. There a minor insurrection was in progress and the noise of the firing in the streets was more than he could resist. He and Kiazim disembarked. The insurrection proved footling but meanwhile travelling conditions deteriorated. Aubrey wrote to his mother from Uskub:

All my plans have undergone a change. Travelling here is most impracticable. Kiazim and I have had three bad bothers in 24 hours. In the first I hit a man almost in my sleep so that it ought not really to have counted . . . Kiazim has become very much more fastidious. He went to look at a hotel for me at this place with another Albanian. I asked him if it was clean. No, he said, but the other one said it was all right. Kiazim shouted 'No, I have been in London' . . . I regret to say that I found out that my servitor is much 'wanted' where he is known . . .

In February, when Aubrey arrived in Constantinople, he found the season in full swing and a displeased Ambassador. Sir Nicholas O'Conor was a tolerant chief but he thought the time had come for Aubrey to do some work. He forbade further travel and told him to prepare a memorandum on Macedonia. Aubrey was gloomy about Macedonian prospects. He wrote to his mother: 'Anything that weakens the Sultan's rule produces only worse anarchy, and it can only be strengthened by terrorism. It is only from a distance that it is all opera bouffe – it is grim and tragic enough on the spot.'

At the same time his attitude towards Turkey and the Turks was changing. The year before he had written to Raymond Asquith, 'Don't ever be a Turko-phil', and to his mother, 'I'm getting more anti-Turkish every day, though I like the Turks themselves immensely'. Now, though he wrote to Bron saying 'I want to see this swinish government knocked out', he was becoming no longer anti-Turkish but only anti-Sultan. His personal liking for the people and his growing knowledge of the Ottoman Empire began to change his political judgment. In the days that he kept the Butcher's Book of Macedonia he had been surprised to find that many of the worst atrocities were committed by the Christians upon their own kind. More Bulgars were slaughtered by Greeks than by Turks during Aubrey's book-keeping days. As he now delved deeper into the mire of Macedonian politics he found his distaste for the cringing, bloodthirsty Christians growing and his abhorrence for the genial, if ferocious, Turks decreasing.

This gradual move towards greater sympathy with the Turks was hastened by some new friendships. Through Kiazim Aubrey had been brought in touch with the more ruffianly element of Turkish life; and he found it to his liking. Now a new friendship with Damad Ferid Pasha brought him in touch with a more polished circle. Damad Ferid was the brother-in-law of the Sultan, Abdul Hamid, and was thus able to entertain foreigners with impunity. Aubrey dined often at his palace at Balta Liman and sometimes stayed the night. Damad Ferid was a civilised and thoughtful man, 'well read,' wrote Aubrey to his mother, 'in Victor Hugo, Shakespeare and Antony Hope', whose unheroic role in the eventual downfall of the Osmanli dynasty has earned him the undeserved contempt of Turkish historians. Aubrey never despised him and the two became fast and loyal friends. They always conversed and corresponded in French although Aubrey's Turkish was by now fluent.

Aubrey formed another life long friendship at the Balta Liman palace. This friend, Rifat Bey, was unusual among Turks of that time in that he spoke and even wrote English. Flowery epistles in improbable phraseology came regularly from Rifat until the day Aubrey died. Both Damad Ferid and Rifat talked politics openly and fearlessly. There was everywhere a sense of foreboding. No one knew how, where or when the crash would come but all were sure that come it would.

Meanwhile, as Aubrey became more immersed in Turkish politics and life (he had taken up wrestling again but found the Turks slow and heavy compared with the Japanese and complained 'they don't fall down out of politeness'), Elsie's thoughts were straying in other directions. She was wintering in France and Germany with Mervyn, who having got his first was now brushing up his languages for the Foreign Office exam. She wrote to Aubrey in March proposing that he should come home and study law, while waiting for a suitable seat in Parliament to become vacant. Aubrey was not tempted by the law. He was enjoying Constantinople and was busy planning a journey in Syria where he hoped his mother would join him. However, he replied accommodatingly, 'Of course, my dear, anything you think best. I know it's never a subject at which I shall be good. But doesn't it take years and years? Ever since I've known Belloc, seven years I suppose, he seems to have been reading for the bar.'

The Ambassador was not accommodating about Aubrey's Syrian plans. Aubrey agreed to stay on in Constantinople until after the Persian Festival. The Persian Festival took place on the anniversary of the martyrdom of Hussein, son-in-law of the Prophet, at Kerbela in Southern Iraq and remains the great day of the Shi'ite Moslems. Aubrey wrote a description to his mother:

As the dusk falls they begin their procession, with their green flags waving and scimitars showing pale. Then when night falls they come in, raving in chorus 'Hussain and Hasan', with great torches and horses clothed in white, with pigeons on them. When the frenzy has reached a certain point they begin cutting themselves with their huge Persian swords that are as sharp as razors. I took the glasses Bron gave me and focussed on one man, just under a torch. It was rather horrible, as the glasses seemed to bring the face so close, that one felt as if it was almost inside one's head. The eyes and mouth looked hypnotic; the eyes absolutely fixed and the mouth only sobbing mechanically. Then he struck himself with his sword on the head and his face was blotted out, as he became red from head to foot. After a time, men go behind them and interpose sticks between the heads of the fanatics and their swords. The horses and the doves are covered with blood, and the whole place smells of it. It was rather unpleasant going out as we got caught in the passage by the crowd and jambed against these bloodstained men. They were carrying a good many out, one looked to me dead. It is very interesting but I don't think I want to see it more than once.

Aubrey did not leave Constantinople after the Persian Festival because Elsie wrote cancelling the Syrian expedition on grounds of expense. Periodically Elsie would indulge in bouts of economy. She was not herself an extravagant woman. She dressed unfashionably and even wore darned gloves. Her extravagances were all charitable. She founded village schools and technical training centres where the villagers were taught how to cobble their shoes or weave blankets for the winter. At the same time her manner of living, though modest and unsmart, was expensive. She maintained three large houses, Pixton, Teversal and Portofino, and a London house. Management was one of her gifts. She was never careless or slapdash. She held in her tidy mind, and teeming notebooks, accounts of all her financial affairs. When, as at this moment, she found the outlook unsatisfactory, she took precautionary measures and instituted systematic economies. The Syrian expedition was a luxury which could if necessary be done without.

Aubrey himself was not so much extravagant as careless about money. Although he lived cheaply, his money was always running out and unlike Elsie, he never knew where or why it had gone. He found the bazaars of Constantinople irresistible, and he fed daily various packs of street dogs. But his lodging cost practically nothing. Kiazim had found a large room fifty feet long for Aubrey and a small room for himself in a hotel which provided them both with breakfast, all for the price of six francs a day. Later it emerged that the hotel was a roulette den and the proprietor had let the rooms for this derisory sum in the hope that a resident official from the British Embassy would afford him protection from the police. Aubrey returning late one night from a dance found the hotel cordoned off and himself under arrest. He was released but his cheap lodgings were forfeit.

Travel, on the other hand, was expensive. In the remote corners of the Ottoman Empire to which Aubrey was addicted it was often necessary to hire not only guides but also military escorts. Aubrey gave up his Syrian plans sorrowfully, but concurred in Elsie's alternative proposal that they should meet in Crete and travel back to England together by way of Greece, Montenegro and Portofino.

There remained the problem of the future. The study of law had few attractions, while Constantinople still had many. On the other hand Aubrey was unenthusiastic about diplomacy as a career. He wrote to Bron: 'I am not sure it is a life I should always care to go on with. At most posts the ministers are simply glorified telegraph clerks and it is a service which has made an idol of that filthy thing the status quo.' However the choice was not entirely in Aubrey's hands. Elsie had decided that there was little to be gained in staying longer in Turkey. She wanted Aubrey in England. Aubrey was reluctant to resign his post. He discussed the matter with the Ambassador and reported to his mother: 'He [Sir Nicholas] has made what seems to be a good suggestion if I understand it, only one never knows where one is. If I like I can go back to England

and have this place simply as a sinecure. He says it would probably do one good if one was working for Parliament to be attaché at this place, like having initials after one's name. Well for a little I don't see how that can hurt.' So ended Aubrey's diplomatic career. Henceforth his connection with the Embassy was informal and loose. For five more years Aubrey still had a desk in Chancery and still wrote the occasional memorandum or report. But though his Embassy connection weakened with the years, his ties with Turkey grew in strength.

In May 1905, a month after his twenty-fifth birthday, Aubrey left Constantinople to join his mother in Crete. Leaving Kiazim behind was the greatest wrench. He wrote to Elsie the day before he left, 'I shall never see his like again as a servant.' He may not have seen his like, but he was to see a great deal more of Kiazim.

4

Arabian Journey

Aubrey found life in England agreeable but not wholly satisfying. The glittering London gatherings, the long country-house parties and the perpetual whirl of family and friends soon began to pall. The match-making and breaking, the strict conventions of social intercourse, the absence of the element of surprise and the grave and almost intellectual regard for games and gossip contrasted ill with the life of rough travel, unexpected encounters and eastern intrigue that he had known in the Ottoman Empire. England seemed tame and trivial. Aubrey was impatient to be away. The abundant lovingness of his family, though a strength and joy, was also a restraint and reproach. He knew that his mother longed for him to settle down. He had been almost continuously abroad since leaving Oxford three years before. He was now twenty-five, an age for responsibility.

Elsie, however, for all her stern sense of purpose and duty, could never deny Aubrey anything he really wanted. She agreed that before he seriously set about finding a constituency and entering Parliament he should go on one last long travel. The idle plan, made with Leland Buxton the year before, to try and reach San'aa, was resurrected and ratified.

Various papers and periodicals were approached. Aubrey optimistic-ally hoped to finance his journey with journalism. *Blackwood's*, the *Morning Post* and the *Daily Mail* showed interest. Aubrey's articles were unsigned, for which he was rebuked by Reginald Farrer who wrote:

damn your pusillanimous undeceptive and possibly vulgar anonymity, — damn it, and damn it. If you are going to write things unworthy of your name, better not write at all. Also, it deceives no one. Also it helps to perpetuate the old superstition that literature is a cad's trade, in which no gentleman must take any part, unless he shields his own name from the horrid contamination, by adopting anonymity or pseudonymity. Mary Cholmondeley's relations told her they would die if they saw their name on a book: and that quintessen-tial snobbishness is not yet dead: and men like ourselves can help to kill it by shewing a finer appreciation of things.

Aubrey was unrepentant and continued then and later to write either under a psuedonym or anonymously.

Leaving his mother in Paris, Aubrey travelled out to Egypt. There he was met by Leland Buxton. Few were sanguine about the young men's chances of reaching San'aa. Everyone to whom they spoke offered only discouragement; and indeed it did seem a hopeless quest. The Yemen, which at the best of times was an inaccessible and remote territory of the Ottoman Empire, was at the time of Aubrey's journey in a state of war. The year before had seen a serious revolt. San'aa was besieged for four months by rebel Yemenis. The Turkish garrison inside the town had been reduced by famine from 11,000 to 2,000 men. In April 1905 the town had been relieved. By October the war of reconquest was finished and its septuagenarian victor, General Ahmed Feizi Pasha, who had marched across Arabia from Baghdad in order to subdue the Yemen by a mixture of diplomacy and military leadership, remained in charge.

Little news of the war in the Yemen had reached Europe. The Sublime Porte had done its effective utmost to keep the events of the war secret. There seemed little likelihood that the authorities would allow two stray young Englishmen to roam through the devastated land. Nevertheless, undeterred by the advice of their elders, Aubrey and Leland Buxton set sail from Suez. They were seen off by the Governor, an affectionate and talkative man who had only two words of English, 'Damn fool', which he used often and inappropriately. The boat was filled with pilgrims from every corner of the Islamic world on their way to Mecca. In Jeddah everyone disembarked. Aubrey had a letter of introduction to the British Consul from FitzMaurice, the dragoman at Constantinople. FitzMaurice had warned Aubrey that the Consul 'was peculiar and his wife more so'. Although Aubrey and Buxton stayed the night with him they never saw his wife, who sent a message through her husband that she had a swollen face. Apparently she always had a swollen face when visitors came to the house.

After Jeddah the pilgrim passengers departed, leaving Buxton and Aubrey alone on the boat as it slowly steamed down the Red Sea. At Hodeidah they too disembarked. The chief spectacle of the town was an old man who had been chained to the ground on the same spot for forty years. Now bereft of his wits, he was considered a saint. A few planks had been erected between him and the sun. No one could remember any more the crime that he had committed to earn this punishment. He steadfastly refused to be released. The townspeople brought him well cooked meats and other offerings. Aubrey saw his daughter-in-law and other relations eating these up with relish.

At Hodeidah there was trouble at the customs over Aubrey's

typewriter, swiftly followed by trouble from the authorities over the
projected journey. Aubrey and Buxton called on the Mutesarrif, Hifzi
Pasha. To allay suspicion they made themselves out to be rich and stupid
sportsmen on their way to India to shoot big game. 'Nous allons faire la
chasse aux tigres' Aubrey explained. Buxton, silent to this point, added
to complete the picture 'et lions' whereupon the Mutesarrif, a courteous,
sleepy, benign old Turk, woke as from a dream and said sharply that there
were no lions in India. There followed a long discussion in Turkish
between the Mutesarrif and his second-in-command, who was convinced
that the travellers were really British army officers come to spy and sow
dissent among the Arabs. Aubrey, who could follow all their conversation, had to sit placid and unprotesting playing his part of the rich,
stupid sportsman. To lend conviction to his performance he interrupted
to ask which was the best hotel in San'aa. The Turks with difficulty
restrained their mirth at this astonishing enquiry.

The interview ended inconclusively. Although the Mutesarrif, out of
politeness and goodwill, did not wish to return a definite 'no' to their
request, Buxton and Aubrey left despondent. That evening, in a coffee
shop, a Greek approached Aubrey in a conspiratorial manner. He
promised to help and introduced them to a muleteer. They made swift
arrangements. A message was sent to the Mutesarrif that their preparations were complete and they were ready to start the next morning. The
next morning dawned on two intrepid Englishmen, with their medicine
chests, provisions, revolvers and all accoutrements of travel, but no
Greek, no muleteer, no mules, no escort, only the eternal heat.

For three hours they waited in the hot sun and then dejectedly trudged
to the Mutesarrif's residence. He would not see them. The next day
Aubrey had another interview with the Mutesarrif, who promised in
broken French that they should depart within twenty-four hours. Four
days later they were still in Hodeidah. The muleteer was ready and
waiting but the escort was inadequate and insubordinate. It would
neither leave nor permit the travellers to leave without it.

The heat and the repeated disappointments proved too much for
Aubrey's temper. He went to see the Mutesarrif in a rage. Abandoning
all pretence, he broke into furious and voluble Turkish. 'You gave us
your word,' said Aubrey. 'Yes,' said the Mutesarrif, 'I gave your exalted
presence my word, but now we take it back again.' It seemed the end.
Yet the Mutesarrif had been taken aback by Aubrey's sudden flood of
Turkish and in fact it was the beginning of a thaw. The interview, which
had begun without honorifics, ended amicably. They drank coffee and
smoked. The next day Aubrey called again. This time, according to
Aubrey's diary, 'we both soaped each other. I told him I was descended

from Charlemagne. One becomes quite shameless.' After an hour Aubrey took his leave. The Mutesarrif had again promised that they should depart next day. 'Go quickly and quickly come again,' he said. 'You must not keep those tigers waiting. We have recommended you to God.'

This time the Mutesarrif was as good as his word. The next morning an escort of a hundred and fifty men was waiting. For forty hours they marched and rode, changing mounts and stopping only for three hours' sleep. Aubrey walked and rode alternately. It was on this march that his love and admiration for the Turkish race blossomed. Hitherto his dislike of the Ottoman regime had dominated his feelings for the Turks. But now his admiration for his companions, far from their homeland, stolid and sturdy in their suffering, generous in their poverty, and comradely to the stranger, won him to their cause, and he became henceforth their champion and defender. Leland Buxton who had started the journey brimming with anti-Turkish prejudice from his experiences in Bulgaria, also found his attitudes altered. These Turkish soldiers, although legally absolved from fasting (it was then the month of Ramadan) did not avail themselves of this dispensation and neither smoked nor ate nor drank until the sun set. And even when that hour arrived, before they broke their fast, they offered Aubrey and Buxton their brackish water and unleavened bread and meagre olives. Once when Aubrey's mule went lame he asked that it should be sent back with a soldier who was not fit to march. The wizened sergeant major replied, 'Such talk is not for the Yemen. Here men and animals, sound or lame, go on because they must. What is thy beast? A mule. What is that man? A private soldier. Mount, Lord. Hurry, you rascals.'

Once free of the hot, low-lying, fever-infested plain, and into the green mountains covered with flowers, and intersected with fertile valleys and streams, the frenzied haste of the journey was abandoned by common consent. Travellers and soldiers dawdled. Through Obel, Hedjilek Atara, Menakha, Beht-i-Mehti, Ijiz, Betli-Ajiz, Menfaak, Suk el Hamis, they passed amidst devastation and poverty. Once they came across a circle of skeletons of men who had died fighting; flowers were growing out of the eyes and mouths of the skulls. Everywhere there was painful evidence of the war, deserted villages, skeletons and ravaged buildings. In Menakha they were told that two thousand Jews had died in the famine. In village after village dogs and children fought over scraps of decaying food.

On November 13th, after six days on the march, they reached San'aa. It was a tragic city. Before the siege the inhabitants had numbered about seventy thousand; now the population was a mere twenty thousand.

Nine thousand Ottoman troops had died of starvation. Among the civilians the large Jewish community had suffered most. Aubrey wrote, 'The famine had fallen like a hammer on the Jews. It was visible in their faces and in their homes.' Of the thirty-two synagogues of San'aa only four remained open. About a quarter of the community survived but in wretched condition. Aubrey had to abandon another prejudice. He knew the rich, sleek Jews of English society and its fringes and he knew the prosperous and grasping merchants and usurers of Europe and the Near East. He liked neither. But in San'aa he met quite another sort of Jew and his heart was melted.

Aubrey and Buxton walked round, dazed, distributing charity, and being followed by a crowd 'greater than even the Pied Piper drew after him'. Aubrey wrote, 'The houses are tall and old. They are embroidered with white stucco, and ornamented with great doors of wrought iron, heavily clamped. The windows are circular and paned with thin slabs of pure alabaster, which gives them a grey, shrouded unwinking look.' Few Europeans ever came to San'aa and none had been since the famine. The Turks, instead of boasting of their heroic defence during the siege, had censored all reports to the outside world. Aubrey was able to report for the first time accurate facts and figures. For an amateur journalist it was a great piece of luck.

The heroic old Turkish general, Ahmed Feizi Pasha, was away from San'aa, pacifying outlying districts and hunting the Imam Yahia, leader of the revolt. In his absence Aubrey and Buxton called on the Temporary Governor, Mahmud Nedim Bey, who received them courteously. He explained that had Ahmed Feizi Pasha known of their coming he would certainly have prevented it but since they had arrived they were welcome. He refused them permission to go on to Aden and said they must return speedily to Hodeidah. Nevertheless they managed to linger six days in San'aa, while arrangements were being made for their return journey. They followed the same route and were greeted as old friends at their stopping places. At Bajil, Aubrey drank from an infected well, which was to have dire consequences.

Having exhausted the limited pleasures of Hodeidah during their earlier enforced stay both Leland and Aubrey were anxious to move on. Within two days they found a Khedival boat going to Aden. At Aden, the acting British Resident, Captain Hancock, was astounded to hear that they had been to San'aa. He presented Aubrey with a packet of letters from his mother which had been steadily piling up. She wrote urging him to be diligent in his diary writing, expressing her longing for him, 'I hunger for the sight of your blessed face', and providing news of her own life. Mr Monypenny had been to stay, researching among Lord

Carnarvon's papers for his life of Disraeli; Elsie commented, 'I am more and more puzzled why he was selected to write it. He seems very much bored by it and does not give the impression of an able man in any way.'

Growing bored in Aden, Aubrey and Buxton decided to travel to India, after all, in search of some big game hunting. They engaged a young Arab boy, Abu Salaam (Father of Peace), as their joint servant. Aubrey boarded the French boat for Bombay feeling unwell. He was in fact extremely ill with a virulent typhoid. The infected well at Bajil had exacted its toll. The crossing to Bombay passed in a haze. At Bombay, the ship's officials, anxious to get rid of a doubtful invalid, helped him ashore before the other passengers and put him in a taxi for the General Hospital. Through a dream Aubrey heard his enterprising Parsee taxi driver reciting imaginary titles of his client to hard-faced English doctors. He was put in an enormous ward, next to a Chinese seaman and a dying Japanese. There Buxton found him, too ill to make much sense, but with one clear wish – that Kiazim be sent for. Buxton passed on the message to the Embassy at Constantinople.

After a week in the hospital Aubrey began to be aware of his discomfort. The noise, the rough, unfriendly attentions, the unceasing face washings made him long for peace and quiet. He knew there was no hope of a medical discharge so he summoned his useless servant, who for once rose to the occasion. Abu Salaam erected screens around his bed, brought in clothes and helped him to dress. Quietly they walked out of the hospital unnoticed and drove to the Hotel Taj Mahal. Aubrey lay in his hotel room in comfort but too weak to get to the bell to summon attention. The service was poor and Aubrey soon regretted his move. Swallowing his pride he sent a message to the friendliest of the hospital doctors who forgivingly came to his bedside. The doctor explained to him that he had suffered a very serious attack of typhoid. Up to this point Aubrey had been ignorant of his illness and had only guessed at its gravity. The doctor strongly advised him to return to England as soon as he was fit to travel. Aubrey, however, was convinced that in winter the Persian Gulf offered better prospects for recuperation and when Leland Buxton returned to Bombay they set sail together for Muscat in the SS *Africa*. Christmas Day was spent at Muscat. Then they rejoined their ship which unfortunately ran aground six miles from Bahrein on a coral reef. The shipwrecked passengers were lowered into Arab barques, rowed to Bahrein and then carried ashore on the backs of groaning men. There, huge white donkeys with scarlet henna-dyed chests awaited them. The passengers were deposited on the donkeys, with no bridles, no stirrups and no reins. The donkeys set off at full gallop for their respective homes amid the shrieks of protest and fear from the passengers.

When Leland and Aubrey eventually found each other again they made their way to the British Residency. There they found the Resident, Captain Prideaux, on a verandah dispensing justice to prisoners tied by chains to a bench. Only when Aubrey and Leland clamoured louder than the prisoners, demanding food, did he abandon his duty and take them inside.

They passed New Year's Day 1906 in Bahrein. Captain Prideaux, who had been a reluctant host at the outset, unbent, and entertained them lavishly. They stayed in Bahrein for about ten days. Leland, meanwhile, was becoming restive. He was sceptical about Aubrey's plans to cross the Arabian desert from El Hasa by way of Ojair, and decided to leave Bahrein once the ship SS *Africa* was righted. On January 8th he left, bound for Basra, Baghdad, Damascus and home. Aubrey recorded in his diary, 'Sorry to part with B. We don't care about anything in common hardly, but we got on very well if unenthusiastically together and he is a very good fellow indeed.'

Buxton had been right to be sceptical about Aubrey's expedition. Captain Prideaux refused all official help. Undeterred, Aubrey pressed ahead with his plans. Abu Salaam, the Father of Peace, reluctantly agreed to accompany him. Another servant, with knowledge of the hostile Saudi coast was advised, so Aubrey engaged a villainous pock-marked Arab, named Ali. Through the offices of this unsavoury individual he also hired a dhow to transport him across to the mainland. On embarking, he found the boat, hired for himself alone, teeming with humanity. 'I can't think why I started without better preparations', he wrote in his diary, 'this nation of traitors has done me again.'

After five stormy days at sea, they landed on a bitterly cold morning at Ojair. Officials, both Turkish and Arab, greeted Aubrey with friendliness. However, he was told there was no question of proceeding to El Hasa. At Ojair there lived one European, an old Greek chemist named Gabriel Mikhalaki. He had almost forgotten his own language and never seemed aware of what tongue he spoke. Aubrey, whose Arabic had improved steadily, now scarcely needed the aid of an interpreter but the old Greek offered his services. Aubrey obligingly accepted the offer. He said something in Turkish to be put into Arabic. The chemist repeated his words, with enormous emphasis, still in Turkish, sometimes adding a Greek or Arabic termination.

Aubrey was given a cell in the garrison and there he remained a virtual prisoner. He spent his days planning escapes, with the enthusiastic support of Gabriel Mikhalaki. One day the old chemist brought word to Aubrey that a caravan would be watering at a well five miles from the fort that night. Aubrey decided to make his escape. His servant, Abu

Salaam, whom Aubrey invited to carry his heavy bag of Maria Teresa dollars, flatly refused to leave the safety of the fort. The keeper of the gate and Chief of the Customs accepted the rather inappropriate bribe of a bottle of port which Aubrey had brought with him. Aubrey said goodbye to the trembling Father of Peace and quietly passed through the unlocked door of the fort, clutching his bag of money.

The moon was bright and Aubrey walked fast and furtively, transferring his load from one hand to the other, pausing sometimes to rest. His spirits were high. However, he had hopelessly misjudged his strength. The typhoid attack had left him weaker than he realised. A sudden collapse came upon him and he knew he must return. He turned back, hoping to creep back into the fort as quietly as he had left it. All went well until he came to the walls. There he was set upon by a savage pack of pariah dogs. The noise of the attacking dogs woke the garrison. Aubrey heard a voice shouting loudly from the roof but could pay no attention as he was too busy trying to beat off the dogs. Eventually he drew his revolver and shot one. The others were frightened and withdrew a distance. Meanwhile the great door of the fort opened and soldiers poured out. The Captain greeted him grimly, 'The sentry on the roof has orders to shoot after shouting three times,' he said. 'He disobeyed those orders tonight; he shall be punished tomorrow.' And Suliman, the Circassian with whom Aubrey had made friends, accompanied Aubrey to his cell, saying: 'Oh my lamb, what wild deeds are these?'

The next morning Aubrey went to see the Captain to plead the cause of the imprisoned sentry. The Captain unsmilingly refused to relent saying he knew his duty towards all men, guests, enemies or subordinates. Aubrey replied that he had no desire to instruct him in his duty, but asked a favour as one gentleman to another. The Captain replied, 'Your pleasure is my will' and the sentry was released. However the Captain never forgave Aubrey, and remained stern and unbending for the remainder of his enforced stay.

It gradually became clear to Aubrey, as wearisome day followed wearisome day, that he was never going to get to El Hasa. He decided to return to Bahrein. He feasted the garrison on some goats brought in by the Bedouin and said his farewells. Accompanied by Abu Salaam, Aubrey arrived in Bahrein five uncomfortable days later. He had been away exactly three weeks. After a brief and happy stay at the Residency, he took the next British India boat to Bushire, leaving behind Abu Salaam who had turned against travel and now wanted a life of peace and quiet.

On boarding the ship, Aubrey was asked by the Captain if he spoke

Turkish. He was told there was a Turkish Pasha aboard, travelling in the second class, who was bargaining for some carpets but needed the help of an interpreter. Aubrey went below. There he found Kiazim, dressed up to the nines, playing the part of a Pasha with great verve. Kiazim fell on Aubrey, kissing his hands again and again, 'Oh, the wonders of God that thou and I should meet upon a strange sea.'

Kiazim had left Constantinople, his fare paid by George Lloyd at the Embassy, as soon as Aubrey's summons had arrived from Bombay. He had travelled to Bombay and sought his master unavailingly there. Finally he had heard a rumour that Aubrey was somewhere in the Persian Gulf. Thither he had repaired confident that fate would contrive to bring them together. Aubrey was overjoyed at this masterly stroke which fate had indeed contrived. He wrote in his diary, 'The relief of having him once again is very great.'

At Bushire Aubrey and Kiazim disembarked. Aubrey's first impressions of Persia in his diary ran 'An immoral people; dirty streets; liars'. Sir Percy Cox, the Consul, invited them to stay. It was a comfortable house despite the household pets which included ten cats, a dog, a parrot and many monkeys. Sir Percy, famed throughout the Gulf, was not what Aubrey had expected, 'He was quiet not talkative, rather attractive, and did not give the impression of being weak. We went over a fairly big space and disagreed on nothing.'

From Bushire Aubrey and Kiazim set sail again for Basra, where they had letters to the English Consul, Mr Crow. Their ship anchored outside Basra. Aubrey, impatient to go ashore and ignoring the quarantine rules, took an Arab sambuk. As the little boat came up the mouth of the river there was a challenge and they saw a black soldier on the bank with a rifle pointing towards their boat. The soldier ordered the Arab rowers to halt. Aubrey drawing his revolver ordered them to proceed. Kiazim, uncharacteristically, intervened on the side of peace, 'Be calm, my two eyes; leave this important business to me. Upon my head be it.'

With impotent rage Aubrey found himself a prisoner in the quarantine station until a boat from the Consulate arrived. Then, after a little soothing diplomacy, they were conducted back to their ship to await the lifting of quarantine restrictions.

A few days later they legally disembarked and went to stay with the Consul. There Aubrey found a large bundle of letters from home. Lady Carnarvon wrote with unaccustomed hysteria, 'Revolution is upon us', an allusion to the 1906 General Election which had resulted in a Liberal landslide. She had visited the House of Commons and reported, 'It is a melancholy spectacle and our depleted and decrepit front bench made me long for the sight of your beloved face to fill the gaps. Austen looked very ill and is going abroad at once. Mr Balfour spoke in a nervous stuttering manner – so much so it might have been his first speech in the House. Mr Chamberlain was not there. It seems a case of very few followers and no leader worth mentioning.' Austen Chamberlain did not escape abroad before he had been button-holed by Elsie, who sought his help in procuring a seat for Aubrey. She reported, 'He advised waiting until the Conservative Office is reorganised.' Aubrey had every intention of waiting. He was now planning, with Kiazim as companion, to cross the Syrian desert from Baghdad to Damascus.

While staying in Basra with the Crows, Aubrey visited the Garden of Eden and camped in the marshes. Unlike subsequent travellers, he failed to see the beauty and romance of the marsh Arabs; he wrote, 'The country quite flat; the people a very low type, hideous, very savage looking, always shewing their teeth in a canine smile.' Kiazim felt even more strongly on this subject. He detested and despised the Arabs and thought their bitter coffee in tiny cups a mockery of hospitality. No one, however, could fault the hospitality of the Crows. Aubrey, who knew how meagre were the salaries earned by consuls in distant places, felt guilty about their generosity; he wrote in his diary, 'Here people are more or less forced to entertain everyone who comes. They are very hospitable but one feels a brute accepting it and it threatens to become a real source of poverty to them.'

An English firm, Lynch, operated steamers on the Tigris. Aubrey and Kiazim boarded one for Baghdad. The skipper was a Captain Cowley, a valiant man whom Aubrey met again during the Mesopotamian campaign in 1916, when Cowley made a doomed but heroic attempt to relieve Kut, for which he was awarded a posthumous VC.

There were some odd passengers on the steamer, but the oddest by far was a Miss Christie. A spinster well embarked on middle age, she had, on receiving a bequest late in life, abandoned her native West Country village, where she had lived all her life, sheltered and respected, and started out on a life of travel and adventure. Miss Christie's tastes in travel and adventure were extreme. She was only happy courting death and disaster. 'She takes her risks without winking', Aubrey wrote in his diary and in a letter to his mother he described her as 'one of those women like Gertrude Bell but minus her cleverness and also, thanks be, without her temper'. She spoke no foreign tongue but put her trust in Providence and the English language. Rosy cheeked and gentle in manner, she seemed to Aubrey 'the archetype of courageous British womanhood'. Nonetheless he did not want her as a companion on his travels in the fanatical country round Baghdad. He recognised in her a spirit more intrepid than his own. He shunned the responsibility of protecting her as she shook one hostile hand too many. Miss Christie, on the other hand, was eager to share her adventures with what she regarded as a fellow spirit. In Baghdad they were both guests of the British Consul, Colonel Newmarsh, whom Aubrey found 'a queer old thing. He gives one an uncomfortable feeling, like a huge great clock that's going to strike with a bang.'

Aubrey was determined to visit the Shi'ite shrine of Kerbela during the time of Muharram when the Shi'ites honour the memory of their saint and martyr, Hussein. The fanatical reputation of these Shi'ite devotions stirred Aubrey's curiosity. Naturally Miss Christie was even more determined to expose herself to the dangers of Kerbela at the season of Muharram. When Aubrey discovered that both their carriages had been ordered for four o'clock one morning, he decided to postpone his start by an hour and a half. Kiazim was shocked by his master's lack of chivalry. Aubrey's explanation that it was not the custom in his country for a gentleman and lady to travel alone together was instantly seen through. 'This is an error, surely, my dear,' said Kiazim. 'Have I not been in England?'

As it happened all Aubrey's subterfuges were in vain. When he arrived at the gates of Baghdad he found Miss Christie's carriage arrested. The Turks had refused to let her proceed alone. 'Our two cabs crawled like courting insects across the plain,' wrote Aubrey. Miss Christie's proud and independent spirit was hurt by this compulsory chaperoning. That evening they stayed in Babylon, the guests of German archaeologists. Aubrey recorded in his diary that after dinner Miss Christie 'brought down a twopenny ramshackle revolver which she wanted loaded in such a way that it would not go off. If it had to go off, she said, there must be a number of preliminary clicks to give her time to think whether she really meant to kill the man. I suggested it would also give the man time to think if he wanted to be killed. Anyway she is not likely to hit anything.'

To Aubrey's relief the authorities refused Miss Christie permission to proceed to Kerbela and the next morning Aubrey bid her a warm farewell and set out alone, but for Kiazim. Aubrey and Kiazim were met everywhere with scowls, and sometimes with open hostility. In none of the villages could Aubrey get food or water. Kiazim as a Sunni Moslem was permitted food, although the people broke his plate after he had eaten. He was forbidden to bring any food for his Christian master. The magnificent mosques of Kerbela were difficult to see because of the lamenting devotees. After one night Aubrey thankfully returned to Baghdad, where he had a happy reunion with Miss Christie, who was no doubt secretly contemptuous of Aubrey's slight appetite for the hostility he and Kiazim had encountered.

Aubrey's last days in Baghdad were pleasant. He now felt recovered in health and renewed in strength. On Saturday 3rd March, accompanied by Kiazim, a muleteer named Mahmoud, who rode a tiny donkey, two pack horses and two riding horses, Aubrey left Baghdad for Damascus. The journey from Baghdad to Damascus was a well-established endurance test. The distance was over seven hundred miles, largely through desert. It was not dangerous, merely strenuous. Aubrey soon found that he had many hangers-on – two Persians and an assortment of Arabs.

They established a routine, rising before dawn in the bitter desert cold. They then rode or walked for ten to twelve hours. By mid-day the heat became fierce and blistered their faces and lips. They lunched in the saddle and in the evening made a fire. Kiazim cooked rice, his only culinary accomplishment, and sang sad or ferocious Albanian ballads. Aubrey cooked boiled eggs, his only culinary accomplishment, and listened.

Kiazim proved to be a difficult travelling companion. His contempt for the Arabs, matched only by his conceit in himself, led to misunderstandings and occasionally violence. He developed a mania for secrecy. In front of Turkish-speaking Arabs he insisted on addressing Aubrey in what he thought was Greek in order to baffle the onlookers. Unfortunately Aubrey had forgotten most of the Greek he knew and Kiazim had never really known any; the result was general confusion and amazement. Kiazim would then resort to a furious and exaggerated dumb crambo which in as far as it was comprehensible was comprehensible to all. And with the increasing frustrations of the journey, so Kiazim's manners became rougher and more ferocious. After a time Aubrey found it better not to question Kiazim too closely. Chickens, and on one occasion, a lamb, were mysteriously procured. At the stopping places other travellers were ejected from the best hovels and Aubrey and Kiazim installed. Kiazim could not speak Arabic and, like many a bad linguist before and since, resorted to shouting louder and louder in his own tongue. As Aubrey put it, he believed that 'hullabaloo was a great ally of lucidity'. His hatred of the desert grew daily; 'God give this desert trouble', he repeated monotonously and his reproaches to both his master and his God became a litany. 'Yesterday', wrote Aubrey in his diary, 'as punishment, I spoke no word to him. He was quite miserable and implored pardon in the evening. This I gave after a little demur. He takes too much on himself.'

One of the bones of contention between them was Aubrey's habit of dismounting and walking for long periods. Aubrey always enjoyed walking and in this particular case had good reason. 'My beast', he wrote, 'is the most irritating I have ever ridden. He has a romantic eye and anything from a camel to the shadow of a palm tree in the desert appears to him in the shape of an Arab mare.' Rather than struggle endlessly to control the phantom passions and rough paces of this disagreeable steed, Aubrey preferred to walk. Walking in Turkey, however, was the habit only of vagabonds and Kiazim felt his master's dignity was impaired when he took to his feet. And anything that impaired his master's dignity also impaired his own. In the end a compromise was reached. Aubrey agreed to ride in and out of villages and only dismount in the secure solitude of the desert.

Another source of disagreement between them was Aubrey's softheartedness. Kiazim, and indeed the whole band of hangers-on including the Persians, were furious with Aubrey for releasing some robbers. A peasant came to them, not far from Baghdad, complaining that some thieves had beaten him and stolen his corn. Aubrey and the better mounted members of his caravan gave chase. They had an exhilarating ride and cornered the men in an angle of the river. After the thieves had been disarmed, every able-bodied man set about beating them. Aubrey called a halt and insisted on letting them go. Kiazim sulked mightily.

Nevertheless the bond between master and servant was strong and enduring. Kiazim's devotion and loyalty were total, and Aubrey for his part loved his servant. He could listen forever to Kiazim's tales. The poetry of his language and the mixture of mystic philosophy and improbable anecdote delighted him.

Some extracts from Aubrey's diary serve to give the flavour of the journey:

March 5 Roumada
Stopped last night at Feluja, a huge dilapidated khan . . . insects like sharks . . . found a couple of Arabs waiting for me here in order to attach themselves to me for protection . . . Kiazim like an Albanian sees an enemy in every man. I should like to go bang bang bang with my revolver he says with indignation when he sees the light-hearted Arabs.
March 7 Hit
. . . a horrible day. 5 hours in a sandstorm. Kiazim's horse kept falling. I can hear his yells of Oh blind! blind! blind! and at last in a frenzy he banged it with rifle and revolver. The sand was frightfully painful to the eyes and yellow as London fog. K and I were separated for five minutes and the fear of being lost came upon us both . . . The dens for sleeping were nauseous. My head and feet touched either side of the room, and the floor was greasy.
March 9
Anah. A very long town all by the river, a great sense of peace about it . . . The olives made me homesick for Portofino.
March 10 Ghayim
16 hrs march, the hottest day we have had. After 9 hrs I determined to give up

abstinence and drink. I needed it. No water. K. had drunk and the rest spilt. Persian fell off, and seemed very ill. I gave him my remaining half flask of brandy and moistened my lips with the rest. Nearly drank from a green stinking puddle, but refrained and prevented Kiazim by cajolery. I reminded him of the Imam David. Earlier I had told him the story of David and how, when his three captains brought him water, he had poured it out upon the sand saying 'Shall I drink the blood of my people'. Kiazim had applauded saying, 'Finely done. Thus will a king and a man act'. Now he said 'I am not a king, neither are these circumstances mine.' I answered that I knew now what to believe of Albanian manhood. And so he resisted the water. The Arabs sucked it up. We longed to. Afterwards Kiazim said 'The world is like a melon, but oh the stairway of the universe', ie the ups and downs of things.

March 11

At last I got a great quantity of camels milk. The comfort of it was I think greater than anything I have ever felt. It seemed to soak all over one . . . The two Persians got ahead of us and took the only room. K. turned them out . . .

March 12 Miadin

9 hrs journey. 4 eggs from dawn till then. Tomorrow we arrive at Deir, a place flowing with milk and honey . . .

March 13 Deir

Land of milk and honey but not much else; no meat. Kiazim cooked our food in the Persians' room so as to avoid having smoke in ours. They are highly annoyed . . .

March 17 Bir i Jedid

Gloom in the caravan they think I am going to stop at Palmyra but I shan't. The old postman is my favourite amongst them. They come and go. Only the Persians have been with us all through. A jolly negro came yesterday. Two bedouins with us today, nice fellows. Some scarlet anemones on the way . . . I find I cannot go on living on hard boiled eggs . . . Mahmoud's little donkey is pathetic. It is so tiny and yet it does such an enormous amount. Mahmoud is angry with me because I took away his knife with which he prods it.

March 20 Tadmor, Palmyra

14 hrs. march. Tempest of wind, torrents of rain. Sent Zaptieh ahead to see if he could get mattresses as ours were wet. Followed him with the Persian. Desert became slippery, then a marsh. Night fell. It was like being dressed in eels wearing my buckskin breeches . . . To complete the disaster we lost the caravan and the road . . . Finally we came to ruins which we could see against the sky; these we came to several times so we must have journeyed in a circle . . . We reached through pitch darkness a kind of habitation, from where children led us somewhere else. It was very rough. I fell and was nearly walked on by my horse . . . I ordered the Persian to do something, but he only wailed piteously. I was on the point of going to the Mudir's to ask for help when to my infinite relief K, Mahmoud and the caravan arrived, with chattering teeth and making noises like ghouls. K. very distressed at having lost me . . . The sheikh's brother turned up and offered a room. Very politely I said j'y suis, j'y reste.

On Friday 24th March, exactly three weeks after their start, they rode into Damascus. 'Everybody laughed and talked and sang. The sky was pure blue, there was peach and almond blossom everywhere and the tinkle of water.' Aubrey rode at the head of the column of bedraggled travellers. Kiazim rode jealously behind to keep the Persian merchant in his place among the humble and the unpretentious. Arriving at the best hotel, Aubrey, in the face of fierce protests from Kiazim, gave away all his remaining money. To Mahmoud the muleteer he gave the most but all received a little charity. After a brief farewell speech he was cheered, sympathetic onlookers joining in.

Then, penniless, filthy and heavily armed, Aubrey and Kiazim entered the hotel and marched into the dining room. Silence fell upon the room. They ordered a huge lunch. Fortunately, lunching at the hotel at the same time was Edmonds, the British Consul, who backed Aubrey's name on a piece of paper for any money he might require.

For three days Aubrey and Kiazim revelled in the luxury of the hotel, indulging in hot baths and delectable meals. Damascus in those days was a hospitable city and invitations were showered on Aubrey. Meanwhile poor Kiazim, whose sufferings on the journey had been augmented by toothache, took himself off and returned having had five teeth extracted in half an hour. He shrugged off Aubrey's condolences saying that the day was a good day, the teeth had undoubtedly been bad teeth and the operator was a man of education.

Regretfully leaving Damascus and their comfortable hotel, they moved to Beirut. There Aubrey met his friend George Lloyd, on leave from the Embassy at Constantinople.

George Lloyd (later Lord Lloyd) came from a prosperous middle-class background. At Eton he had been a year older than Aubrey but they had been friends. Later he followed Aubrey to Constantinople as an honorary attaché. It was an improbable friendship. The two men could scarcely have had more contrasting characters. George Lloyd was hard working, ambitious and wonderfully thorough: he seldom changed his views. He was jealous of success but generous to failure. He was never flippant. Yet the friendship was close and lasting. Aubrey often began his letters to Lloyd 'Delicious George' and he remained one of the few men who could tease Lloyd with impunity.

Aubrey did not like Beirut. He went to Cyprus, came back, and persuaded George Lloyd to accompany him to Jerusalem for Easter. That year the Latin and Orthodox Easters coincided and Jerusalem promised to be a memorable spectacle. First, however, there was a difficulty. George Lloyd's servant, a huge and fierce Armenian, and Kiazim were not compatible companions. Both were born to lead and neither to follow. Since the prospect of the Moslem Kiazim at loose among the Holy Places seemed at best incongruous, Aubrey despatched his servant to Constantinople and proceeded without him to Jerusalem.

Jerusalem at Easter was not an edifying sight. Christian fought Christian in the crowded chruches and dubious Holy Places, while the Turkish soldiery looked on, occasionally spitting at the passing of a cross. In the Church of the Holy Sepulchre Aubrey found himself in the centre of three contending groups, Latins, Greeks and Armenians, who were beating each other with crosses, sticks and ikons. A Turkish captain, sitting above the tumult, sent in a few soldiers to break up the fight. They pulled Aubrey out of the mêlée and he joined the captain. After the old soldier had reminisced for some time about his many campaigns and battles Aubrey said, 'If it isn't a rude question, how did you lose your eye?' The captain replied, 'Ah, that was no honourable scar. I lost my eye doing what I sent my man to do for you today, preventing Christians from killing each other.'

After some misadventures on the Egyptian-Palestinian frontier Lloyd and Aubrey decided to abandon their projected ride and travel to Egypt by a boat from Jaffa, 'Aubrey in great deshabille' according to George Lloyd's diary. In Egypt they were received by Lord Cromer who was anxious to hear news of Constantinople from Lloyd and of the Yemen from Aubrey. Although he was sceptical of Aubrey's imperial designs which included the annexation by the British Government of the whole Persian Gulf, he listened with interest to what the young men had to say. Aubrey wrote to his mother, 'He fires questions like bullets but to my surprise I found him very pleasant and interesting.'

Aubrey returned with Lloyd to Constantinople. Constantinople had changed little in the interval. FitzMaurice had written to Aubrey the month before, 'We seem to be carrying on here as of yore – all of us grouped around the Grand Old Spider who unceasingly weaves cobwebs as meshes to strangle the interests and prestige of the British Lion.' Aubrey caroused with his friends, Turkish and English, disrupted the life of Chancery not a little, and felt happy and at home. His love and knowledge of the city was deep. Later, in an article, he wrote: 'Nearly all travellers distinguish some spot among their journeyings as the object of a special enthusiasm.' Constantinople was Aubrey's 'special enthusiasm' with 'its squalor and its glory' and its doomed history. 'Coveted by the world', he wrote, 'it has always been its destiny to bring misfortune to its owners, and itself to be the capital of a decaying race, whether Latins, Greeks, Franks or Turks.' Many years later Ataturk was to hold this view so strongly that he transferred the capital of his new republic to Ankara.

At the British Embassy at this time there was, as well as George Lloyd, another honorary attaché, Mark Sykes. Mark Sykes was a remarkable man. The heir to a baronetcy and vast estates in Yorkshire, his early life had been spent in adventurous Eastern travel. His upbringing had been curious. His parents hated each other. His mother, young, warm-hearted, unconventional, promiscuous and drunken, lived apart from his father, Sir Tatton Sykes, who was old, harsh and unpleasant. Mark Sykes was the only child of this unhappy union. Warm-hearted and unconventional like his mother, he had the additional gifts of a keen brain, great charm and an overriding sense of humour and fun together with a talent for mimicry and caricature. Aubrey loved Mark Sykes from the start. They were kindred souls, although holding wildly divergent views. These three honorary attachés, Mark Sykes, George Lloyd and Aubrey shared a fascination with the Levant. The threads of their lives were to tangle and entwine again and again. All three were in Constantinople together, all three became Conservative members of parliament and were part of the same political group, all three were to be closely involved in Arab/Turkish affairs during the Great War. At the Arab Bureau in Cairo during the war they were nicknamed 'The Three Musketeers'. Yet they were not a united trio. Mark Sykes and George Lloyd did not in fact like each other. They were bound together in close friendship with Aubrey and common interests but between them there was no real friendship. George Lloyd mistrusted Sykes's flamboyance and wit. He thought him essentially shallow; while Mark Sykes thought Lloyd pompous and rigid. Each, in their letters to Aubrey, often included barbed remarks about the other. During the war Sykes would sometimes write letters to Aubrey beginning 'Dear Pompey' and ending 'love Caesar'. In those letters he would refer to Lloyd as 'Crassus'.

At the end of May, Aubrey reluctantly left Constantinople for home. His greatest problem was Kiazim. Lady Carnarvon wrote: 'Have you settled anything for poor Kiazim? I scarcely think it would do to have him in London and it would be rather expensive to have a servant only as a friend.' As the time of Aubrey's departure grew closer, Kiazim reminisced longingly about his time in the servants' hall at Pixton: 'There was Anne,' he would say. 'Such a one was Anne, by God, verily such a one, Allah make her eyes radiant. She admired me greatly. How fares she, oh my dear?' Aubrey often found these questions difficult to answer, and would earn the rebuke 'Behold, Bey, is not Anne a girl of education and under thy protection. Inform thyself of thy handmaiden.'

Kiazim had in Albania a wife and two children. Even Aubrey, impractical though he was, could see both the unsuitability of importing the whole family to England and the impropriety of separating them for ever. So, amid many protestations of undying loyalty, Aubrey and Kiazim parted.

Aubrey was, as usual, reluctant to return to England. His reluctance on this occasion was strengthened by the fear (unfounded in the event) that these travels could prove his last for some time. He had embarked on this travel on the clear understanding that afterwards he would settle down and devote himself to politics and English life. Aubrey found the prospect chilling. The nomadic life, the sounds and smells of the East, had entered his blood. Aubrey left Constantinople with dutiful intentions, but he could no more stay away from the decaying capital and its wild empire than a moth can stay away from the light. In less than a year he was back in Turkey.

5

Irish Courtship
and Turkish Revolt

The next few years, from 1906 to 1910, were busy ones for Aubrey. There were to be further travels in the Ottoman Empire, adoption for a constituency, elections fought and lost, a voyage to Australia and deaths in the family. But, most important of all, he met, and eventually married, Mary Vesey.

Mary Vesey had just celebrated her eighteenth birthday when Aubrey met her in Florence in April 1907. She was six foot tall, a severe and splendid beauty, with flashing eyes and regal carriage, proud, clever and unconventional. Not yet launched on the world, she was staying in Florence with her mother, Lady de Vesci. Aubrey already knew and admired Lady de Vesci; indeed she was known and admired throughout English society. Born Lady Evelyn Charteris, the eldest daughter of the tenth Earl of Wemyss, she married in 1872 the fourth Viscount de Vesci. His mother had been Lady Emma Herbert, a daughter of the eleventh Earl of Pembroke, which made Aubrey and Mary Vesey distant cousins.

When Aubrey met Mary, Lady de Vesci had been widowed for five years. Like Lady Carnarvon she always wore black, but not the darned and dowdy black favoured by Elsie; Lady de Vesci's black was exquisite and sumptuous. Mary Vesey was her only child, not just the apple of her eye, but the pivot of her existence. While the world worshipped Evelyn de Vesci, she worshipped her daughter. From the age of three Mary had been drawn and painted by every celebrated artist of the time; Burne-Jones designed a suit of armour for her when she was five. For Lady de Vesci was a member of the group known as the 'Souls' and thus knew and was known by the literary and artistic world of the day, which stretched outside conventional 'society', and was in touch with all the arts. In her bedroom at Abbeyliex there was a shelf in a bookcase exclusively filled with books that had been dedicated to her.

Lady de Vesci's passion for her only child was remarkable even in an age which made a cult of motherhood. There was a reason. Lady de Vesci had been married for seventeen years, childless and apparently barren. In 1888, accompanied by a friend, Lady Wenlock, who also had been long and fruitlessly married, she went to Bayreuth ostensibly to listen to Wagner. There the two ladies visited a German doctor who had made a discreet international name for himself in the treatment of barren women. Within a year both ladies had borne a child. In both cases the children were daughters, not the sons and heirs to the peerage that their parents had desired; but Lady de Vesci did not repine. She looked on her daughter as a gift from heaven, a treasure beyond treasures.

Many children might have become spoilt as a consequence of this rarified and adoring atmosphere; Mary did not. She reacted against the excessive flattery which surrounded beauties like her mother and the current absurdities of female vanity which fed on this flattery. Her nature was forthright, direct and strong; she was uninterested in her own appearance. Impatient of compliments, unmoved by admiration, she disregarded her own beauty, left it unpampered, and was unconcerned when its season passed. Nor were her looks universally admired. There was a school of opinion that held that she was too tall and too thin and, later, too ungroomed.

To this latter school Aubrey, most emphatically, did not belong. He thought her magnificent in mind and body. Unlike many girls of her class and generation, Mary's education had not been left exclusively in the hands of foreign governesses. She had attended a school, Northlands, near Englefield Green. Lady de Vesci bought a house nearby so that Mary should be able to go by day, and avoid the rigours of boarding. The school was the creation of a remarkable woman, Miss Weisse, and, though predominantly musical under the direction of Donald Tovey, it provided a broad education in the arts and modern languages. The school served Mary well. She read widely and deeply.

Aubrey and Mary soon struck up a friendship in Florence. Thenceforth they wrote to each other regularly but infrequently. Mary's letters began 'Dear Mr Aubrey'; his began 'Dear Miss Vesey'. Though formal in address these letters are intimate in manner with an undercurrent of mild flirtation. Mary regarded Aubrey as a dear friend. He regarded her as something more. As yet unready for marriage himself and realising that her extreme youth made necessary a long courtship he was content for the time being to woo her imperceptibly. In the same year, 1907, that Aubrey met Mary Vesey, his great friend Raymond Asquith married. He wrote to Aubrey, 'I am going to be married to Katherine Horner at the end of July. I am in love with her and I think this is the best thing to do . . . I fear you will always draw the line at monogamy in a cottage. My temperament as you know is less versatile.' The Horners were close family friends of the Veseys and Lady Horner, Katherine's mother, like Lady de Vesci was a prominent 'Soul'.

Raymond had expected his news to elicit reproaches from Aubrey. In fact Aubrey's prejudice against monogamy had been dealt a mortal blow by his meeting with Mary Vesey. He was not yet deeply in love nor was he completely reconciled to marriage. The losing of his heart was a slow process. His feelings for Mary Vesey were strong, his admiration warm. She filled his imagination, but only every now and then. Other pursuits and interests took up his time and energy, and besides, he recognised his suit as hopeless. As time went by, he caught delicious glimpses of Mary at balls, and parties and country house visits. They exchanged letters; argued about politics, books and personalities; the friendship flourished. But Aubrey was hampered in his suit by a real sense of his own unworthiness and by Mary's obstinate refusal to lift their relationship out of the realm of friendship into that of courtship. A year after their first meeting Aubrey wrote her a poem entitled *E Poi*; which made his position clear:

The wind is lazy on the sea, the ripple sleeps below the vine;
The world's a dream for you and me, a dream that will not long be mine;
But for this hour let us together find on the cliff a sheltered place
Where I can lie on thyme and heather, and hear you speak and watch your face.

         *   *   *

The perfect days are very few, and rarely happiness as near,
So I'm content to be with you, and watch your face my dear, my dear.
This dream is all that we shall share, I will not risk my golden hour,
For once in life I will not dare, unless you bid who have the power.

         *   *   *

When Mary received this poem in the spring of 1908 she was no longer a cloistered girl fresh from the schoolroom. She had a London season behind her, admirers by the score, and all the confidence of a conquering beauty. Her cousin and contemporary, Cynthia Charteris, listing the beauties of her time in *Remember and be Glad*, recalls her vividly in her first season:

> Mary Vesey's beauty glowed in the ballroom, blazed, I might say for I have seen no other eyes of the same jewel-like lustre. Emerald green, yet deeply grey, they flashed – fiercely at times, beneath thick black brows. Her brilliant colour came and went; her superb neck rounded like the shaft of a column was of a dazzling whiteness. Aquiline, strikingly tall, untamed looking, she was the very antithesis of the trivial, fluffy, white-tulle variety of debutante. An almost Roman splendour of feature proclaimed an inescapable nobleness of nature . . .

Mary accepted Aubrey's love poetry critically; she read in it no personal message. She liked Aubrey and was proud of his friendship. He was older than her other friends, known as the 'Slips', the children of the 'Souls', later mildly notorious as the 'Coterie'. There was a certain aura surrounding his name, his climbing exploits at Balliol, his balloon flight with Charlie Meade and his travels in the East. His disreputable appearance had given rise to many stories, most mythical. But she steadfastly insisted on treating him as a friend rather than a swain. So Aubrey had to be content with friendship. He found himself going with less reluctance to balls. He stayed more often in the country houses she frequented, Stanway, Hatfield, Althorp, Hewell, Ewehurst and Taplow but his suit remained hidden and undeclared. His friends were in ignorance of his feelings and her friends saw in him no rival.

Meanwhile Aubrey's life continued in its customary whirl. After his return to England in the summer of 1906, he was offered and accepted a constituency in the Conservative interest. Raymond Asquith had done his best to shift Aubrey's allegiance, warning him in several letters of the bleak prospects in a Conservative future. F. E. Smith, he told Aubrey, was the new star in the Tory firmament, 'a most fluent and plausible bounder, the very man they want on that side and certain to lead the party in the end, which makes it quite impossible for you to join it. No, Aubrey dear, you must be a Liberal now: otherwise you will be out of office for 20 years, led by a shit when your beard is white.' Or, on a more fanciful note, Raymond urged him to join the Labour Party: 'I have an idea for when you go in – go in as a Labour candidate – don't you see the theatrical capabilities of that? The young aristocrat with ideals and sympathies which carry him passionately out of his class – a tribune of the people – Gracchus, Rienzi, Tolstoi anyone you like. It would explain your clothes too.'

Raymond's wayward advice did not sway Aubrey. He wrote, 'It is a nuisance being on the other side with you and Bron Liberals.' It was in these personal terms he saw party politics. His father had been a Conservative cabinet minister and his mother was a devoted daughter of Toryism. It never seriously occurred to Aubrey to join any other party. Although, later, others often regarded his membership of the Conservative party as an aberration and mistake, he would have been no better suited elsewhere. When he entered politics Aubrey's attitude to the British elector was one of benevolent feudalism and so it remained. In practice his interest in politics was mainly concentrated on foreign affairs and here party politics had little bearing.

The constituency which invited Aubrey to be their candidate was South Somerset. Its chief town was Yeovil, and it was the neighbouring constituency to Pixton and therefore convenient. There was, however, one serious drawback. It had been a safe Liberal seat from its inception in 1885. The sitting member, Sir Edward Strachey, had comfortably held the seat since 1892. Aubrey disliked both the man and his politics. He therefore threw himself with enthusiasm into the work. The electors of South Somerset were an independent people with a strong non-conformist streak. Aubrey's lack of convention appealed to their sturdy, and sometimes surly, individualism.

While Aubrey was in Yeovil, at the beginning of November word came of the death of his Uncle Auberon. Elsie hurried to the death bed. This, coming only two months after the unexpected death of his beloved Aunt, Eveline Portsmouth, was a blow. Uncle Auberon's obituary in *The Times* was severe: 'His place in contemporary history might have been higher if he had been more in touch with the spirit of the age . . . He followed his bent with an absolute disregard for convention and author-ity. If he had come of a less aristocratic stock it is possible that the respect for the opinion of others which checks eccentricity among the middle classes might have induced a greater soundness of judgement.'

Aubrey had much of his Uncle Auberon in him. He was a gentler, less arrogant, more humorous version, but undeniably of the same stock. Nan, Auberon's daughter, recorded in her diary a few years later, 'Aubrey is, I think, exactly what Dods must have been as a young man.'

Only three months later Alan Herbert, the doctor, died in Paris. Again Elsie was at the death bed. And so in the space of six months the elder generation of Herbert uncles and aunts was wiped out, leaving only his maiden aunt Gwendolyn, a lonely survivor of a dead generation. Aubrey attended his Uncle Auberon's funeral but was unable to go to Paris for Uncle Alan's because he was laid low with mumps.

After his attack of mumps, Aubrey planned a visit to Albania. Inspired by Kiazim he had long wanted to see the homeland of his henchman. Originally Reginald Farrer had agreed to come too, writing: 'I cannot conceive of anything to which I am less fitted than to carry comfort into snowy blood-stained mountains. However if I am to be the martyr of your sense of humour, I will not shirk my doom.' When the time came, however, he did shirk, in a fit of pique with Aubrey over some minor matter. So Aubrey arrived companionless in Scutari at the beginning of May 1907, fresh from his encounter with Mary Vesey in Florence. He found a town after his own heart. Behind the fortifications and high garden walls the place seethed with bloodthirsty vendettas. While Aubrey waited for Kiazim, whom he had summoned, he heard word in the bazaar that a revolution was in progress in neighbouring Monte-negro. He immediately made his way to the scene of action but was disappointed. In Podgoritza (now Titograd) he was arrested as an

IRISH COURTSHIP AND TURKISH REVOLT

Italian spy. He had made the mistake of talking Italian. Aubrey was unaware that two days before his arrival the Italian Tobacco Monopoly at Antivari had been blown up by Montenegrin patriots and the night before his arrival the chief of police had been killed and the Governor grievously wounded by a man thought to be an Italian sympathiser. The place was in an uproar and Italian agents were suspected under every bed.

It took Aubrey two days to convince the authorities that he was a harmless English traveller. Slightly sheepishly he made his way back to Scutari where he found an ecstatic Kiazim waiting for him. It should have been Kiazim's triumphant hour; the chance to conduct his master over the homeland he had so often extolled in song and ballad. Alas, it turned out differently. The Turkish authorities refused Kiazim a passport and they refused permission or an escort for Aubrey's projected ride across the mountains to Uskub (Skopje). There Aubrey proposed to meet Mervyn who had just finished his Foreign Office examinations.

In the end Aubrey decided to risk the consequences and travel as planned. It was a foolhardy decision. The Turks had refused permission because the country Aubrey wished to traverse was at that particular turbulent moment outside their control. But Kiazim was unhappy. He lost his usual swagger, only occasionally recovering it in his dealings with the Christian muleteer, whom he despised and resented. Aubrey wrote in his diary 'Can't make out what has come to K. Nerves I am afraid.' The truth was indeed that Kiazim was nervous. It was all very well for Aubrey to flout the dangers of the journey. His position was very different from Kiazim's. If Aubrey were taken by Albanian bandits the chances were that he would either be held to ransom or used as a bargaining counter with the Turkish authorities. Kiazim was neither worthy of ransom nor of use as a bargaining counter. Moreover he was an Albanian and had many enemies of his own in the country. The expedition later led to his arrest and imprisonment by the Turkish authorities.

Mervyn was not at Uskub when Aubrey arrived. After an exchange of telegrams the brothers agreed to meet in Salonika. From Salonika they rode, with a now cheerful Kiazim, by way of Galatza and Polygero to Ayia Nikola. There they took a boat to Mount Athos and spent a happy fortnight, staying at monasteries, before returning by sea to Salonika.

Elsie meanwhile was in England and as usual demanding Aubrey's return. There was, she claimed, constituency business that urgently required his presence. Aubrey replied on 1st June from Constantinople that he was very reluctant to come back and was worried over Kiazim: 'K is very happy, but the government is being tiresome about him and I am afraid he may get oppression when I leave.' As indeed it happened. Aubrey had been back in England only a month when he received a letter from FitzMaurice of the Embassy: 'Your trusty henchman Kiazim has sent me a couple of missives through the Embassy cavass Feizullah inquiring whether I am looking into his "case", viz. that I should induce the Sultan or some other such dignitary to release him from durance vile in the salubrious town of Dibra-bala. I told Feizullah to ask him how it was that an eagle like Kiazim can be caged by wretched Turkish hawks . . .'

Aubrey was upset by this letter but a fortnight later FitzMaurice wrote reassuringly, 'He may be shadowed at present at Dibra for having "broken bounds" with you in Albania but that is bound to blow over and you may trust to his native wit and resources to get himself out of any temporary scrape of the kind.' Aubrey, quite rightly, had a guilty conscience about Kiazim. On the other hand, as all his friends in Turkey realised and Aubrey only half realised, Kiazim was a seasoned old scoundrel well able to look after himself.

After his return from Turkey, Aubrey dutifully plunged himself once more into constituency politics and English social life. By the New Year of 1908, however, he was again off on his travels, this time at the behest of his mother.

Lord Carnarvon had bought, while he was Colonial Secretary, large properties in Canada and Australia to show his faith in the Dominions. Elsie had inherited these properties and had become perturbed by the reports from her agent in Australia, Sir William Manning. He advised her to sell. There was a strong probability that the Australian government would bring in a heavy absentee land tax. Also many of the properties, whole streets in the centre of Sydney, had become slum dwellings, something Elsie could not countenance. She asked Aubrey, therefore, to go out to Australia and sort out the whole business in person. The usual chorus of disapproval that greeted Aubrey's departure on a travel was led this time by female friends. Gertrude Bell wrote, 'Your presence makes more difference to me than to a wretched gang of colonials.'

Aubrey left in January on the R.M.S. *Ophir*. Reginald Farrer came with him. Reginald had become a Buddhist and wished to study both the religion and the flowers of Ceylon where he proposed to disembark. Aubrey was glad to have his companionship. He found the other people on the boat uncongenial. He wrote to Elsie 'the first class are only fit to play chess with . . . the majority of them are not even Saturday to Monday.'

In Melbourne Aubrey met the acting Prime Minister Kirkpatrick and was impressed by him. He was embarrassed however by the social lionising he received. 'The club rang with "the honourable" until I perspired.' In Sydney the lionising continued. 'Next Sunday I am to go to the richest heiress of Sydney who apparently is very lavish and is to send two or three motors to fetch me.' He sent his mother detailed advice about her business interests. He recommended selling Hunter Street, Bourke Street, Forbes Street and Victoria Street while retaining a great deal of other property. He said the slums, though very wretched, were not a quarter as bad as those in England. And so having ordered the family affairs, and bought a quantity of boomerangs, he set sail for home, meeting his mother in Portofino on the way.

A few months after his return to England the news came at the end of July of the Young Turks' revolt in Salonika which excited Aubrey greatly. Turkish friends wrote joyous letters, confident that all would be well. Even Damad Farid, brother-in-law of the Sultan, was delighted by the turn of events, though he alone of Aubrey's correspondents struck a warning note. He wrote, 'C'est trop beau pour que les dieux n'en soient pas jaloux.' Aubrey wrote to Mervyn in August 1908:

> I wish them luck, the young Turks. It's very fine but it's only the beginning. The trouble will begin when, after they have elected their parliament, the committee is called upon to give up their power, to dismiss itself. Also equality is charming as a sentiment but Turkey will find it just as impracticable in their Empire as we have in ours. *Civis Romanus sum* is all right where all are Romans, and though we are Romans in theory, when our Indians claim equality in Canada or Australia, they not only don't get it but they can't even get in. You are bound to have trouble and exclusion or inequality where one class is ready to live for a quarter of what another will take. The Turk can't compete with the Syrian, the Armenian and the Jew. He is the dominant race, and in the interests of peace he should show that straight away, or blood will run in thick rivers in Constantinople.

Aubrey was not content to pontificate, however shrewdly, from a distance. He naturally wished to be there. This was the Revolution that he and his friends had so eagerly anticipated in night-long discussions in Constantinople. There were, however, some pressing engagements which were impossible to escape. His territorial army obligations encompassed the whole of August in camp at Westward Ho! and there were dates already forfeit in September and October for constituency events in Yeovil. Some speeches he delegated to his sister Vera who had become an enthusiastic party worker, although, as Aubrey wrote to Mary, 'She writes her speeches on blue paper with a blue pencil and then tries to read them in the twilight.' Aubrey was also, he thought, on the threshold of making his fortune. Even the cautious and practical Elsie was persuaded to participate in the scheme. The enterprise hinged on a new splash-proof bottle, invented by an Australian whom Aubrey had met on his travels. Aubrey wrote to Mervyn: 'The company will of course be limited . . . I have got to pay the Australian. He has sent me a sort of prospectus. It's a wonderful bottle, quite simple. I can't think why Galileo didn't discover it at the same time he found out the other thing. Nothing will ever splash again. There really is no knowing how much money we mayn't make: only write at once.' Aubrey always believed that he possessed a flair for business, but he was never rewarded by success in his occasional sorties into the world of finance.

In November Aubrey finally made his escape from England and his entanglements. He arrived in Constantinople on November 28th. He wrote to Elsie, 'I didn't realise how intensely glad I am to have done with Yeovil till I got here. It is a change to come from niggling non-conformists to people who really are ready to sacrifice all they have for their creed.' He found Constantinople still ablaze with fraternal revolution. Later he described the mood of the capital. 'The city was glowing like a rose, and tense with excitement. Where before there had been silence, crowds wandered singing. Christians had their arms round the necks of Moslems; the old order and the new mingled. There were high hopes for the future. Murder ceased; there was no thieving; baksheesh was refused; the millennium reigned.' The millennium's reign was brief. Already anxiety was taking over from euphoria. In October Bulgaria had proclaimed her independence and Austria had annexed Bosnia and Herzegovina. The Balkan countries were beginning to realise that a strong reformed Turkey did not suit their nationalist aspirations and the Young Turks were beginning to realise that the European powers who had for so long preached reform in fact preferred the old corrupt ways which gave them an excuse to meddle in, and extort economic concessions from, the creaking Ottoman Empire. 'Europe', Aubrey wrote, 'wanted a client and not a competitor.'

Aubrey was wholeheartedly behind the revolution and keenly resented the attitude of the British Government, as represented by the Embassy. The Ambassador, Sir Gerard Lowther, had been the object of enormous enthusiasm and popularity in the first days of the revolution. A mob had unharnessed his carriage horses and cheering Turks had themselves pulled the carriage up the steep hill to the Embassy. In November pro-British sentiment was still rampant. Anything English was revered. Moslem and Christian looked to the Mother of Parliaments for help, advice and support; but the help was not forthcoming, the advice heavy handed and the support grudging.

It was not in fact the policy of Sir Edward Grey or even of the Ambassador, Sir Gerard Lowther, that prevailed in the Embassy at Constantinople. The *eminence grise* of the situation was Aubrey's old friend FitzMaurice, now the senior Dragoman. A Catholic Irish gentleman of immense vitality, attractive, clever, subtle and passionate, he knew and loved Turkey deeply, spoke the language perfectly and dominated Embassy thinking. All his official life, whether serving in the Arabian Gulf or at Constantinople, FitzMaurice had dealt with, and indeed struggled against, the old Ottoman Turk, but he could not stand aside and see the old order crumble away. Aubrey, although in the opposing camp, could understand FitzMaurice's views and wrote years later:

> He could often talk the Turks' language as well as the Turk; he used the same silences and gutturals as deep as the Pashas, some of whom he had grown to respect. He was the ivy that supported the tottering Ottoman oak . . . Now in the place of the old pashas, with their stately presence, their high honorifics, their venerable beards, he was called upon to meet a miscellany of Jews from Salonika, of Turkish Boulevardiers, and moustachioed Syrians from Lausanne, who spoke to him, not in Turkish but in the French of Pera.

Aubrey also was susceptible to the courtesy and polish of the old ruling class, but this did not blind him to the qualities of the new order. He admired the courage and patriotism of the Young Turks and sympathised with them in their difficulties. The heroes of the revolution, men like Talaat and Enver, whose swagger and vulgarity disgusted FitzMaurice, Aubrey found convivial and likeable. He met Talaat for the first time the day after his arrival in Constantinople and described him in his diary: 'His face oval and sallow, with a wide forehead and very thick hair, heavy eyebrows and a hawk nose; a light in his eyes, rarely seen in men but sometimes in animals at dusk'. Aubrey met Enver a few days later. Friends at the Embassy had warned Aubrey against him, emphasising his vanity. It was said he could never pass a mirror without looking in it. Aubrey wrote in his diary, 'Saw Enver Bey this afternoon. Expected to find him posturing. Very agreeably surprised . . . He certainly strikes me as one of the most statesmanlike of the Turks. He has no desire whatever to put himself forward.' A week later they dined together. Aubrey wrote in his diary: 'Dined with Enver Bey. He goes as an attaché militaire to Berlin. I told him that I thought it was a pity . . .'

At the Parliament Club Aubrey found the old philosopher he had met in exile in Koniah, Riza Tewfic, now a deputy, and still talking of Spencer and Stuart Mill with undiminished enthusiasm. Aubrey also in his first week dined with Kiamil Pasha, the Grand Vizier. Kiamil was a puppet of FitzMaurice, and owed his position to Embassy influence. Aubrey's new friends among the Young Turks were not in sympathy with Kiamil and resented his appointment. Aubrey shared their views. He wrote in his diary 'His friends say he is seventy-eight and his enemies eighty-four. An impartial observer would on first impression say he is gaga . . . He is a Jew or said to be.'

Almost everybody to do with the revolution was either a Jew or said to be. Aubrey always maintained that the Jewish role was greatly exaggerated but the general impression that Jews, or at any rate unbelievers, were in control of the revolution contributed to the strength of the eventual reaction against it. The members of the Committee of Union and Progress were certainly not devout Moslems but then the Committee was not a cohesive body. Its members came from different classes, backgrounds and nationalities. There were idealists, rascals and preferment seekers. They were united only in a general detestation of the old regime. Aubrey wrote to his mother, 'Things don't lose their interest for a moment here; but it's rather like being a mole, there are so many ways and all of them underground.'

A little later he wrote to Mary Vesey:

> The young Turks here are utterly divided. The best men have gone back to the Army and politicians have come to the top . . . the power is going back to the Sultan. All these ministers are his men. Most of them have had his money in the past, some are said to take it now . . . I feel as if I was watching someone whom I liked very much and who had no experience of climbing, trying to get up a horrible cliff. . . I wrote to Violet [Asquith] drawing a piteous picture of things but I don't believe that Old Father [the prime minister] knows or cares very much. Grey, whom an old Turk spoke to me of, probably with dim reminiscence of an English dinner, as Greyvy, I believe does care.

In the excitement of the new dawn Aubrey did not forget old, unfashionable friends. He went and stayed the night with Damad Ferid, who was cautiously optimistic about the turn of events. The next day they lunched together at the Pera Palace Hotel. They were joined by Prince Sabah ed Din who warned them there was a man behind a screen next to their table. Aubrey pulled back the screen and the eavesdropper who had been taking notes on their conversation ran away. Ferid swore he was a German. It was a breath of the old Constantinople.

A breath of the new was felt on 17th December 1908 when the Sultan opened the revolutionary parliament. The Young Turks had taken the engines from his boat so Abdul Hamid trembling for his life and throne had to go by carriage. Crouched low in his victoria, he was forced to drive through the huge mixed crowds on his way to the Parliament which stood in the shadow of the great dome of Santa Sofia. Aubrey watched the scene and described his emotions in his diary. 'In spite of the extraordinary gentleness of the people, one knew how they all had suffered, how many had lost everything in life worth having through him, how he had made a horror of the life of a whole generation, and I, and I suppose everybody, wondered, will no one take revenge? And if they do where will it be? On the old bridge with the glitter of the golden horn or in the sordid street of Pera . . .'

Aubrey had been presented with one of the much coveted tickets for the ceremony. He watched the arrival of the Sultan and stayed for the speech from the throne. The Sultan never took off his overcoat but showed some unexpected courage in refusing to swear allegiance to the constitution. He made a reference to the oath he had made on his accession and with this the deputies had to be content. Aubrey wrote a long and eloquent account of the occasion for the *Spectator*, through which his own romantic attachment to the new constitution shone:

It seemed to me that behind the Deputies there were ranged, rank upon rank, the shadowy hordes of the constituents; that the stillness of the House reproduced the hush of Anatolia, where the long-suffering, stolid Turk waits for the news of life or death that will filter through to him by obscure channels. For in no idle, rhetorical sense, but in very truth, the destinies of the nation lie in the hands of the men that it has chosen, nearly all of whom are without experience of responsibility and statecraft. [The article ends] Will these men from the country who have done so much, be able to hold their own against European intrigue and the rapacity of the West? *In shallah*. God builds the nest of the blind bird, says the Turkish proverb.

In December Kiazim 'thoroughly constitutionalised' except for an unacceptable desire to kill Bulgars, turned up unbidden in Constantinople and returned to his former duties. Aubrey left Constantinople with Kiazim on 23rd December to visit his friends Bonham and Steven of the Gendarmerie in Drama for Christmas. After Christmas they moved on to Salonika to stay with the Consul and from there penetrated once more into Albania, riding in bitterly cold weather over frozen lakes and streams from Mitrovitza to Ipek. The Albanians were uncharacteristically enthusiastic about the constitution but nevertheless Aubrey foresaw much trouble ahead.

By late January 1909 Aubrey was back in England, but not for long. In February Mary Vesey and her mother came to stay at Portofino. By now Aubrey was deeply in love with her. In 1907 his letters had begun Dear Miss Vesey, by 1908 he had progressed to Dear Miss Mary and in 1909 after the Portofino visit he was writing Dear Mary. However the letters were not love letters and his relationship was still only that of a privileged friend. There seems to have been a convention that love could be expressed in poetry but not in prose, for while he was writing light impersonal letters he was bombarding her with love poetry:

> It's air without the sunlight, and sea without the tide,
> It's Mary without mercy, and a king who's lost his pride,
> A broken golden harpstring in a shrine that's filled with night,
> The life I live without you, and the day that lacks your light.

Aubrey had scarcely returned to England from Italy when news broke of the counter-revolution in Turkey. Aubrey hurriedly returned to Constantinople. He arrived a few days too late for the fighting but in time for the political battles. The counter-revolution had been brief. On 13th April, a mob bribed by the Sultan had collected outside the Chamber of Deputies and murdered several of the prominent members of the Committee of Union and Progress as they left the building. The Constantinople garrison of Albanians had been persuaded or bribed to revolt against the Constitution and for a brief space the city was in the hands of counter-revolutionary forces while former ministers went into hiding. However on 24th April, nine days later, troops under Enver, loyal to the Constitution, arrived from Salonika, and after some fierce fighting, prevailed. The Committee was reinstated and the Sultan, Abdul the Damned, finally deposed in favour of his brother Mohammed V. Aubrey was present when, for the first time in Ottoman history, a Constitutional Sultan was girt with the sword of Osman. Again he wrote an account for the *Spectator* comparing the ceremony with the one he had described in the same paper only four months before:

> Though it is summer now, there was nothing of the gaiety that marked the people upon the clear December day when Abdul Hamid swore for the last time that tyranny should cease. Then there was silence that held the attention as much as the spontaneous surge of cheering, but three days ago there was never perfect quietness, nor irrepressible shouts of gladness. The comparative stillness that fell as the Padishah drove past seemed rather a pause of sad reminiscence than of hope, a contemplation of the past rather than a prayer for the future. For much has happened since the opening of parliament. High expectations have failed; Sultan Hamid has once again smirched his great office . . .

Aubrey was among those whose high expectations had been dashed. He bitterly resented the role of the Embassy in the late events. He wrote to his mother, 'Four months ago when I was here there was nothing in the world the Turks would not do for an Englishman. All that is changed now. Our Embassy have snubbed them whenever it was possible, have supported the people they most disliked . . .' Aubrey blamed FitzMaurice and their friendship foundered, never completely to recover.

The second half of May and early June Aubrey spent travelling in Southern Albania. He left behind Kiazim, who had at last found some employment, taking instead an Austrian servant, named Joseph. His travels were disheartening. The fraternal spirit of a few months before was dead. Aubrey wrote to Mervyn, 'They keep on hanging people and before breakfast too. It creates a bad impression all round. I feel it myself', and about his servant Joseph he wrote, 'If only he was swarthier he would do'.

Meanwhile in England the political situation was in crisis. At the end of November 1909 the Tory Lords took the unprecedented step of throwing out the Budget. An immediate dissolution followed. Aubrey was not in Yeovil to do battle but laid up at Stanway with an injured ankle. He had indulged in a wrestling bout with the son of the house, Ego Charteris, and in the process had broken a small bone in his ankle. Arthur Balfour who, as so often, was also staying in the house, seeing Aubrey writhe in pain on the floor, thought he was watching a charade and applauded vigorously. Partly through the incompetence of the local doctor, the recuperation proved long and painful. However, for Aubrey there was a silver lining. Cynthia Charteris, a daughter of the house, and her cousin Mary Vesey took turns at his bedside, reading aloud and administering morphia. By the time Aubrey could walk again he had made a considerable impression on the affections of his 'Santa Ghiacciata' (holy icicle), Mary Vesey.

Aubrey lost the election in January 1910, but only just. He reduced Sir Edward Strachey's majority from 1,917 to 511 (the electorate in those days was very small and majorities correspondingly so). Aubrey had not expected to win and was more encouraged than dejected by the result. After the election party politics became unaccustomedly bitter. Aubrey, for once, was distracted from the affairs of the Ottoman Empire and immersed himself in the English political scene. Reginald Farrer, staying at Pixton shortly before the election, detected a change for the worse in Aubrey's character and wrote to tell him of it.

It is an impossible letter, an embarrassing document for both the writer and the recipient. Letters between friends in this period seem cloying to the modern mind. It is not their lack of reserve or their intensely personal nature that is distasteful but the extravagance of the flattery used between equals that is hard to swallow. But even in the context of the times this letter of Reginald's went beyond the limits of convention and plainly showed the extent of his unhappily suppressed homosexual yearning. The letter began without greeting:

> I am puzzled about you just now. I've never had quite such an unsatisfactory visit, seen so little of you, been made to feel quite so remote. Do you know you have the most curious isolating effect on me: it works doubly: first of all, I am swamped and put away on a shelf by the violent realisation of all your innumerable friendships, activities, manifestations in which I obviously have no share: in the second place I am always being reminded of the enormous and ever increasing divergence of all our thoughts, ideas and aspirations.

Aubrey's ideas, thoughts and aspirations are then examined in detail, likewise the thoughts and aspirations of Reginald, who with each passing year had become more self-absorbed. He was jealous of Aubrey's new enthusiasms and painfully jealous of his new friends:

> How whole-hearted is your allegiance to the men whose claim upon your admiration is that they are 'hard as nails'? Because it would not be a good thing if you too indistinguishably confused my ideas with me . . . my attitude, as opposed to your 'practical' heroes deserves a further consideration. In other words, though to live among ideals is ridiculous and unprofitable, sometimes you seem to me, in your views, to steer a middle course between shallowness and depth, to concentrate on the immediate and to ignore underlying principles . . . As for the practical men, who are hard as nails, with definite material aims in view, it is not perhaps possible to value their aims and their characters too highly, but it is possible to value them too exclusively. . . I mean these people talk a different language. Don't you learn it of them so completely, that I shan't be able to talk to you any more! I don't want, just yet, to be sent off alone on that grim hill journey which you poetically admire, while resolutely clinging to the fat grasslands beneath.

Pages more follow of convoluted prose in recrimination, self-abasement and self-analysis, ending up at last on a wounded, huffy note:

> You've prevented me for a long while to come from coming to you for help and encouragement. And I wanted to which makes it so boring of you to have patted my horns tight back into my shell! Perhaps you have only a faint conception of how enormously I value you and revel in you and take refuge in you. There it is, and that will always be. Thank you most kindly and with all my inmost heart, for being in the world and being my friend. But all the same you've shut me up on this occasion: I rather wonder at you for you know how

my nature works: and you've never done such a thing before: but now it'll take me a long time to uncoil to you again.

      – which leaves me as it finds me,

            Yours v. affly
            Reginald

Even so Reginald seemed unable to finish his letter and added a postscript of another two pages of extravagant devotion and wounded reproach, beginning: 'How very damnably ungrateful and carping is all this' and containing passages like: 'At your call I would still come and go like a two year old: for the possibility of your approach, yours alone among mortals, would I keep my aged bones out of bed after midnight: your voice has power to smooth my fur and retrench my claws in a manner nothing short of miraculous . . . But the fact is, you're the best person to be with in my world: the worst to visit . . .'

The criticisms that Reginald levelled at Aubrey seem on the whole wide of the mark. It is true that Aubrey was not an idealist in the sense that he neither subscribed to nor followed any set of high-minded ideas, although he was all too susceptible to causes. He was never, however, a materialist, never interested in material success and singularly indifferent to material comforts; he cannot justly be accused of 'clinging to the fat grasslands'. However, there was some substance in Reginald's real grievance, Aubrey's uncaringness in personal relations. Aubrey had the gift of inspiring devotion, a dangerous gift in unheeding hands. Throughout his life he treated those that loved him, and they were legion, cavalierly. His own nature was open and affectionate but he never understood or attempted to understand more complicated natures and passions. Poor Reginald suffered accordingly.

At this time, too, Aubrey's attentions were fully taken up with his pursuit of Mary Vesey. In April 1910, after travelling in Morocco with Charlie Meade and visiting Mervyn in Spain where the latter was en poste, Aubrey went to stay with the widowed Lady de Vesci at Abbeyleix, the Vesey family seat in Ireland which, in the absence of a Vesey son, had now passed by entail to a cousin, but which Lady de Vesci always took for a few months each year. There Aubrey proposed to Mary and was turned down. However the refusal was not definitive. When Aubrey left Abbeyleix he was confident that in time he would prevail. Mary's devotion to her mother, and deep sense of responsibility towards her, lay behind her refusal. Aubrey had succeeded in winning her affections, although in a tentative and insecure way.

On his return to England Aubrey confided his hopes to his mother. Lady Carnarvon and Lady de Vesci were on terms of formal friendship. Lady de Vesci had been to stay at Portofino and Pixton and Lady Carnarvon had borrowed Lady de Vesci's town house, 28 Bruton St, on one occasion. No two women however could have been more different in character. Elsie was serious, high-minded, organised. Her reading was government white papers, treatises on education or co-operatives or colonial affairs. All her pleasures were found in service to her family, to the community, in helping the less privileged. She had little humour, no instinct for beauty or comfort, no taste. Houses and clothes to her were simply places one lived in and things one wore. Her attitudes were strictly practical. None of her houses was comfortable or pretty inside. Her clothes were dull and dowdy. Evelyn de Vesci, in contrast, was worldly, frivolous and charming. She loved music and pretty things. She had an instinct for beauty which was apparent in all she touched. Her houses were delightful, temples of taste and discrimination. Her pleasures were in friendships, parties, music, intellectual games. Her reading was novels and poetry. Her attitudes were light-hearted and warm. She laughed often and easily. She was sympathetic, a good listener. Where Elsie Carnarvon was universally respected, Evelyn de Vesci was universally loved. Yet these two widows had one thing in common: both were adoring mothers.

Elsie wrote to Evelyn de Vesci to press Aubrey's claims. Elsie, though a possessive mother, was always in the important things of life generous and open-hearted. Aubrey's marriage would rob her of that which was dearest in her life but she espoused his cause with all the vigour of her nature. Lady de Vesci replied:

> Dearest Elsie,
>   Your little note *touched me very much*. I was startled . . . I still always feel Mary to be a child – an eager darling brilliant sort of a child – and I loved Aubrey's friendship for her and I honestly like him so much better – so differently – to any other of Mary's friends . . .
>   What are we to do?
>   *She is too young*
> I don't want selfishly to keep her – but I feel you would say as I do were she your girl – it is too soon to speak – if only Aubrey could feel that it would be possible to leave everything as it is for some time longer – to give her time to know more what she really feels. One thing is clear to her that she would feel deeply giving up her friendship with Aubrey . . .

Elsie wrote again. Lady de Vesci replied in the same illegible scrawl and breathless style: 'I am standing aside . . . I could not dare to influ-

Aubrey Herbert with his father, the Earl of Carnarvon

Aubrey Herbert, boy and man

Mary Vesey

Mary Herbert

Pixton

Kiazim

TANCRED CONINGSBY HERBERT
FINALLY THROWS
IN HIS LOT
WITH
YOUNG ENG
LAND.

wo caricatures of Aubrey Herbert,
ght) by Mark Sykes,
elow) by Margot Howard de Walden

Aubrey Herbert in the
trenches at Gallipoli

Mark Sykes

Aubrey Herbert in uniform

Aubrey Herbert
with his daughter Gabriel

Electioneering, 1918

Aubrey Herbert at Portofino

ence her, not even if I could do so. I could not dare it for either of their sakes . . . I know nothing, because I feel truly that now Mary does not know herself and in my heart I wish that it had come a little later.'

In fact when Lady de Vesci wrote these letters Mary had just had her twenty-first birthday and Aubrey had already waited three years before proposing. Elsie herself did not share Lady de Vesci's concern about Mary's age. She wrote to Aubrey, 'I do not think her too young. It is far better to marry at 21 than later but her dear mother has scarcely realised that she has grown up and is naturally startled at learning it in such an unmistakable way. But her youth has and will make you additionally tender and careful of her.'

Meanwhile Aubrey was writing to Mary: 'Till I hear from you everything is unreal. You will marry, lovely one, but no man who loves you as much as I do. Without you I am speaking in dreams and moving in shadows.'

In May Aubrey again went to stay at Abbeyleix and this time won a sort of uncertain secret acceptance from Mary. No engagement was to be announced and time must pass before anything definite could be settled. Aubrey nonetheless was well satisfied and returned to England elated. He went, as usual, to summer camp at Westward Ho! to fulfil his territorial army obligations with the Royal Devon Hussars. From there he wrote daily to Mary. Every letter began with a different endearment – My wild thyme, My delicious nun, Meraviglia mia, My gold and silver lily, My benediction, Rosalila, My proud spirit, My morning glory, Incomparable, My Cypress girl and many others in strange languages. His love letters were ardent, poetic and moving. Mary was duly moved. In her letters she gradually unfurled: 'How utterly the veil of a few weeks ago seems to have disappeared', she wrote, 'I feel such a sure and impregnable protection.' Aubrey replied, 'Getting letters from you after the tramp and business of these two days is like hearing clear songs and the wind in trees after the rattle of machinery, it's like being in a garden of roses and dew after you have been working at the architecture of drains.' Mary wrote, 'I don't feel anyone could carry off a typewritten love letter but you.'

Meanwhile Aubrey was anxious that no whisper of the engagement should reach the outside world and destroy the precarious position he had gained. He wrote to his mother forbidding her to mention it, even within the family: 'they would all intend not to say a word and very likely they wouldn't, but still a secret shared by a number of people is fairly sure to leak out and I think there are quite enough who know as it is. I am most perfectly content with things as they are at the present moment, and I hope you will be. I want to marry Mary and I know the

best way to do that.' And he did. By the end of June Mary's last reserva-
tions had been swept aside and on 1st July 1910 the engagement was
formally announced.

Mary's friends were horrified that this lovely girl should throw herself
away on a half-blind, disreputably dressed man with curious foreign
friends. Aubrey was not an ornament of society, he was a well-
connected rough diamond. There were murmurs of 'Beauty and the
beast'. Nor did Aubrey's friends greet the news with pleasure. Leland
Buxton wrote:

> I never congratulate people on these occasions if I can help it, because
> matrimony usually makes people selfish, indifferent and unenterprising, but
> as you are an original person you will probably be a brilliant exception . . .
> You've had some great moments, and I suppose the shades of the prison house
> will be a new experience. I was very surprised to hear of it. It is not a bit like
> you and I have a terrible fear that you must have changed, and that I shan't
> like you any more. I suppose being in politics on the fashionable and correct
> side is enough to destroy anyone's soul. I didn't mean to be rude when I began
> . . .

But while bachelor friends might be excused for venting some traditional hostility to the institution of marriage, even close married friends
like Raymond Asquith thought Aubrey had done better than he
deserved. He wrote: 'Your luck amounts to genius. To be frank with you
a more glittering prize was never awarded to a more mis-spent life than
yours.' But Raymond, at least, was delighted by the engagement – his
letter continued:

> For a very long time nothing has pleased me so much (nor you either I dare
> say) as this news. Both of you are now firmly secured within the particular
> little plot of society which also contains Katherine and me. Whereas either of
> you might so easily have strayed into some alien and inaccessible orbit. Mary
> was capable of marrying an Irishman and living on an island: you might have
> been entangled either with a dowdy aristocrat or with a flashy cosmopolitan,
> a Hapsburg or a Levantine; but you have secured breeding without dullness
> and beauty without vice. This shows that it is possible to rise, as well as to
> fall, between two stools.
> [The letter continues in a lyrical paean of praise to Mary's beauty] She is
> superb, one of the jewels of the universe. I well remember the day when it first
> occurred to me that Mary was one of the most beautiful women in Europe. It
> was last August when Katherine and I were at Venice. Mary had just come
> down from the Dolomites and we went to take her out to dinner. I walked
> with her from our hotel across the Piazza to the 'Vapore' and it was like
> walking with an archangel: there was a depth of radiance in her beauty which

beat back the twilight as a strong swimmer divides the waves: it was as if the brightest star were reflected in the darkest sapphire; the church of St Mark was enriched as she passed: and as I led her through the tables of Florians I was thrilled with a sort of celestial snobbery, a pure racial pride which Kipling and Nelson and Tariff Reform and all the rest of our Imperial assets have never been able to stir in me.

[The letter ends] Bless you, my dear Aubrey. I wish we were drinking together to this great exploit of yours.

As the engagement progressed Mary became more confident and wilful in her dealings with Aubrey. First she tackled the vexed subject of his clothes.

I must tell you a thing which will make you furious with me. I am going to take you to a tailor myself and choose a stuff and make you have a brand new country suit for Gosford. For you must take it for granted that clothes are important and some day you will grow to understand and agree for that side has never been put before you. Grandpapa rightly or wrongly sets great store by dress, and judges by it, so for the sake of future peace you must let me have my way. I don't want to turn you into a fashion plate. I want you to look like a brigand, especially in the country, but I want the brigand to be prepared by the best tailor. I also don't mind the Latin Quarter student effect in London, but the one thing I can't stand is any suspicion of a Mr Hoopdriver [an H. G. Wells character] effect and an out of fashion Norfolk jacket is always liable to do that. It couldn't with you because nothing could but it's too great a risk. So we will visit the tailor next week and not the tailor that made for Dr Johnson and Dickens.

Every grand-daughter of Lord Wemyss had to pass the ordeal of presenting her prospective husband at Gosford. Lord Wemyss (nicknamed the brigadier within the family) was born three years before the death of Napoleon and was the oldest living peer in the land. He was a beloved and splendid figure but ugliness, awkwardness or untidyness distressed him, while turned-up trousers reduced him to speechless rage.

The next defect in Aubrey that Mary set out to remedy was his indiscriminate hospitality at Pixton. In August she wrote: 'I can't and won't cope with overflowing promiscuous parties. You must curb your generous hospitable instincts – with you it amounts simply to self-indulgence and it is only the wonderful self-sacrifice and nobility of your women folk that has submitted to your hordes of drunken consuls all these years. Now I am neither self-sacrificing nor noble. I come of a supremely selfish, worldly, ambitious stock, and I cannot waste my youth, health and beauty on drunken consuls.' However she ended the letter, 'Under this rather militant suffragette tone there is, as you know, all the most dutiful feelings of a Greek slave.'

Mary did not win the battle of the consuls. They continued to come and go at Pixton in increasing numbers, mingling harmoniously and unharmoniously with the fashionable and beautiful that she imported. Nor did she win the battle of the clothes. Aubrey briefly looked respectable for his visit to Gosford. Thereafter he relapsed into his usual tramp-like disarray.

These were trivial skirmishes. Mary had no real desire to change Aubrey but she did have a burning desire to come first with him. Although she herself was a loving and dutiful daughter, she resented Elsie Carnarvon's hold on Aubrey from the beginning. During her engagement Mary suppressed this feeling and genuinely tried hard to please and love her prospective mother-in-law. Elsie for her part had no need to dissemble. She loved Mary as an automatic extension of her love for Aubrey.

Elsie was briefly distracted from Aubrey's forthcoming nuptials by the behaviour of Mervyn. Mervyn was in love with Lady Letty Manners, one of the three beautiful daughters of the Duchess of Rutland. Elsie, in common with most mothers of the period, strongly disapproved of these girls, or 'the Hot House' as they were called. Aubrey wrote to Mary about Mervyn, 'the fact of my going to be married has apparently made him want to also.' Mervyn had gone to tea with Letty and stayed till 5.30 in the morning. Mary replied putting the Hot House in its proper perspective:

> I am very much amused by Mervyn's tea-party. I am sure it was fun there and you shouldn't grudge it him. For they are much more amusing than other people – and Letty I swear to you is a good girl . . . Besides you are much too suspicious of her intentions. Why, the Hot House is one of the few places in London where people can frolic without having to look out for meshes at their feet. It's in such respectable houses as the Strathmores and Dartmouths that really perilous traps are laid. Even if Marjorie [Manners] does lay traps they are as limpidly obvious as daylight and Letty never intrigues. She leaves it to her mother, who weaves wonderful artistic gossamer webs that people can just trample through. It is the good and conscientious mother who weaves them of hemp so that they cannot be broken down. But even if for once the gossamer web held, why is it a tragedy? Letty would make Mervyn a very ornamental and amusing wife. She would always keep him amused and do what he liked for she really is a good girl but then I am nearly certain that the trap is trimmed for another bird, and that they have not given up hope, for he's very shy. But beware of Diana [Manners], she is wicked I am sure . . .

Mary was quite right about the trap being trimmed for another bird.

To Mervyn's great disappointment, Letty was married before the year was out to Mary's first cousin and great friend Ego Charteris, soon to be Lord Elcho, a more eligible suitor.

Both Aubrey and Mary found their engagement trying. They were rarely together and even then seldom alone. The wedding was fixed for October 20th. In September they both set out in different directions to go on solitary holidays with their mothers. Mary took Lady de Vesci to Germany to see the Passion Play at Oberammergau. Aubrey took Elsie to Constantinople. Kiazim materialised from nowhere and remained in attendance. The visit was not a success. The authorities had massacred the huge dog population and deported the survivors to an island. Aubrey minded quite disproportionately. He was, he wrote to Mary, 'haunted by the ghosts of dogs and the stories of cruelty to them', and he fretted at his separation from her. He wrote, 'I want to fill your white hands with moonstone and pomegranate seeds' and 'It has been a mistake having this damned absolute separation, and yet things were very difficult in England too, weren't they?'

The wedding, which took place on 20th October 1910, was a grand society affair. St James's, Piccadilly, was filled to overflowing. The bride was given away by her aged grandfather, the Earl of Wemyss, and attended by fourteen grown-up bridesmaids, all children of Peers, like Aubrey and Mary themselves. The reception was held at 29 Grosvenor Square, lent by Mary's aunt, Lady Bath.

The society papers were filled, column after column, with accounts of what each guest wore for the occasion and lists of the wedding presents. These were lavish: silver, diamonds, rubies, motor-cars, furniture and furs. Aubrey's gift to his bride, tucked incongruously, in the *Morning Post*, between a large silver box from Princess Victoria of Schleswig Holstein and a diamond rivière from the Marquis and Marchioness of Bath, was two thoroughbred wolf-hounds.

6

Marriage and Parliament

Few honeymoons can have been better chronicled than Aubrey's and Mary's. Each wrote almost daily to their respective mothers and several times to their new mothers-in-law. Aubrey's original wish had been to go to the Scilly Isles. This whim Mary had resisted, writing to her mother, 'Thank God Aubrey has forgotten about the Scilly Islands. I should have felt branded with ridicule for life if we had honeymooned there.' She was not, however, uncritical of Highclere where they went instead and its 'prosperous English park'. She found it a place 'without enchantment', and though she wrote of 'cloudless times together' she could not share Aubrey's love for his boyhood home and complained of 'hideous ivory curios that Aubrey adores'. Despite these carpings there is a clear thread of joy running through her letters to her mother.

Her letters to her new mother-in-law on the other hand are more laboured. Elsie had written asking Mary to find a 'little name' to call her by. To Mary this seemed an impossible sentimentality. Eventually she wrote uncompromisingly 'Darling Lady Carnarvon' and left open the question of a name; 'Aubrey,' she wrote, 'pacing the library like a panther, has annihilated all my suggestions and insists that Turkish is the only true language for endearment but I don't think somehow that either you or I would feel much reality about Turkish.'

From Highclere, the honeymooning couple moved on to Picket's Post, Bron Herbert's house in the New Forest. Mary found Picket's Post much more to her taste than Highclere. She wrote to Lady de Vesci: 'Picket is a paradise', and she praised 'the proud democratic life here, utterly free and utterly unbourgeois'.

For the third leg of their honeymoon, they moved to Holnicote, the Exmoor home of the Aclands, distant cousins of the Herberts and large West Country landowners. Although famed as a magical spot Holnicote pleased Mary no more than Highclere; she wrote, 'The house is Morris in parts but downstairs it's uncomfy and awkward and there are nothing but bookcases of unreadable ten-year-old novels mixed up with small dusty religious works and gems from English poetry.' Her view may have been jaundiced by the arrival of Lady Carnarvon who came over for one night from Pixton where she had been clearing out the last of her small personal clutter. Mary wrote to Lady de Vesci, 'Lady Carnarvon came for Monday night; it was no better . . . I immediately felt a waif as usual, for in spite of a wish not to be she is obstinate and commandeering and does impose her will . . . if we were much together it would end in a dogged pull of wills. As it is she took command of Aubrey and talked and things became dry powder in her hands as she spoke . . . anyhow it has been very blissful since she tootled away yesterday afternoon.' The dogged pull of wills was postponed, but there was little possibility that two such powerful women could forever put off a major engagement.

After Holnicote, Aubrey and Mary returned briefly to London to take possession of 28 Bruton St, Lady de Vesci's magnificent Mayfair house, which she had generously made over to them. Then on Saturday 12th November they took a train to Pixton.

The people of Dulverton, Bury, Brushford and Kings Brompton had made elaborate preparations for this homecoming. The tenantry of Pixton were feudally exuberant. Earlier in the year they had staged an overwhelming welcome for Aubrey on his return as the defeated candidate for Yeovil. They were determined on this occasion to outdo all previous efforts. A committee and two sub-committees, one for lighting and one for decoration, were formed. Detonators had been placed along the railway track which were discharged by the approaching train to warn the waiting crowd of the imminent arrival. The station was decorated with streamers and flags and laurel bushes. A carpet and triumphal arch saying *welcome* were on the platform. Amidst loud and prolonged cheering Aubrey and Mary descended from the train and walked between a guard of honour formed by the Royal Devon Hussars to their carriage. There, the white horses had been taken out of the shafts and ropes attached, so that the carriage could be pulled by the tenantry and employees of Pixton Estate. A torchlit procession formed, led by the Dulverton Brass Band, followed by the two led carriage horses, unencumbered of their load, then four mounted Hussars, then the carriage dragged by tenantry, then more mounted and unmounted Hussars, then the Dulverton boy scouts, then the station-master and assistant station-master and bringing up the rear a huge crowd, singing, cheering and, according to the local paper, 'emitting hunting cries'. All this rowdy enthusiasm was apparently undampened by a prolonged downpour. Bedraggled but still cheering they made the one and a half mile journey to Pixton, up the station drive to the house, where more illuminated arches bearing messages *God bless the happy pair, Thine own wish wish I thee* and other such sentiments greeted them.

Aubrey and Mary were unable to spend much time basking in their local popularity. Parliament was dissolved on 28th November 1910 and once again the country found itself in the throes of a General Election. Aubrey and Mary left Pixton for Yeovil. They made their headquarters at Coker Court. In January Aubrey had been forlornly fighting a 2,000 majority but that he had reduced to 511, and in December for the first time victory seemed possible. Hopes were high in the Conservative camp, but Aubrey again lost the contest. The figures were: Sir Edward Strachey 4,784; Hon. Aubrey Herbert 4,317. Sir Edward's majority of 467 was down a further 44 votes but it was still a disappointing result.

Aubrey meanwhile was running into financial difficulties. Elsie as usual came to the rescue. Aubrey wrote to her, 'I can't bear having taken that thousand from you. But it really has made more than a thousands difference to me. I hope it hasn't in another sense to you my dearest.' Aubrey hated sponging off his mother and was perpetually on the look out for independent ways of supplementing his income. He turned his mind towards business. Undeterred by the failure of his splash-proof bottle, he now gave his enthusiasm to a new cork. His old friend from Constantinople, the rising young diplomat Eric Phipps, now en poste in Paris was recruited to persuade Perrier to promote the new cork. Phipps wrote from Paris, 'We still hope the corks will sell, but it's a long business persuading dull people that they are the only possible corks (chiefly because there is no cork in them).'

In another quarter, Aubrey's hopes of financial fortune had once more been raised by an invention which was the brainchild of an Albanian shepherd whom he had met in a remote region of that country. It was a machine for perpetual motion that worked without electricity, oil, water or coal. It was made of wood. Aubrey, who liked to share his prospects of prosperity with his friends, wrote to Charlie Meade and invited him to participate. Charlie replied: 'I hope the man with the substitute for the steam engine will not require the whole of our fortune.'

The same year, still optimistic, and on what might if pursued have turned out to be an altogether more profitable tack, Aubrey wrote to Mary from his territorial camp at Minehead with another money-making plan. 'I have developed my Arabian oil scheme with St Hill. He is to do the fighting while I interpret with an umbrella behind. It really would be a fine thing if we could make a fortune.'

Mary was expecting a child. Aubrey was not elated at the prospect. He wrote to his brother Mervyn, 'It's very provoking. I have never looked on children as anything but a misfortune – like public speaking a duty and a bore – but there it is.' Aubrey was at this time going through a crisis of nerves. While Mary struggled to make Pixton pretty ('Come quickly and restore my shreds of taste,' she wrote to her mother. 'I have a sort of terror that my eye is growing into the passion flowers and gold curtains, I notice it less and less'), Aubrey struggled against the domesticity he felt encircling him. Mary in turn feared that country life was swamping her and wrote to Lady de Vesci, 'I really am beginning to get worried about my propensity for Marthadom. Aubrey really must get into parliament quick and I must return to the irresponsible life of society and quick movement or I shall degenerate into a provincial hausfrau . . . I spent an hour this morning with Hutton (the butler) pinching Baskerville (the chauffeur) so as to see how badly his clothes fitted. I discussed for another hour butter-making with Marguerite in a disgustingly prolix way. You must save me from all the layers of wrinkles and double chins and dreary clothes that these symptoms point to.'

Aubrey was displaying more serious symptoms pointing to more serious ailments. In March his hair started to fall out in round patches. He was suffering from *alopecia*. Mary explained to her mother, 'It is an insidious disease that spreads like wild fire, a microbe that eats the hair till the head is reduced to a perfectly smooth pink surface. Paraffin is the only cure. We douche Aubrey's head with it and I am thankful to say it shows no progress. He must also eat enormously as it is a matter of nerves and worry. I couldn't bear to have a completely pink-headed husband especially as his hair was so jolly and Aubrey is panic stricken . . . If I see any signs of a new patch I shall send him straight up to London . . .'

New patches came and Aubrey set out on a cheerless round of doctors and nerve specialists in London. New hair began to come in the bald patches, but it was snow white. Soon Aubrey's head presented a speckled appearance which it retained for the rest of his life. His depression took longer to cure. Mary and Elsie fought over him. The warfare between these two strong-willed women, both of whom he loved deeply, exacerbated his condition. Gradually Mary won the battle, which though undeclared had been bitter, and Aubrey for his part gradually recovered his nerves and spirits. As for Elsie, she was content in her son's recovery and genuinely delighted in the evident strength and happiness of his marriage. Her nature was neither sensitive nor suspicious. She never bore grudges. She truly loved Mary as Aubrey's wife and never realised how close she had come to alienating her daughter-in-law irrevocably.

In the summer of 1911, Blackwood's published a slim volume of Aubrey's verse, entitled *Eastern Songs*. Aubrey used the nom de plume Ben Kendim (Turkish for 'I, myself') which he had used many times before in his casual journalism. The book was dedicated to his mother and gave her great pleasure. The verse is varied. The collection ranged over many years and many travels. One, 'Damascus Gate', written in 1906, is particularly pleasing.

> She went to bargain in the city,
> And passed a beggar by her gate,
> And he was wretched, so from pity
> She gave, because his need was great.
>
> And this was like her, that she gave
> In charity without a thought
> A coin of gold, for 'gold can save'
> (She said) 'What gold has never bought'.
>
> The beggar followed where she went,
> Forgot his hunger for a star,
> And when at last, her money spent
> She could not buy in the bazaar,
>
> He said, 'Take back your gift, I pray,
> Do me this honour, once my due.'
> She bought with it red silk, and grey,
> And that was very like her, too.

In July Reginald Farrer came to stay at Pixton. Initially the visit went well, but soon his prickly, difficult nature overcame his good intentions. Mary though pleased to exploit his gardening knowledge, did not like him. She described him to her mother as 'a malevolent gnome, with a wish to be fascinating but an ill-restrained bitterness of tongue'.

In August Aubrey and Mary moved to London to await the birth of their child. On 29th September 1911 Mary was safely delivered of a daughter. The baby was christened Gabriel Mary Hermione. Aubrey chose the names but was not present for the christening, as almost immediately after the birth he left England for Constantinople. Affairs in Turkey had reached an interesting stage. The rule of the Committee of Union and Progress was not running smoothly. Martial law, established after the counter-revolution, had not been lifted and the Committee had resorted to a regime of terror little better than that which prevailed in the bad old days of Abdul Hamid. And Turkey was now in open conflict with Italy. Aubrey was saddened by the state of his beloved city.

By chance, as Aubrey walked through the streets on his first day in Constantinople, he met Kiazim who promptly returned to his duties. At his hotel, Kiazim talked volubly and despairingly of the state of Turkey. To distract him Aubrey asked him to sing a ballad as he unpacked the clothes. Kiazim sang. Others were less easily distracted. All Aubrey's friends were gloomy; the idealism of the revolution was dead. Turkey faced humiliation on every side. Aubrey on this visit consorted more with the opposition parties and less with the Committee men. He saw a great deal of Riza Tewfic and Hilmi Pasha and Damad Ferid. He wrote daily to Mary. His letters were a jumble of love and politics. His endearments were exotic. Letters begin 'My Lightly Treading Marazion', 'My Black Browed Kara Kash', and other totally incomprehensible salutations. 'I don't think any man has ever been made so little aware of limitations by his wife as I by you,' he wrote. 'You have made my life' and 'Constantinople is to me among cities what you are among women.' In one letter he lists the main characters in the drama.

There is the poor old Grand Vizier Said, covered with flies like a mummy in age, who vacillates from side to side, gravitating more and more to the Committee; old Kiamil, ninety-three, mouthing like a dotard, yearning for power and for his brigand son in exile, but refusing to take office unless he is quite free of the Committee and meaning to break that machine when he does; and Hilmy, with twenty years of life in spite of the assassins of the Yemen, sitting like an intelligent Arab Shagpat at Shish where I shall see him this afternoon. And behind all these people Javid and Jahid, pulling strings, loading revolvers, in any dark place between the Ghetto and the Palace or the Porte. My little creature, it is interesting. This is still Byzantium. One thinks the next years must open a new chapter but the same refrain runs through all the chapters.

Interesting though it undoubtedly was, Aubrey was unable to stay long. Sir Edward Strachey had accepted a peerage in the Coronation honours list and the Yeovil by-election was called for November 21st. Aubrey was back in time to fight a brisk three-week campaign. When the votes were counted Aubrey was found to have won by the slender majority of 138. There were tumultuous scenes of rejoicing. In London when the news of the Yeovil result came through, dealing was briefly suspended on the floor of the Stock Exchange to allow members to give voice to their enthusiasm. For it was a famous victory. What only two years before had been considered one of the safest Liberal seats in the country had fallen dramatically to the Conservatives.

Meanwhile the Conservative Party had suffered a major upheaval. On 8th November, Balfour, bored by the intrigues against him, resigned the leadership. On 13th November at a meeting at the Carlton Club, the Party elected, unopposed, an outsider as his successor, Mr Bonar Law. When Aubrey therefore took his seat in the House of Commons at the end of November 1911 his leader was no longer the familiar figure of Arthur Balfour, whose subtle and discerning mind had delighted the drawing rooms of the Souls and earned the affectionate respect of Aubrey's and Mary's generation, but a total stranger, Bonar Law, contemptuously dismissed by Asquith as 'the gilded tradesman'. Bonar Law, the son of a Presbyterian minister of Ulster origins, was born in Canada and spent his childhood in Glasgow. There was nothing in this austere and obscure man, one would suppose, to appeal to Aubrey. Bonar Law represented the hard-headed capitalist, unsentimental side of Toryism which had little in common with Aubrey's romantic feudal brand. And yet, surprisingly, from their first meetings Aubrey liked and respected his leader.

Among the newer, younger Tory members, there were some exceptional and gifted men. To these Aubrey naturally gravitated. Foremost among them were two old friends from Constantinople, Mark Sykes and George Lloyd. Mark Sykes had won a by-election only a few months before Aubrey but George Lloyd had been returned in the first election of 1910 and so had nearly two years' parliamentary experience behind him. All three of them were chiefly interested in foreign policy. They each had considerably more understanding and knowledge of the Eastern Question, in particular, than their elders on either of the front benches, which the House was quick to recognise and appreciate. However, domestic politics can seldom have been more compelling and it may seem strange today that these three clever and versatile young men should have shown so little interest in the momentous struggles of the day on the home front. Of the three, Aubrey was the most indifferent. While Lloyd George was pushing through a radical programme of social reform which was to change the whole structure and direction of English life, heralding the Welfare State and a fairer if less sturdy society, Aubrey's eyes remained fixed on the Balkans. The great increase in industrial unrest, the savage fight for women's suffrage, the economic battles between Free Traders and Tariff Reformers, scarcely engaged his attention. Like most of his class, he feared the land valuations Lloyd George sought, resented the income tax, and half believed revolution was round the corner, but he seldom spoke in the house about such matters. Although from Turkey he had written of that 'stinking thing the status quo', in England he generally supported the stinking thing. He even voted against women's suffrage in the free vote in the House of Commons in 1912.

Within a month of his election, on 14th December 1911, Aubrey made his maiden speech. At the time it earned him much praise and congratulation, not only from old friends like Belloc and Bron Herbert, but also from that seasoned parliamentarian John Redmond who declared it the best maiden speech he had heard for many years. The subject of the speech was, needless to say, Turkey and its theme a plea for understanding and sympathy for that country in its current difficulties.

Soon after his debut in the House Aubrey and his friend Mark Sykes were invited to join a dining club. This club, which became known as the Tuesday Club because it met on Tuesday evenings in a small room off the Terrace of the House of Commons, was at the heart of Aubrey's parliamentary life. It was founded by Sir Ian Malcom in succession to the 'Hughligans', a group which took its name from Lord Hugh Cecil.

The club had little political significance, but Aubrey derived much of his pleasure in membership of the House from the company of this convivial band. One rite always observed before the evening broke up was the drawing by Mark Sykes of a caricature in the Club Book. Aubrey was a favourite victim of Mark's pen. The book is now lost and so the only caricatures to survive are those published in Shane Leslie's book on Mark Sykes. One entitled *The Apotheosis of Aubrey Herbert* and captioned *Tancred Coningsby Herbert finally throws in his lot with Young England* is reproduced between pages 90 and 91.

Few of Aubrey's friends in the House of Commons, with the exception of the Cecil brothers, were national figures. Aubrey's closest cronies, after Mark Sykes and George Lloyd, were Lord Alexander Thynne and Lord Henry Cavendish-Bentinck. Alex Thynne was killed in the Great War and Henry Bentinck's politics were always too wild for serious consideration.

Within his own party, Aubrey knew all the prominent people but was on terms of intimacy with none. Among the Liberals he was more naturally at home. He was bound to the whole Asquith family circle by ties of warmest friendship. He lunched and dined often at Downing Street, weekended at The Wharf, saw Raymond, Beb and Violet continually. His wife Mary, like many other beautiful young women, was a favourite of the Prime Minister's. However, as time went on, and political tempers ran high, Aubrey was subjected to increasingly hostile pressure from his own party about his familiarity with the Asquith circle. By 1914 his whips were suspicious and distrustful of his contacts with Downing Street. Aubrey, in May, records in his diary his own uneasiness: 'Asked down to P.M's. Have refused. Think it is too difficult. They chatter, the women do, about things of great importance, as if they were talking of daisies. They are intelligent, inconsequent, informed and partisan; and one is liable to be either a spy in their camp, or untrue to one's party.' Much as he was amused by the company of Margot Asquith (his nickname for her in letters to Mary was The Old Curiosity Shop) he was well aware of the dangers of her irresponsible gossip.

It was not only with the Liberals that Aubrey felt uneasy in 1914. His relations with his own party had become severely strained. The activities of Carson in Ulster and Bonar Law's connivance in these activities, led Aubrey and his friends seriously to contemplate resigning the Unionist whip and forming a new party of moderates. Their plans came to nothing, but by happy chance Aubrey, who seldom kept a diary in London, adopted the practice during the spring of 1914.

The diary is too long to quote in full but some extracts will serve to illustrate the prevailing mood. The following background will make the extracts more comprehensible:

Redmond, for the Irish Nationalists, had in the two elections of 1910 unexpectedly achieved Parnell's dream of holding the balance of power in the House of Commons. His price for support of the Liberal Government was home rule for Ireland. In 1912 Asquith had introduced the Third Home Rule Bill. The recent removal of the House of Lords' power of veto ensured the enactment of a bill after two years' delay if it passed the House of Commons a second time during the same parliament. This was now imminent and the Unionists, infuriated by their powerlessness to stop the Bill, encouraged Carson's campaign of incitement to disorder in the North for the exclusion of Ulster and connived at mutinous feelings in the British Army. In March 1914 came the Curragh mutiny followed by the resignation of Seely, the War Minister. Aubrey and his friends believed that the unity of Ireland could be preserved by a federal system within a Dominion framework and strongly disapproved of Carson's behaviour and Bonar Law's support. In his diary that year, Aubrey wrote:

April 19
Told Mary I thought of resigning my seat and fighting on a peace platform. She received this news rapturously, but wanted to know if it would interfere with my giving her a horse . . . Saw Mark [Sykes] again after dinner, suggested careful selection of patriots . . . We decided to have small nucleus dinner at Bruton St or Buckingham Gate. No servants. An enormous table, crab, lobster quails, plovers eggs, Yquem, champagne, hock. A traitors' party: who are loyal to the Empire.

April 26
Lord Roberts' interview with the King was apparently a command to him to apologise to Seely. Lord Roberts said on the telephone to French, 'that swine Seely' and French reported him. The Federal Ferdies have been getting into deep water, I expect the other side, the Conciliation Cuthberts, have been doing the same. The Whips have said they do not approve, and our people have left us; a few faithful.

This morning Mark and I went to Lord Edmund Talbot. We asked him why he had put an embargo on Federalism, he said Bonar had told him to. I said that if Bonar meant civil war I could not follow him. Mark said the same. Ld E asked us to go and see Bonar.

April 30

Had a federal meeting in the House in the afternoon. Devlin came and talked to Mark and me. He said they could give no further concessions . . . He also did not definitely say they would not accept Winston's proposal, but he spoke of it as this Churchill business and said Winston and F. E. Smith had come together over it. FE is said to be toying with the instinct of fear . . .

In the evening dined with the P.M., Mary [Herbert], Margot [Asquith], Violet [Asquith], [Edwin] Montagu. Never had a more curious dinner. Margot whispering on one side of me, Violet on the other. Nerves visible everywhere except the P.M. who looked tired and worn. People's hands spilled their wine, at least mine did mine. Violet began by asking if there had been a plot. I said of course there had, this led off merrily. We got through dinner somehow, Margot, Mary and Violet left. Violet returning like an ADC to give her father some papers. He then settled down to catechize me. I readily gave my impressions of the danger of the situation but mentioned no names . . . I told him I was afraid of the Japanese spirit on our side: that people were worked up to such a pitch, that the sacrifice of their lives at a price was beginning to appear glorious. That a number of back benchers wanted to settle, and that if the Gov. failed to meet Carson's moderation in the same spirit we should all be driven into the ranks of the extremists. Montagu spoke in silky, Jewish, vindictive tones, like a man who is only getting fifty per cent when he expected eighty. Once or twice the PM said 'I take a broader view than that', when he (Montagu) was attacking Ulster . . .

May 15

. . . Went to H of C. Told whips I had paired and should be away for 3rd Reading of Home Rule Bill but would stay and vote against Home Rule, if they would let me make a speech in favour of it. Left them annoyed . . . Dined Kuhlmans between Baroness Kuhlman and Lady Cunard. The last is a dreadful little wart on civilisation. Her profile is as disastrous as her full face. Vulgar, stupid, not over kind, boring. I accepted all her invitations and pressed for more. Advised Mary to do same, and then write notes saying how obstinate are the obstacles that prevent acceptance . . .

May 28

. . . Walked to his house with Mark. Quarrelled vehemently on Turkey and made friends violently. In the afternoon in the House, Lloyd George in the smoking room came up and put his hands on one of my knees and Winston on the other. I fled as I saw the Ulstermen looking at me stonily . . . Yesterday I had a horrible thing happen. I went into the bathroom and meant to fling a lot of lotion on my head instead I poured on it almost pure carbolic acid. I spent several hours in great agony, wondering what had happened to the follicles of my hair. Oddly enough it did not make my temper bad . . .

At the end of May Aubrey left England with Mary to spend a month in

Portofino. They left behind at Pixton, Gabriel now nearly three years old and the new baby Bridget who had been born on 22nd February 1914. Although Gabriel had wriggled a little way into his heart, Aubrey still remained aloof from the nursery world. Announcing Bridget's arrival to Mervyn he wrote: 'Mary is well and the baby is as well as a child can be that looks as like Lord Haldane as it does'; while to his mother he wrote, 'I am afraid you will be disappointed that it is not a boy; personally I don't mind, in fact I rather prefer it as it is.'

7

The Sanjak of Novi Bazar – Albanian Adventures

From the time of his election in 1911, Aubrey had embraced English parliamentary life with enthusiasm, but the greatest part of his energies and interests were given to Balkan affairs. During the three years between his election and the outbreak of the Great War, Aubrey worked tirelessly both at home and abroad for the cause of Albanian nationalism. These were dramatic years in the Balkans as the grip of the Ottoman Empire trembled, finally to be broken bloodily in the first Balkan War in 1912.

It was not until August 1912, a full ten months after his last visit, that Aubrey managed to return to the Balkans. There was in particular a corner of Albania in the North East that Aubrey had never visited. This area, known as the Sanjak of Novi Bazar, was not really Albania but, as Aubrey put it, 'a no-man's land, occupied by the Turks, held precariously by the Albanians, ruled by none'. Today it is part of Yugoslavia. Then, in August 1912, it was in its usual turbulent condition. Albania as a whole was in a state of uneasy peace, awaiting the concessions, won by force of arms, in the revolt against the Turks of 1911–12, and negotiated by the Archbishop of Scutari.

Aubrey kept a diary of his journey, beginning in Vienna on 20th August. From there he went to Sarajevo, the town that two years later was to be the scene of the assassination that led to the Great War. Then, however, it was a peaceful backwater, enjoying the tolerant rule of the Austrians who had liberated it from the Ottomans in 1878. It was not altogether to Aubrey's liking. He wrote in his diary: 'In the town the West is conquering the East, the mean hotel crowds out the mosque, and the ostentation of the synagogue is blatant.' He found everyone extraordinarily helpful, all vying to give advice on his proposed journey to the Sanjak. The diary continues:

Different counsels were given to me in Sarajevo. The first advice, Austrian, was, 'Do not go to Sanjak; it's a desperate place, since we left it'. Some of the

Moslems said to me, 'Do go there. It used to be very dangerous because the politicians were brigands, but now the brigands have become politicians and it is quite safe'.

When I took my ticket, the Austrian at the guichet said to me, 'be well armed' and added, 'don't talk Turkish whatever happens'. A man in the crowd, a Serbian, hurried forward and said, 'on your life, don't talk Italian; it is more unpopular than Turkish and German is even worse'. A poor Turk in the train said, 'Above all things, don't go armed. Rely upon the merciful government and hide your weapons.'

At Priboi there was news, by telegram, of fierce fighting near Berana. Djevad Pasha, the Turkish Commander, was rumoured to be on the march from Mitrovitza. The Deputy for Akova, whom Aubrey had befriended in his hotel, suggested that he and Aubrey should go at once to Berana and see what was happening. Aubrey fell in with the suggestion.

They were supplied with an escort of gendarmes and soldiers. As they rode along the soldiers talked ceaselessly of the exploits of Issa Boletin, the Robin Hood of the Balkans who was said to have 20,000 men at his command. When Aubrey had last been in Albania, he had crossed the tracks of Issa Boletin. Then he had been shown a hill that Issa had held in a snow storm against an overwhelming force. He was credited with killing a hundred men with his own rifle, and was greatly admired by both soldiers and gendarmes. Aubrey had a weakness for romantic brigands and would have dearly liked to meet him. This wish was soon fulfilled:

Saturday August 24, Sienitiza. This morning we went out with an unusually big escort, forty or fifty men, a charming Turkish officer in command. He gave me his horse to ride. I am not quite sure if this was an act of courtesy or if he was glad to have someone else on its back. The horse was a very hot bay. When he bucked rather too close to the precipice the Turkish captain said genially 'He plays; he likes playing; it is his nature . . .'

We passed through a very changing country. After a time conversation stopped. We met some dishevelled soldiers on the road and they made a communication to the escort which was not passed on to me. Anxiety and gloom fell upon our party, and we went on in silence. We were going down a road between two hills in the evening, as we came to Sienitiza. Suddenly a crowd of bashi-bazouks came to meet us, and on the right flank there was a rush of, I suppose a hundred or more armed men. I tried to gallop round to join my escort, but they seized the reins of my horse, making him rear, and told me to dismount. I got off and walked in the middle of the throng in a savage rage. then stopped and said I was accustomed to ride when I wanted to ride and to walk when I wanted to walk. They answered me 'If you wish to, ride'. Then as I was mounting, my saddle came round. It was a moment of affliction and humiliation where in the West people would certainly have laughed. They offered no help and made no comment. Johnny *[his servant] came up, and I put the saddle straight and tightened the girth. I mounted and we went into the confused and angry town. The escort had disappeared. There was a lot of shooting going on. We were taken to the Khan (Inn) of the town. I was unceremoniously pushed upstairs and Johnny was hustled and roughly handled. The crowd kept back. We were taken into a fairly big room and about twenty five armed men crowded in with us. I was anxious to keep control of the situation and, as their host, I invited the twenty five to sit down, and began talking about general things.

Meanwhile they had torn open my luggage. Johnny had remained calm throughout. He now came to me and said indignantly, 'Do you see that man? He has taken your brushes and is brushing his moustache with them'. This giant had a moustache like a walrus. I spoke to him in a friendly way and said, 'You should not do that'. He said 'Why not, pray?' I answered 'Well, if you come to my country, I should not break open your bag, nor use your brushes'. 'No,' he said, 'I suppose not. I have no bags like yours nor are my brushes made of ivory'. Another man, of about six foot four, armed to the teeth, came up and spoke angrily to me, while the others listened. He said, 'You are an Austrian, and you have come to take our land'. I said 'I am not. I am an Englishman a Dere-bey (landowner). I have too much land of my own and don't want yours. It is a bad business being a landlord today. Land brings you in practically nothing'.

All this time the shooting was going on outside. Another very tall man, called Ahmed, who became my friend, came up to me. He said, 'Fear nothing, my lamb; these men lack civilization, but I have been in prison at Smyrna for five years and in prison at Monastir for seven, and I know what civilization is. These men are wild'. The conversation became general and rather more friendly. They told me that they had just taken the town and that the people had killed the Kaimakam of Berana, who was being buried at that moment. I gave them cigarettes and showed them my Mauser pistol, my patent razor and a big clasp knife. I said to them 'What is all this shooting going on outside? Are they killing the Christians? I can't have that'. They said 'No it is only the boys, in their excitement firing off their guns'.

Later Aubrey was able to walk in the town and see for himself the state of affairs. His captors telegraphed Issa Boletin in Mitrovitza to ask what they were to do about him.

Sunday August 25. When I got up this morning, Ahmed came to tell me that a telegram had arrived from Issa Boletin, saying that if injury of any kind was done to me, dire vengeance would fall upon those responsible, so my status has now entirely changed and Johnny and I are the heroes of the moment.

So they left Sienitiza in triumph escorted by a large band of warrior citizens. Some miles outside the town they halted and made a ring and everyone made speeches – Aubrey's diary continues, 'I do not think I have ever seen such fine men physically. We all said what we would do next time we met, and they said that if trouble came they would come and seek my *bessa* (protection) in England. They looked like kings in rags.'

By evening Aubrey had reached Novi Bazar. The next day he set out at six in the morning for Mitrovitza. Mitrovitza was still held by Turks so Aubrey's escort of Albanian bandits melted away before they reached the town. In Mitrovitza he lingered a few days. He knew the town from his journey across Northern Albania in 1908. Here there were Austrian and Russian consuls who asked him to dinner and to play bridge and a charming Kaimakam, Halid Bey, and the general, Djavid Pasha, who put a room at Aubrey's disposal. On Aubrey's second night in Mitrovitza, a mysterious message was brought to him in the middle of dinner with the Austrian consul. The message told him Issa Boletin was waiting in a Khan outside the town and wished to see him. Aubrey left the dinner table and was led through the town until he reached the Khan. There he was conducted by a great crowd of wild, heavily armed mountaineers to an upstairs room where he found Issa Boletin 'a very tall, lithe, well-made Albanian, aquiline, with restless eyes and a handsome fierce face'. Issa turned out all but one of his followers and sat down with Aubrey on a low divan and discussed politics. Their discussion, however, was interrupted by shots under the window.

> I was interested in the conversation and paid no attention. Issa pulled back a little curtain and looked out into the moon-light. As he did so, a dozen shots rang just outside. Instantly his clansmen swarmed into the room, taking arms down from the wall. They walked upon dancing feet and their eyes glittered. Issa jumped up with a rifle in his hand and said to me 'The house is surrounded by Turks, I am going to fight my way out'. I said to him 'This is not my quarrel, but I will come with you, as if you are taken the Turks will not shoot you if I am there'. He said 'No, you are my guest. My honour will not allow this thing. You protect my son'. Issa and his men poured out. Some stayed and kept me in. They were back again almost at once. It had, apparently, been only a brawl outside – Turks they said – and nobody hurt. I am very glad that I saw it. It was wonderful, the way in which the clansmen formed round Issa Boletin. They were like men on springs, active and lithe as panthers.

The thread of political discourse was snapped by this interlude, so after some general conversation Aubrey returned to his municipal room provided by Djavid Pasha. He was left, however, with a feeling of warm admiration for the bandit chief, while Issa Boletin, in the simple, direct way of his fierce countrymen, counted Aubrey as a friend and brother. Their next meeting was to be in London, a more bizarre setting for Issa Boletin than the Khan in Mitrovitza had been for Aubrey.

Still elated from these Albanian adventures Aubrey met Mary in September in Constantinople. Constantinople also provided excitements, not the physical thrill of danger always present in Albania, but the stimulation of political intrigue and gossip. Mary was scornful of the politics, and wrote to her mother, 'All the most important ministers bring childish schemes to Aubrey for making peace [with Italy] and ask him to urge the English government to force the Italians to agree. It is all very amusing to watch but tragic for them, poor dears, as they are quite fatalistic about the future and think Bulgaria must march on them in a few days.'

Though a little baffled and bored by the politics Mary enjoyed being taken to stay with Ferid in the harem of his palace on the Bosphorus. Here too the talk was all politics but at least it was in French. Mary wrote, 'The Turks are very funny about politics, they expect espionage at every corner but their expedients for guarding against it are childish. For instance Ferid was determined that our coachman was a spy and listening to our talk in French, but he was completely reassured directly the man denied any knowledge of French.' Ferid then took them to stay on the island of Prinkipo in the sea of Marmara, but he was very depressed by the local Greek holidaymakers in satin dresses and ostrich feather hats. Mary reported, 'it made him nearly ill to sit at meals amidst such company.'

Kiazim, who appeared to be able to sniff Aubrey's presence in Constantinople, and had briefly reattached himself to Aubrey's service, shared Ferid's prejudices. He had accompanied his master to Prinkipo and complained often and vehemently about the class of person to be found on the island.

Before Aubrey and Mary arrived back in England (they lingered on the homeward journey in Greece, Venice and Portofino), the first Balkan War had broken out. The four independent states of the Balkan League – Montenegro, Serbia, Bulgaria and Greece – attacked Turkey which was already weakened by the Italian war and Albanian insurrection. Albania, which declared itself neutral, became a battleground. Turkey suffered swift and crushing defeats. Aubrey suffered with the Turks. He wrote to FitzMaurice in November, 'I am feeling very sad about the whole thing and am very anxious for my friends.' One friend about whom Aubrey was anxious was Kiazim. At the outbreak of war Kiazim joined the Albanian Volunteer Battalion, bringing with him 270 recruits from Dibra. Kiazim regarded any opportunity to kill Bulgars as a treat, but he soon found that army life was disagreeable and the army just as quickly found Kiazim and his undisciplined band more trouble than they were worth; the battalion was disbanded. Kiazim returned to Constantinople but his employer, Philip Graves, a *Times* journalist and friend of Aubrey's, refused to re-employ him. Using the services of a professional letter-writer, Kiazim wrote to Aubrey in England, 'Your poor Kiazim Bey, volunteer for military service. He is suffering from hunger, without money or employment.' Mr Graves was made the villain of the tale: 'he did not treat me with a gentlemanlike manner.' Aubrey wrote to Philip Graves and got an indignant reply:

> I am sorry but wild horses wouldn't drag me to take him back. For fellows who throw up their jobs, run about with 'Dibra fedai' in their caps and get drunk, refuse to do ordinary jobs, e.g. accompanying my wife to Kandilli for 2 hours, in an impudent manner on the grounds of alleged military duties, I have little use, the more so when the heroic volunteer returns from the front after 15 days having resigned his job . . . Still I'll see he doesn't starve. If you know of anyone who wants a useless if highly ornamental retainer let me know. Excuse my irritation but I am still sore when I see how he has imposed on me over financial matters – I now live 25% more cheaply.

Aubrey sent a placatory letter to Philip Graves. He put up only a thin defence of Kiazim:

> He has been part of deeds and wanderings that have given much pleasure. For that reason I have been fond of him. I never expected to find in him, any more than you might have, virtues with which literature is accustomed to endow all highlanders and in particular the Albanian. But please believe me, when I heard that he had left you it never for a moment occurred to me that he was not at fault. I knew how generously you had treated him in the past, and I was certain that you would in the future. I feel no responsibility about Kiazim, only the kind of weakness that I have described. Also perhaps that there is the extenuating circumstance that I do not believe that we ever completely understand that type of man, – at least I don't.

It was not strictly truthful of Aubrey to claim he felt no responsibility. When he returned to Constantinople in February he found work for Kiazim rescuing starving horses from maltreatment for an English charity. Later he found him other jobs and at various times he sent money to tide over the numerous crises in Kiazim's unpeaceful career. He always remained fond of him.

The first stage of the Balkan War, in which Kiazim had played such an inglorious part, ended in December when the Great Powers imposed an armistice. Delegates arrived in London for a peace conference from the victorious Balkan allies, from the Turkish Government and from Albania. Albania, invaded on all sides, had born the brunt of the war. In the north the Montenegrins committed many atrocities; in the south the Greeks embarked on a murderous policy of forcible Hellenization and the Serbian army of occupation maintained, even after the armistice, its siege of Scutari. The country was filled with starving refugees. In London Aubrey founded the Albanian Committee. This helped to guide the Albanian delegation in its negotiations with the Great Powers who, Aubrey considered, 'were animal in their lusts, Pharisees in their aspirations'. The Committee also acted as a pressure group drawing attention to the appalling situation in Albania and raising money for the refugees. Aubrey was its President and it proved an arduous task. Apart from the many difficulties in dealing with the various squabbling factions of the Albanian delegation, the Committee itself was as disparate in its views and unhomogeneous in its composition as the delegation it was attempting to aid.

The delegates represented the many strands in Albanian life – Moslem, Catholic, Greek Orthodox and Vatra, the federation of Albanians in America. It was difficult for them to present a united front. At their head was Ismail Kemal Bey who had set up the provisional government in Valona a few months before. Aubrey was fond of the old man, though aware of his many faults. 'He was like', Aubrey wrote, 'a wise and benevolent tortoise. He had in him a real liberalism that never faded, but which became encrusted with the slovenliness of his own nature, and the weary deviations from straightness to which circumstance forced him. He was canny and he was able; and he had the power of phrasing his canniness crisply.'

Another delegate was none other than the picturesque illiterate old bandit Issa Boletin. Aubrey was delighted to see him again. Issa was miserable in London, bullied by the politicians, confused by the city, and homesick for his mountains and clansmen. He spent long hours drinking Turkish coffee at Bruton Street. Often Aubrey would receive agitated telephone calls at the House of Commons from Mary and come home to find them sitting together, speechless, but bowing to each other at short intervals. Aubrey took Issa under his wing; he brought him to the House of Commons, where his startling appearance caused a considerable stir.

Aubrey thought that one politician who would certainly enjoy Issa was Lloyd George, the bandit of English politics. He asked Lloyd George, then Chancellor of the Exchequer, to lunch to meet him. The two villains took an instant liking to each other. Aubrey was asked to translate flattering sentiments like 'Tell him that I am a mountaineer, as he is, and that I know his heart is kind to those that suffer', but Issa's parting message was more characteristic, 'Say that when Spring comes, we will manure the plains of Kossovo with the bones of Serbs, for we Albanians have suffered too much to forget.'

In October 1913 not long after Issa's return to Albania Aubrey read in the newspapers that he had been captured by Serbs in a guerrilla fight. Knowing the habits of the Serbs, Aubrey was certain that Issa would be murdered in prison. He hurried to the Foreign Office. His friends there told him that interceding for Albanian bandits was outside their province, but suggested that Aubrey should find some great man to plead his friend's cause. Aubrey went to Lord Cromer. Lord Cromer said, 'Is it politics, or is it a case of helping a friend of yours? If it is a friend of yours I will do what I can.' There and then he drafted a telegram to the King of Serbia. The next day Aubrey was glad yet embarrassed to read in the morning papers: 'Yesterday it was stated that Issa Boletin had been taken prisoner by the Serbs. The contrary appears to be the case. The noted leader of banditry has inflicted a heavy defeat upon the combined forces of the Serbs and Montenegrins.' Lord Cromer took the blunder in good part merely telephoning Aubrey with, 'Why did you get me to appeal for this conqueror?' However, in the end Issa Boletin met his death much as Aubrey had predicted. He was murdered in a Montenegrin gaol. He killed eight men before he was captured and brought, badly wounded, to the prison at Podgoritza (Titograd).

When the peace negotiations were broken off at the end of January 1913 after little more than a month, the Albanian delegation although it had lost much had also achieved much. Austria had persuaded the great powers to recognise the principle of an autonomous Albania. By February war had again flared up between Turkey and Bulgaria and Aubrey hurried out to Constantinople, pairing in the House of Commons with Noel Buxton who was also bound hot foot for the Balkans to succour the other side in the affray. Aubrey felt strongly partisan. He wrote to Mary before he left, 'The Turks will probably disgrace themselves with massacres etc. But they will ride out like Paladins and Saladins to mop up those intriguing, bomb-throwing, swine-eating, queen-disembowelling cads . . . I have resigned my judgement, I am angry not logical.' In the event the Turks, half starved, equipped with sophisticated weapons they could not use, attacked by a fifth column of Christians within their midst, mopped up no one, but reeled from defeat to defeat.

Aubrey left London on 15th February and arrived in Constantinople four days later. 'Bosphorus bleak and cold,' his diary reported. 'Many apathetic Turks. Guns on the point. Passengers silent. Arrived at Pera Palace. Saw many people. Impression is Constantinople may be lost.

Quarrelled with waiter about gold fish. Opened his eye against electric light to show how it must hurt the lidless eyes of fish. Row.' Later the diary becomes more cheerful.

On this visit Aubrey fell out yet again with FitzMaurice. Aubrey had welcomed the coup of the Young Turks in January, although deploring the murder of Nazim: FitzMaurice deplored the coup, in which his aged puppet, the liberal Grand Vizier Kiamil had been ousted. Aubrey wrote to Mark Sykes, 'I gave great offence in certain quarters, by seeing the Young Turks, dining and lunching etc. Why shouldn't I? The Ambassador (Lowther) didn't mind and I am equally friends with the Kiamilists, and the third party, the anti-everyones . . . Fitz will catch a cold whispering behind doors and die the death.' While to Mervyn he wrote more strongly, 'FitzMaurice loathes Turkey and after that England. He is the Irish Catholic of the really bitter Dillon-Lynch type, cunning as a weasel and as savage', and in his diary, after dining at the Embassy, he wrote, 'FitzMaurice cannot be loyal to any chief. He hates Lowther alive now as much as he hates O'Conor dead.'

Aubrey returned to London in a savage frame of mind. The English newspapers continued to extol the deeds of the Balkan allies. Pro-Turkish letters were not printed. In a mood of anger and bitterness Aubrey gave vent to his feelings in a poem:

There falls perpetual snow upon a broken plain,
And through the twilight filled with flakes the white earth joins the sky
Grim as a famished, wounded wolf, his lean neck in a chain
The Turk stands up to die.

Intrigues within, intrigues without, no man to trust,
He feeds street dogs that starve with him; to friends who are his foe
To Greeks and Bulgars in his lines, he flings a sudden crust
The Turk who has to go.

By infamous unbridled tongues and dumb deceit,
Through pulpits and the Stock Exchange the Balkans do their work,
The preacher in the chapel and the hawker in the street
Feed on the dying Turk.

The Turk worked in the vineyard, others drank the wine,
The Jew who sold him plough shares kept an interest in his plough.
The Serb and Bulgar waited till King and Priest should sign,
Till Kings said 'kill, kill now'.

So now the twilight falls upon the twice betrayed,
The Daily Mail tells England and the Daily News tells God

That God and British Statesmen should make the Turks afraid
Who fight unfed, unshod.

On 26th March Adrianople (now Edirne) surrendered to the Bulgarians. Five days later the Sublime Porte accepted the terms of the Great
Powers for a cessation of hostilities. The first Balkan War was over. The
peace conference was resumed in London and Aubrey's friend Mahmud
Shevket Pasha, Grand Vizier and Minister of War, was compelled to
accept the humiliating terms that had provoked the coup against Kiamil
and the return to power of the Young Turks.

The Treaty of London which was the result of the peace conference
was signed on 30th May 1913. Twelve days later Mahmud Shevket was
murdered in Constantinople. The assassination was more an act of
retaliation for the murder of Nazim in January than a result of the
peace treaty. Nevertheless the Treaty of London was a disaster for the
Turks who lost most of their European empire including Adrianople.
The Albanians, also, regarded the treaty as a disaster. Alone among the
Balkan countries Albania lacked the backing of any of the Great Powers.
She had no newspaper support and few propagandists save Aubrey and
his friends on the Albanian Committee. The loss of fertile lands in the
North to Serbia was bitterly resented, by none more than their inhabitants. Yet all in all, Albania might have fared worse. Although the
boundaries remained undecided the Great Powers had committed themselves in principle to Albanian independence and had agreed to
despatch an international force to compel the occupying Balkan armies
to retire.

Aubrey was not dissatisfied with his work. He longed to go back to
Albania with the returning delegates to see for himself how effective the
International Committee and forces would prove to be, but the parliamentary session did not end until August 15th and Aubrey spoke often
that summer session on the plight of Albania. He was kept fully informed
by his Albanian friends of the desperate situation, where thousands
were homeless and starvation and disease were rife. Aubrey himself was
too enmeshed to view the matter dispassionately; he wrote to his mother,
'I feel as if there had been a click in my brain, like there was in my watch
– it ticked quite gaily but remained unmoveable. My mind has been
moving so much in a circle of massacres . . .'

Meanwhile the second Balkan War had broken out on 29th June 1913.
While Bulgaria was occupied in fighting her former allies (Roumania,
like a hyena at the feast, had joined Serbia, Greece and Montenegro),
the Turks under the command of Enver Pasha, retook Adrianople.
Aubrey unashamedly rejoiced at these events, but his chief preoccupa-

tion remained Albania. As soon as the parliamentary session ended he hurried out. Mary, pregnant again, stayed behind.

Aubrey was by now a national hero in Albania. The help he had given the Albanian delegation in London had won him many new friends and his persistent questioning in the House of Commons on Albanian matters was known and appreciated throughout the land. Everywhere he went he was applauded, feasted, made to make speeches. He stayed a month, dividing his time between talking international politics in Scutari, internal politics in Durazzo and riding round the country.

The burning problem of the hour in Albania was the refusal of the Catholic tribes of Hoti and Gruda in Northern Albania to acquiesce in the annexation of their lands by Montenegro as stipulated in the Treaty of London. Aubrey hoped to write an article for the *Morning Post* on the issue. In Scutari he stayed in a hotel but took most of his meals with Admiral Burney, who commanded the combined fleet despatched by the Great Powers. Aubrey wrote to his mother, 'Things are going badly. Our admiral is not well served and he makes very stupid and unnecessary mistakes, though he tries very hard. Poor man he told me he had been talking French in his delirium. I wonder what it was like. His normal French is like this, "Avait il un decision unanimos?" ' Colonel Phillips, the commander of the land forces (the Yorkshires), was a man of different calibre. He loved the Albanians and got on well with them. He was imaginative in his dealings and a great raconteur.

Aubrey's time was not exclusively taken up with the military missions. He met for the first time Edith Durham, whose name was already a byword in Albania for her work among the sick and refugees. Aubrey was to have many dealings in the future with this formidable English spinster and to be the recipient of over five hundred letters from her. He described his first impressions of her in a letter to Mary, 'She cuts her hair short like a man, has a cockney accent and a roving eye, is clever, aggressive and competitive but she has really done a lot for these people.' Later, in England, Miss Durham became secretary to the Albanian Committee and Albania's most tireless propagandist.

The day before Aubrey's meeting with Miss Durham he had met the old chief of the Catholic tribes of the Grey Mountain, Ded Gion Luli. A man of immense age and dignity, he was in some ways the Catholic equivalent of Issa Boletin. All his life he had fought against the Turks but he was now preparing to lead his people against the Montenegrins. He invited Aubrey to his mountain for the Feast of the Five Banners. The Five Banners were the five tribes: Hoti, Gruda, Skreli, Kastrati and Klementi and they met together each year for the feast of St John. These were the tribes whose lands had been given to the Montenegrins by the

Treaty of London. Aubrey accepted the invitation with alacrity. His diary takes up the tale:

Saturday August 30th. Left early this morning. Galloped along fairly quickly by Bardanjoli, past Montenegrin graves, past burnt Kopliko and a stretch of land, to hedges and fields sweet as English meadows. The destruction of houses and waste of war seems more unwarrantable and extravagant in these circumstances than in the hills. We stopped at the house of Miraslonca where they were digging up ammunition hidden in the ground to fight Monte-negrins. Children walking about stark naked. We came to a cool cave in the hills with water. There we talked and they showed me their sashes, simple red and black. 'That,' they said, 'was the only way we could show our allegiance to our country: the Turks never noticed that.' They sang patriotic songs on the way up. Every village had its story, each peak a memory. The spirit of vengeance has woken from hibernation. All the houses are roofless. This is the work of the Turks except in the plain which the Montenegrins destroyed.

Below Rapsha we met the mountaineers, and twenty five of us sat down to drink beer. They drank beer, mastik raki, and let off revolvers. All very polite . . .

We arrived at Rapsha at six, a high mountain village in the full glory of the evening, having been about eleven hours on the road. There were two priests, Padre Sebastian, a kind, good man, the other one was sulky . . .

I was given Father Sebastian's room, which was full of rifles, breviaries, raki bottles and books of holy sermons . . . All the talk was of Hoti and Gruda. The arguments were as fiery as the raki that the Albanians drank.

During the meal the priests served their guests. They gave them drink and food and cigarettes, and occasionally went out to fire a revolver-shot in answer to another one in the valley. They joined in all the jokes and seemed to have a tremendous grip upon their fierce flock. The priests were generally Albanian by nationality, but most of them had been educated in Austria. It is to her they look, for they are supported by Austrian money. They wear moustaches, according to Eastern custom . . .

This morning was perfect. Later the heat became fierce. All this Sunday a loud hail of revolver shots rained up and down the valley. The rocks acted as telephones; news came and went. There had been an uncomfortable atmos-phere at breakfast of sulkiness, a rare occurrence amongst Albanians. I dis-covered later from Don Sebastian that the reason of this was the presence of Nikol Miras Incas who was with me. Three or four years ago the Albanians had sworn an oath upon the Cross to fight alone against the Turks, without the Montenegrins, and Nikol is said to have betrayed them at Podgoritza. He had also behaved badly in the matter of blood-feuds, for he killed one Moslem half a mile from here, which was in order, but knowing that he would be in blood with the relations of this Moslem, he went and shot two others the same afternoon, which was not considered to be playing the game. He deserved death. I said I should be much obliged if they would not shoot him while he was with me. They could tell him to go. They said there was no question of their shooting him, for the truce was on and they were honourable men. If he had killed five of their number, they would not have touched him, but they resented his presence and wanted me to get rid of him. I said I could not intervene in their quarrels when I was without information. It might be as they said – again it might not. If they wanted him to go they must say so themselves. After this the air cleared and they became cheerful. They all sang songs, solos and in chorus, in the house of the priest. The songs were against Montenegro. The chieftains sometimes went outside and danced with the people and the children. We breakfasted at 11 and went to Mass about 12. There were 500 mountaineers of the Five Tribes, men and women, in their fine clothes, all seated under the shade of one enormous plane tree, that stood outside the smoke-blackened shell of a little church, which the Turks had burnt.

. . . After Mass, which ended with a passionate sermon that seemed part of the scorching air they asked me to speak.

The Montenegrin frontier was three miles away and the whole Albanian population was in a state of acute excitement. I was afraid that anything I said would only make the situation worse . . . that I should be accused of having fomented trouble so I said that I would not speak. I was dragged from the shadow of the church into the shadow of the plane tree . . .

At the end of the speech there was loud and continuous cheering: rifles were grounded with a bang; every man who had any kind of firearm then let it off; the smoke was blinding and choking; the leaves from the plane tree fell as if an autumn gale was blowing and a piece of flying bark or a richochetting bullet cut my cheek . . .

We went into the house and my ears were deaf with the noise and my throat dry with the powder that had been fired. We had a draught of cold water and then set off down the mountainside and across the valley for the camp of Ded Gion Luli in a heat that made one wet from head to foot . . .

After a stiff climb we came to the place where the house of Ded Gion Luli had once stood; it, like all the others, had been burnt. A little way off there was a wall and beyond a fringe of trees. My guide gave a long, undulating mountain call, then fired his revolver, and we went a steep way across wild lavander and thyme to his home.

The old man sat upon a carpet under roughly trellised branches, while another ragged carpet was hung as shelter against the westering sun . . . A feast was laid. Ded Gion was ready enough to talk of the past, he did not care to talk of the coming struggle. I think he was afraid of being offered pacific advice . . .

After this meeting in the mountains Aubrey wrote to Mary: 'I wonder if I should have had a different feeling for Carson if he dressed like the Albanians and just propounded their gospel of the village. They don't care a tinkers curse about anything else. It's just the rocks they know and the miserable houses where they were born that they are after keeping.'

Aubrey returned to Scutari, with malaria, but after a few days was well enough to go to Valona. There he was greeted on arrival by Ismail Kemal, the President. Aubrey extracted a promise of five thousand pounds from the wily old man for seed for the starving North. The government put a house at his disposal in Valona. Deputations came endlessly to see Aubrey and complain of the mismanagement of the government. The sons and nephews of Issa Boletin also called with messages from the old bandit.

Aubrey spent longer in Valona than he had intended. He wrote to Mary explaining the delay:

> I leave tomorrow and travel up to see the blackguard Essad. I should have left before. But the day after I got here I went to the prison. I have rarely had such a shock. I have seen prisons in Morocco, and Arab prisons and Arab tortures and all sorts of things, but the place fairly knocked me down. Fifty men in a small room half underground, fifty men where there ought not to have been a dozen in this weather. They stood like phantoms, and salaamed like ghosts and corpses. The smell and the heat nearly knocked me over. I didn't say much but went off to Ismail Kemal. I told him that if that were the way things were run it said very little in favour of the new Albania and that I hadn't the least intention of telling lies to save my friends. I have waited here until I saw with my own eyes that the thing had been put right. I don't know that I have ever talked much straighter to any man than I did to Ismail Kemal but this with the fact of my getting five thousand out of the gov. has not made me as popular as I was.

Nonetheless Ismail Kemal was reluctant to see Aubrey leave Valona. He needed his backing for his shaky government. He was worried by Aubrey's intention to ride to Tirana, the stronghold of his rival Essad Pasha; and he was vexed by Aubrey's choice of companions for the journey, Mohammed Koritza, Mehmed Konitza and Philippe Nogga, none of whom were supporters of his government. The day Aubrey left Valona (10th September 1913) Ismail received a telegram from Essad threatening to set up his own government unless Ismail gave into various demands including moving the seat of government from Valona to Durazzo. Ismail showed Aubrey the telegram. He was determined to resist Essad and tried to dissuade Aubrey from going to Tirana. Aubrey refused to be deflected and set out the same day. Before he left Valona he wrote to Mary. 'It is complete chaos now. Faik Bey * is mustering some thousands of his American Albanians. He told me without turning a hair last night that he had just had the wires cut to Valona, and apologized saying he would have delayed if he had known I wanted to go to Tirana. They are imps of mischief.'

However Faik's wire cutting was ineffective and the lines continued to buzz. Aubrey and his three companions had a delightful ride.

Everywhere they were entertained to huge feasts by the local beys or pashas. Everywhere Aubrey was made to make speeches. Meanwhile Ismail Kemal had not been idle. Along the route they followed he had sacked governors and appointed substitutes. Essad was still officially Minister of the Interior so that Ismail's actions were tantamount to a declaration of political war. At Fieri they stayed with Omer Pasha and were joined the following morning by Feizi Bey who had just heard he had been made Governor of Berat. They all rode on together to Berat where they were greeted by the governor, Mehdi Bey Frasheri, who had not yet heard that he had been deposed. Wherever they passed people attached themselves to their cavalcade. By the time they reached Berat their little party had become a thousand strong, with banners flying and marching songs. At Elbasan, while Aubrey was dining with the Governor, a telegram arrived. It was from Ismail Kemal requesting the Governor to arrest Mehmed Bey and Philippe Nogga. Aubrey said, 'It puts me in a difficult position. I can't leave my friends, you wouldn't.' 'God bless me, no,' said the Governor. 'Of course you want companions; you shall all go off tomorrow, inshallah.'

And so they did, arriving at Tirana the next night. Aubrey stayed in Tirana with Abdy Bey Toptani, a shy and courteous man who reminded him of Lord Lansdowne (Aubrey always claimed that the Albanian Beys were exactly like English squires and was often struck by likenesses to English friends or acquaintances). The next day he spent with Essad.

Essad Pasha was as anxious as Ismail Kemal had been to blacken his rival's name. Aubrey was depressed. He cared passionately that Albania should succeed as an independent nation but the prospect looked bleak. Of the two rival leaders he infinitely preferred the patriotic Ismail but he did not find Essad wholly unattractive. In his diary he wrote, 'It isn't possible to prophesy what he is going to do because I doubt if he knows himself. He, at any rate, is not like the rest of the Albanians, tired of being oriental.'

Having, he hoped, frightened Essad a little, Aubrey returned to Scutari by way of Durazzo. In Scutari he was struck down by another bad bout of malaria. He was ill for a week. He lay propped up in his bed of sickness while deputations came and went, leaving documentation of terrible massacres and deprivation.

On Thursday 24th September Aubrey finally left Scutari, still weakened by fever. His overwhelming feeling as he left was one of dedication and gratitude. In a letter to Mary he wrote: 'It will mean doing a lot I am afraid when I get back to England. I owe it to these people. They were wonderfully good to me, it was a most curious time, riding through the darkness to where thousands of mountaineers came from the shadows to greet me, while I made speeches to the tune of thunder in the hills.'

The port where he embarked for Italy was St John de Medua (now Shenjini), south of Scutari. Aubrey wrote to Mary, 'I never saw such a place in Europe. There are sunken boats in the harbour, houses all ruined, trees half burnt. There are stinking pools alive with insects and great green and white bulbous flowers clouded over with mosquitoes. We eat quinine as if it had been roast beef. We had to drink the water, and the water here is enough to give a duck typhoid. We had to be stung by the mosquitoes and the mosquitoes are enough to give a leech malaria.' His letter ends, 'I am now prepared to do what you want and to shave my moustache as I have grown a beard. It makes me look more intellectual and takes away that coarse look that has done so much to prevent my getting on.'

After a week at Portofino, in which Aubrey finally threw off his malaria, he returned to England in response to appeals from Mary. He came without resentment but with great reluctance for in his brief absence the affairs of Albania had moved towards crisis. Essad had carried out his threat and set up a rival government in Durazzo. Both he and Ismail Kemal telegraphed to Aubrey. However, Mary had written, 'I've just had as long as I can bear without you', and Aubrey, knowing her stoicism, knew the depths of desperation in her appeal. She did not appeal in vain.

So ended what, though Aubrey did not know it, was to be his last such travels in Albania. He wrote to his brother Mervyn: 'The Albanians call me the Paladin of Liberty and say their grandchildren shall bless my name.' These grandchildren eventually grew up in a harsh communist state where the name Aubrey Herbert would have no significance. And Aubrey's next visit to Albania was not as a Paladin of Liberty but as a soldier in uniform in 1918. Nonetheless, for a generation the name Aubrey Herbert was honoured far and wide throughout Albania and many regretted that he had not become their king. Twice Aubrey had the chance to accept the throne of Albania and twice he chose to forgo the adventure.

The first offer was made in May 1913, during the Balkan conference in London, before his triumphal journey to Albania. In those days, at least in the Balkans, it was felt that a nation to be a proper nation, needed to have a king. The Albanians passionately wanted a prince or Mpret. The Great Powers promised to give them one. They wanted an Englishman because they believed that England, alone of the Great Powers, had no interests at stake in the Balkans. The Albanian delegation in London, comprising Moslems, Catholic and Orthodox, under the leadership of Ismail Kemal, approached Aubrey. Ismail Kemal put to him the hypothetical question: if you were formally asked to accept the throne of Albania would you be prepared to accept? The question came as no surprise to Aubrey. He had seen the minds of the delegation working towards the offer for some time. He was in some ways an obvious candidate: an English aristocrat, a Christian, neither Catholic nor Orthodox, with a deep understanding of and admiration for, Islam. He knew the country and the language and he had no great responsibilities or possessions to tie him to England. But when the offer came, he was unprepared. He wrote to his brother Mervyn in May 1913:

I don't know what to do. It would be a very interesting business, but prickly and difficult beyond belief. I know the people pretty well and like them, but that wouldn't mean that one would be a fixture. Of course the Prime [Asquith] and all the rest of them have been ragging about it for an age, but I don't know if I should have their support if it really comes along. The Albanians don't like any of the present candidates. Of course with me money is the trouble. The Albanians have never paid any taxes, and even if they do poor lambs, they can't pay much. I don't think they are likely to get a good Prince. Any prince would be an ass to take it if he knew the difficulties and more of an ass if he didn't.

Aubrey soon found that although the Prime Minister might be prepared to rag him, he was not prepared seriously to entertain the notion of Aubrey as King of Albania. Aubrey discussed the offer in detail with the Foreign Secretary, Sir Edward Grey. Grey was sympathetic but felt bound to dissuade Aubrey from any rash acceptance. He knew that Austria would be extremely hostile to Aubrey's candidature and he was determined that England should not be drawn into the Balkan tangle. Aubrey understood that he could expect no official help. Yet he longed to accept. Mary, always reckless, urged him to let his candidature go forward. She was quite prepared to forsake fashionable London and her home at Pixton for the wilds of Albania. To Aubrey's romantic nature the appeal of thrones, chieftains, bandits, dangerous territory and fierce loyalties was almost irresistible. He could, however, see that the financial drawback was insurmountable. He was, quite simply, not rich enough to be a king. He wrote to Elsie, 'If I had fifty thousand a year, I think I should take Albania', but he had nothing like that sum and so with great regret he told Ismail Kemal that his answer to the hypothetical question was no. Thus it was that the offer was never officially made.

Aubrey's triumphant tour of Albania in the summer of 1913 was in some ways his consolation prize. He was made aware, in all the picturesqueness of his welcomes, of what he was foregoing, but also of the enormous difficulties that the job would have entailed.

Austria had been energetically supporting the candidature of a Germanic Princeling, Prince William of Wied. By a curious coincidence the family of Wied were old friends of the Carnarvons. When Elsie heard of the proposed candidature, her familiarity with the House of Wied did not lead her to approve of the choice. 'I cannot think that any Wied would be a good person for Albania,' she wrote to Aubrey in June. By the time Aubrey returned to England in November the Great Powers had almost agreed to nominate Prince William. The Albanians, desperate for a prince, whose coming they felt would end all disunity in the country, were in the main enthusiastic about the nomination. One of the delegates, Monsignor Nogga, wrote to Aubrey at the end of November, after seeing the Prince and his aunt the Queen of Roumania, 'Nous sommes donc au bout de nos peines. Rule Albania!'

Aubrey himself was less sanguine. He knew and liked the Prince. William of Wied was a man of honour and probably, Aubrey thought, the best the Albanians were likely to get. He could not believe, however, that the Prince understood what was involved. His doubts were increased by his correspondence with the family. Prince William's sister, Princess Louise of Wied, wrote to Aubrey in January 1914:

> Ever since all this has been settled and my brother is preparing himself for this new and not quite simple task I meant to write to you . . . It is good of you to do so much for the miserable people over there, who I fear are not well looked after . . . It is overwhelming to think of all the work my brother and sister-in-law will find to do down there . . . already they are having a very busy time, seeing lots of people, and then the language is pretty stiff work . . . We feel almost like children, learning geography and all sorts of things one has not learnt for centuries. We see heaps of anxieties and dangers for the future but we try to see the beautiful and interesting side as well . . .

Aubrey clearly regarded the Wieds' preparations as inadequate. Princess Louise's next letter thanks Aubrey for 'writing all those interesting details about important people's characters down there' and then moves on to worries about the climate and health: 'it seems that nearly everybody who goes there gets malaria. I believe you had it too.'

Of the two kinds of ass Aubrey had written about to Mervyn ('Any prince would be an ass to take it if he knew the difficulties and more of an ass if he didn't'), Prince William seems to have been the second kind of ass, but there was little Aubrey could do about it. He did his best, however. He saw Prince William in London in February 1914. The Prince was on his way to Albania and full of optimism. Aubrey tried to warn Wied of a few pitfalls and in particular of the untrustworthiness of Essad

Pasha. But the Prince, brimming with good will, showed no sign of understanding the dangers of his position.

The Prince arrived in Albania, complete with a small court, on March 7th. Instead of establishing himself at Scutari where he would have had the support of Colonel Phillips' international force, he landed at Durazzo. It was the first and most crucial mistake of his reign. He remained at Durazzo, a virtual prisoner of Essad's, whom he made General of the Albanian army, Minister of the Interior and Minister for War. Within three weeks of Wied's arrival in Albania, Mehmet Konitza, another delegate and Aubrey's companion in his last ride in Albania and now a close friend, wrote in despair, 'En un mot L'Albanie a fait fiasco – sauf quelque événement imprévu et magique, il ne me reste aucune espoir.'

It was soon clear that no magic happening would save the Wied dynasty. First, fighting broke out between supporters of Ismail Kemal and Essad Pasha. Then in the South of Albania, although the Greeks had reluctantly withdrawn on the insistence of the Great Powers at the eleventh hour from the areas they had occupied since the Balkan Wars, there was a so-called Epirote insurrection. The Greek regular army laid aside its uniforms, and Greek volunteers and Cretan irregulars swarmed in. The inhabitants were terrorised and villages burnt. The fighting continued for months. Meanwhile the Italians and Austrians who had together placed the unfortunate prince on the throne, fell out. The Italians regarded the Prince as too Austrio-phil and plotted with Essad Pasha to dethrone him. In May, Major Sluys of the Dutch Mission, and Commandant of Durazzo, managed to persuade Prince William that Essad was indeed a traitor and, with difficulty, arrested him. Prince William weakly submitted to Italian pressure and failed to take advantage of Essad's arrest. Essad was banished from Albania and made his way to Rome, where he was duly petted and fêted. A few days later the Prince himself took refuge on an Italian warship at Durazzo, fleeing from insurgents from Tirana. This rebellion, in reality a peasant rising against their landowners, had been engineered by Essad to appear as a popular revolt against the Prince. The Prince's brief but panicky flight lost him his remaining support in the country.

That support had already dwindled disastrously. Miss Durham, Albania's sturdy champion whom Aubrey had met in 1913 and corresponded with regularly afterward, wrote to Aubrey from Durazzo in July:

I have little or no sympathy with the King. He is a blighter. Why or by whom he was chosen is a mystery. Surely those responsible must have known he was a feeble stick, devoid of energy or tact or manners and wholly ignorant of the country? They are very Royal – both of them – keep a court and keep people standing in their presence.

It is all ludicrous. The Queen, the few times I have spoken to her, impresses me as a bright young woman, but her only idea is to play the Lady Bountiful, distribute flowers, put medals on the wounded and make fancy blouses of native embroidery.

As for the King he seems a hopeless combine of pretentiousness and incapacity . . . The King might have pulled through if he had a decent entourage. But Heaton-Armstrong is the wrongest man for his post that could have been found. His nickname of the chocolate soldier exactly hits him off. He tells everyone that he only came for the pay. He boasted to me that when he, together with all the Royal party, were invited to dinner at a Bey's house, he refused all the dishes. Said he's sworn not to eat any of their food. I told him if he meant to succeed here he must eat everything and take a pill afterwards if necessary. I learn from Faik Konitza that the whole party behaved very badly and gave great offence by openly laughing at the dishes and at the manner of serving . . .

I am quite unable myself to do anything except see things go from bad to worse . . .

Two months later, in September 1914, and within six months of arriving in Albania to possess his kingdom, Prince William fled the country.

Right up to the last moment Aubrey used all his influence to help the Prince. On the last day of July Aubrey wrote to an English official on the International Commission enclosing a message from him to the insurgents who were threatening Durazzo, the insurgents who finally drove Prince William to flight. In the message Aubrey appealed to the insurgents to lay down their arms. Aubrey had little hope that the message would get through, or that it would make much difference if it did, but as he wrote to his friend on the Commission, 'I can't see what harm it can do anyone except myself' and he added, 'Of course the telegrams reporting Austria has declared war on Serbia are going to make everything outside our own safety irrelevant.'

He was quite right. The fate of Albania and Prince William no longer seemed of any importance as power after power mobilized and issued its ultimatums or declarations in accordance with its treaty obligations. Gradually and inevitably England found herself on the threshold of war. Aubrey and the King of Albania found themselves fighting on opposite sides while Albania herself became once again a battleground.

8

Mons 1914

How did Aubrey, and his circle, view the outbreak of the Great War? Did they have any sense of impending catastrophe, any inkling of the horror to come? Or did they look on it merely as a sporting adventure?

Popular myth represents the young men of 1914 as the blind fools of fortune going off to war much as they might have gone off on a long shooting weekend, while the politicians are represented as callous old men playing with the lives of millions in the manner of a sleepy game of after-dinner bridge. According to popular myth also, war came like a clap of thunder out of a clear sky to disturb a complacent, prosperous upper-class society which had no thoughts beyond its little intellectual games, which had no understanding beyond the confines of its house parties and balls, no interests outside its cosy superiority.

Of course such a picture is a distortion of the truth. The knowledge that one day England would have to fight Germany was something that Aubrey's generation had learned to live with since the beginning of the century. Germany had been blatantly building up a fearsome war machine and had pursued an aggressive and provocative diplomacy. The arms race, in the hands of unscrupulous private profiteers, had become uncontrolled and alarming. The informed felt little complacency, while the politicians, far from carelessly falling into war, fought tooth and nail to avoid it. Asquith and his Liberal cabinet toyed with appeasement because they knew how truly terrible a European war would be. Sir Edward Grey's statement to the House of Commons on 3rd August contained no appeal to the latent jingoism of the House, no diatribe against Germany, no emotional or colourful language, but a rational and despondent account of the events leading up to his reluctant ultimatum, 'We worked for peace up to the last moment, and beyond the last moment,' he said with simple truth.

Aubrey felt no such reluctance. The same evening that Sir Edward Grey made his celebrated remark about the lamps of Europe going out, Aubrey was jubilantly scribbling a note to Mary, 'The millionaires on the Terrace of the House have the faces of souls in Hell.' For Aubrey, and his kind, openly rejoiced at the despondency of the appeasers. It was a

battle of youth and honour versus old age and caution. Aubrey hastened
to volunteer.

Aubrey's elation at England's ultimatum to Germany over Belgian
neutrality was not based on an ignorant or foolhardy misunderstanding
of the magnitude of the event but on many complicated feelings which
he shared with his generation. It was not that they consciously wished
to die; it was not even that they were moved by strong anti-German or
pro-French sentiments; nor was it bloodlust. It was more the result of
their high sense of purpose and honour. They were the flower of Empire
in its zenith. They had been educated to a high pitch. They were men of
talent, some of brilliance, and yet by 1914 Aubrey's contemporaries
were in their thirties and none had achieved great distinction. They had
nursed their promise, not fulfilled it. They were a little tired of themselves, a little tired of life, and impatient of the old men. Something less
than a sense of futility but more than a spirit of restlessness was abroad.
It was as if their whole lives had been a preparation for this moment and
they seized it with eagerness.

And none more eagerly than Aubrey. His haste to volunteer was based
on the popular belief that the war might be over by Christmas. But his
belief was not founded on the ignorant assumption that a military
victory was to be had for the asking, that Germany could be 'knocked
into a cocked hat', as the myth makers claimed the young fools of
fortune believed. Aubrey never underestimated the strength or effici-
ency of the German army. But, equally, he never dreamed that the
whole Empire would be mobilised, and that diplomacy and negotiation
would be discarded. He never entertained the thought that civilised
Europeans would fight to the finish. He feared that, having secured
Belgian neutrality, the old men would move in with their pens and
paper and rulers, and England would retire from the conflict. Hence his
haste and enthusiasm to enlist.

Aubrey, too, had his own ghost to exorcise. He had never forgiven
himself the fiasco of his failure to fight in the South African war. This
time he was determined that nothing should prevent his participation.
Well before the English ultimatum to Germany, before even Germany
had invaded Belgium, Aubrey made his plans. Knowing that his eyesight
would again disqualify him from active service, he conspired with
military friends to find a backdoor entry to the army. The chief conspira-
tor was Tom Vesey, a cousin of Mary's, and a regular soldier in the Irish
Guards. A visit to a military tailor to acquire the uniform of an officer in
that regiment completed Aubrey's preparations.

On Wednesday 12th August 1914, when the Irish Guards marched out
of Wellington Barracks at seven in the morning, Aubrey was lurking on

the pavement outside, dressed in his new uniform. As the ranks marched by, Aubrey unobtrusively took his place among them. They marched along a sleeping Vauxhall Bridge Road to Nine Elms Station where Aubrey got into a railway carriage with Tom Vesey, Valentine Castlerosse and Robin Innes Kerr, all of whom were privy to the plot.*

When the train arrived at Southampton the conspirators successfully smuggled Aubrey on board the troop ship. Once the ship had steamed out of harbour Tom Vesey presented Aubrey to the Commanding Officer, Colonel George Morris.* A blind, if amiable and enthusiastic, volunteer was the last thing the Colonel wanted but he put on a brave face and bowed to the inevitable. Aubrey was given the rank of Lieutenant and appointed interpreter. So it was that Aubrey sailed for France in the first days of the war as a member of the British Expeditionary Force.

Mary had aided Aubrey in all his preparations for departure, but she did so with a heavy heart. She shared none of his enthusiasm or excitement. She was terrified of losing him and half disapproving of his unorthodox approach to military service.

Both Mary and Lady Carnarvon had tried to see Aubrey off. They drove together to Nine Elms Station and watched the Irish Guards board the train for Southampton but they did not catch a glimpse of him among the sea of khaki uniforms. From the boat Aubrey scribbled a note in pencil to Mary, 'Just a line before we start. Blue sea, white seagulls, delicious air and everything exhilarating except the memory of my scaramouch. I am sure you would really rather have had me go, if it hadn't been for the rush. We got to exaggerating things in the rush – the Irishes are very nice. They don't seem to know what it is all about but they don't mind. They have wistful faces. Some come from Abbeyleix.' After this letter there was a long silence. Mary and Elsie wrote daily into the void. 'My darling', Mary wrote, 'it's not to be believed that our perfect life has broken up in this way. I still feel as if it was one of our many small partings and I shall find you in London tomorrow – Oh my dear it's awful the time before us.' In another letter she forgave him for volunteering and wrote that she had changed her mind and no longer thought it an act of 'self-indulgence and war excitement' but added, 'Oh Aubrey, war is abominable. One can hardly imagine the horror of men killing each other.' She filled her days with war work, although she wrote, 'It's such rot trying to do things when there's nothing to do and all one's thoughts are out with you.' She gave Bruton Street over to Belgian refugees and moved in with Elsie who was staying at Vera's house, 5 Stratford Place, so that they should hear any news together.

All the news was bad news. On 20th August Mary wrote, 'I lunched at

Downing Street and the Prime was so depressed and said the Belgians were so smashed and Brussels occupied . . .' Mary spent a great deal of time at Downing Street where Violet Asquith dispensed war gossip. So far the only communication from Aubrey had come in the form of a postcard from a French coal merchant in Arras; it said 'Un officier anglais m'a donné ceci en passant; il dit que c'est pour sa mère! Vive L'Angleterre!' This was the only clue they had of Aubrey's whereabouts and Mary wrote, 'We can tell from our maps that you are north of Amiens. Why can't they tell us? What harm can it do? Violet [Asquith] said the English Army was second line in this battle but you are so far north I don't know what to think.' At Downing Street too she garnered the political gossip and regaled Aubrey with stories of the War Cabinet:

> Violet is funny about Kitchener. She says the P.M. loves him but the cabinet, at any rate Lloyd George, McKenna, Birrell and Bron [Herbert] foam at the mouth when they hear his name for instead of remaining simple war minister as they supposed, he takes enormous pleasure in cabinet meetings, smokes his cigar and talks the whole time. Starting off with, 'I can't see why you want to do away with the Welsh Church or I don't see it's very important if we pass Home Rule now or not', also although he is brilliant at his own ideas he can't understand anyone else's and has to have the difference between the territorial, reserve and special reserve explained every time afresh.

Soon, however, letters from Aubrey began to arrive. They were light-hearted and cheerful. 'The terrors of war so far consist in getting horribly sunbitten'; 'if only one was not so unhappy about you I should not have anything on my mind'. 'I have got a horse but no saddle. She is of the highest lineage but there is a mystery about her somewhere.' Mary wrote, 'You write so happily it makes me happy.' But even as Aubrey's letters arrived disturbing news also began to trickle in. First came muddled accounts of the retreat from Mons; then came the casualty lists. Aubrey was posted wounded and missing.

Mary needed all her reserves of courage in the days that followed. While Elsie wrote and telegraphed frantically to every German of her acquaintance and to all the German friends of all her friends (for the war had not yet severed communications between the two countries, nor had bitterness and bereavement yet broken Europe's old aristocratic networks), Mary dealt with the enormous flow of letters from friends and well-wishers. Margot Asquith wrote, 'My darling Mary, I am haunted by your brave and beautiful face and the knowledge of what lies behind your eyes and in your heart. I am thinking of you with deep love.' But mostly friends wrote about Aubrey's 'charmed life' and the special providence that always seemed to watch over him. None of his friends could or would believe that he was dead. Raymond Asquith wrote, 'All through his risky life Aubrey has had the devil's own luck. It won't desert him. I am convinced of that. Quite soon you will be happy again, dear and beautiful Mary.' And these friends were right. Aubrey's luck had not deserted him. Four days later came the news that he was alive and free. The field hospital where he lay had been abandoned by the Germans, retreating before a French counter-attack. The wounded prisoners were released and despatched to Paris. By the end of September Aubrey was back in England convalescing. Tommy Lascelles, an old friend of Mary's, wrote to another friend of hers, Lady Gwendolyn Godolphin Osborne, 'I saw Aubrey for a minute last Sunday – looking almost beautiful, with a curly titian beard, and his gaping wound healed up miraculously to the size of a shilling . . . He had a capital tale to tell . . .'

A capital tale indeed it was. Aubrey had kept a rough diary and now during his convalescence he wrote a full account. This forms the best part in a book he later published anonymously entitled, *Mons, Anzac and Kut*. It is a pity that the Mons diary is too long to be reproduced here in full. Quotations fail to give the full flavour of the whole, which vividly describes, with humour and charm, the day by day muddle, chaos and gallantry which is impossible to convey in a compressed account. The following are patched-together fragments of the diary which tell the main parts of the story.

On 13th August the 1st Division of Irish Guards arrived early in the morning at Le Havre. The townspeople were hospitable and welcoming, plying the soldiers with wine, coffee and beer with disastrous effects. Many passed out. That night they slept at Wassigny and the next at Vadencourt where again the townspeople threw open their houses, barns and orchards. Aubrey wrote, 'all the people seemed saintly, except the Maire, who was very much of this world.' The men fraternised with the people and, to the colonel's irritation, wore flowers in their hair and caps. They helped with the harvest and there was little soldiering – 'it was more like manoeuvres in the millennium than anything else.'

At Vadencourt Aubrey bought a race-horse. This horse was to be his main preoccupation and joy for the next few days:

Monsieur Louis Prevot came in one day with a beautiful mare, brown to bay, Moonshine II by Troubadour out of Middlemas. He said that she could jump two metres. Her disadvantages were that she jumped those two metres at the wrong time and in the wrong place, that she hated being saddled and kicked when she was groomed: while Monsieur Prevot was showing me how to prevent her kicking she kicked right through the barn door. I bought her for

£40. I think Prevot thought that the French authorities were going to take his stables and that I was his only chance. When she settled down to troops she became a beautiful mount.

Slowly, with no sense of urgency, the Irish Guards made their way northwards to meet the Germans. Ten days after their arrival in France, on 23rd August, they finally faced the enemy.

We marched to a place called Senlis. Dawn came, then an enemy aeroplane appeared over us, which everybody at once shot at. Moonshine broke up two companies in the most casual way. The aeroplane went on . . .

Beyond Senlis we were halted on a plain near a big town which we did not then know was Mons. We were drawn up and told that the Germans were close to us and that we had to drive them back. It was a mournful day in its early hours. We marched on till half past three, through rising and falling land, under a very hot sun. We were getting nearer to the battle. The sky was filled with smoke wreathes from shells.

The first stretch was easy. Some rifle bullets hummed and buzzed round and over us, but nothing to matter. We almost began to vote war a dull thing. We took up our position under a natural earthwork. We had been there a couple of minutes when a really terrific fire opened. It was as if a scythe of bullets passed directly over our heads about a foot above the earthworks. It came in gusts whistling and sighing. The men behaved very well. It seemed inevitable that any man who went over the bank must be cut nearly in two. Then, in a lull, Tom [Vesey] gave the word and we scrambled over and dashed on to the next bank. Bullets were singing round us like a swarm of bees, but we had only a short way to go, and got, all of us, I think, safely to the next shelter, where we lay and gasped and thought hard.

Our next rush was worse, for we had a long way to go through turnips . . . We had not gone more than about 100 yards, at a rush and uphill, when a shell burst over my head. I jumped to the conclusion that I was killed, and fell flat. I was ashamed of myself before I reached the ground, but, looking round, found that everyone else had done the same.

The turnips seemed to offer some sort of cover, and I thought of the feelings of the partridges, a covey of which rose as we sank. Tom gave us a minute in which to get our wind – we lay gasping in the heat, while the shrapnel splashed about – and then he told us to charge, but ordered the men not to fire until they got the word. As we rose, with a number of partridges, the shooting began again, violently, but without much effect. I think we had six or seven men hit. We raced to the trees. Valentine [Castlerosse] was so passionately anxious to get there that he discarded his haversack, scabbard and mackintosh, and for days afterwards walked about with his naked sword as a walking stick.

The wood offered little safety. The Irish Guards were outflanked on the left. Later that night they received the order to retire and so began

the long retreat from Mons. In Aubrey's diary Moonshine's antics are a
recurring theme:

> Moonshine behaved like the war horse in the Bible. She had hysterics which
> were intolerable; smelling the battle a long way off. [The next day] We were
> told that a tremendous German attack was to take place in the evening: we
> disliked the idea as, even to an amateur like myself, it was obvious there was
> hardly any means of defence. We wrote farewell letters which were never
> sent. I kept mine in my pocket, as I thought it would do for a future occasion
> . . . The peasants were flying and offered us all their superfluous goods. They
> were very kind. Then an order to retire came, and in hot haste we left our
> potatoes . . .
>
> The orchard in which we camped (Quevy-le-Petit) blazed with torchlight
> and camp fires and was extremely cheerful. Every now and then a rifle went
> off by accident, and this was always greeted by tremendous cheers. I was very
> tired and threw myself down to sleep under a tree, when up came the Colonel
> and said: 'Come along, have some rum before you go to bed.' I went and drank
> it, and with all the others lay down thoroughly warm and contented in the
> long wet grass, and slept soundly for 3 hours. Next morning we were woken at
> 3 o'clock, but did not march off until 6 o'clock . . .

The retreating army on the whole found the townspeople much less
welcoming than on their outward march. The diary continues:

> This whole retreat was curiously normal. Everybody got very sick of it, and all
> day long one was hearing officers and men saying how they wanted to turn
> and fight. I used to feel that myself, though when one was told to do so and
> realized that we were unchaperoned by the French and faced by about two
> million Germans, it did something to cool one's pugnacity, and one received
> the subsequent order to retire in a temperate spirit. Men occasionally fell out
> from bad feet but the regiment marched quite splendidly. There was never any
> sign of flurry or panic anywhere. I think that most people, when they realized
> what had happened, accepted things rather impersonally.
>
> Hubert [Crichton] and I arrived at Landrecies about 1 o'clock. We went to a
> big house belonging to a man called Berlaimont, which Hubert wanted to
> have as headquarters. Berlaimont was offensive and did not wish to give his
> house. We went to the Maire who gave us permission to take it. Berlaimont
> gave in ungraciously and wrote up rather offensive orders as to what was not
> to be done: 'Ne pas cracher dans les corridors'. In other houses, too, they made
> difficulties. I said: 'After all, we are better than the Germans'. They soon had
> the chance of judging. The troops came to be billeted. At 6 o'clock fire
> suddenly broke out in the town, and the cry was raised that the Germans were
> upon us. I ran back and got my sword and revolver at Headquarters, and going
> out found a body of unattached troops training a Maxim on the estaminet
> that was my lodging. I prevented them firing. Troops took up positions all

over the town. The inhabitants poured out pell-mell. It was like a flight in the
Balkans. They carried their all away in wheel-barrows, carts, perambulators
and even umbrellas. I met and ran into M. Berlaimont, very pale and fat,
trotting away from the town; he said to me with quivering cheeks: 'What is it?'
I said: 'It is the Prussians, M. Berlaimont. And they will probably spit in your
corridors.'

All night the Germans shelled Landrecies. It did not seem as if there was
much chance of getting away, but no one was despondent. At about 1 a.m.
there was a lull in the firing, and I went back to lie down in my room. There I
fell asleep and the shelling of the town did not wake me though the house next
to me was hit.

In the early hours of the morning he was woken and told to search for
some missing officers. As he was blind and it was dark, he was not
successful in his quest. His regiment was by now retiring, but Aubrey
refused to leave without Moonshine who was lost.

My groom and servant had both disappeared. The houses were all locked and
deserted. I battered on a door with my revolver. Two old ladies timidly came
out with a light. They pointed to a house where I could find a man but at that
moment a Frenchman came up, whom I commandeered. I went off to Headquarters to see if a sergeant was left.

There was nobody there. The dinner left looked like Belshazzar's feast. I had
a good swig of beer from a jug. My saddle and sword had gone . . . I determined
to stay, if necessary, and hide until I could find my horse, but the Frenchman
turned up trumps and we found her. We were terrified of her heels in the dark.
As I got out of the town dawn was breaking . . .

The 3rd Battalion of Coldstream Guards remained behind to defend
the town, and suffered terrible casualties. Later Aubrey took a saddle
from another horse and on the swift Moonshine soon caught up with his
regiment. On 31st August they camped at Coeuvre. Aubrey obtained
leave to ride to Soissons to buy provisions, clean shirts and handker-
chiefs as everyone had lost their baggage at Landrecies.

Soissons was like a sunlit town of the dead. Four out of five houses were shut.
Most of the well-to-do people had gone. It was silent streets and blind houses.
The clattering which Moonshine made on the cobbles was almost creepy.
After going to many different shops I found a bazaar like a mortuary, with two
old women and a boy. They said to me: 'Take whatever you want and pay as
much or as little as pleases you. If the Germans come we shall set fire to this
place' . . . It was like being turned loose in Selfridges – boots, scissors, pocket
knives, electric torches, bags, vests, etc. I also bought an alpenstock, as I had
lost my sword and thought it might be useful as a light bayonet.

I then went and had a bath, the first proper one since England. I felt dirty and wanted to shave my beard as the men said every day that I became more like King Edward.

Riding back to Coeuvre, with the Germans close behind, Aubrey fell into conversation with a medical officer and asked him the way.

Then an RAMC Colonel came up and looked at my kit very suspiciously. He asked me who the General in command of the Division was. I said I had forgotten his name; I could not keep my head filled with these details. He said to me: 'You don't seem to know who you are.' I said to him: 'I know who I am, I don't know who you are, I don't want to. I hope to God I shall never see you again. Go to hell and stay there.' This made him angry and he said: 'Your regiment is ahead on the left, but the Germans are in front of you, if you wish to rejoin them', pointing in the direction from which I had come.

All this time I had been waiting for Sheridan and other now numerous stragglers behind me, and at this point I turned round and rode off to see what had happened, thoroughly irritated with the RAMC Colonel. This apparently convinced him that I really was a German, as the engagement in the rear was going on fairly close, and he came after me with a Major of the Rifle Brigade, who was unhappy. He said: 'Will you come with me to my Colonel?' I said: 'I will go with you anywhere to get away from this fussy little man, but if you think that a German spy would come on a race-horse, dressed like the White Knight, with an alpenstock, you are greatly mistaken'. He promised to have my stragglers looked after, and then I rode up to his regiment with him when Dennison came up and shook hands. We had not met since Eton. He cleared my character . . .

Aubrey reached his regiment by nightfall, where both his shopping and the story of his arrest were greeted with delight. The next day, 1st September, they rose at 2 a.m. Before the day was over there would scarcely be an officer in the regiment who was not dead or wounded. Moonshine, as if with premonition, would eat nothing. 'This worried me', Aubrey wrote with some under-statement, 'I had become very fond of her.'

At about 6 o'clock we halted on what I knew to be a tragic plain . . . We sat about on the wet muddy ground for breakfast, while a thin dismal rain fell.

The C.O. called us round and gave us our orders. 'We are required to hold this wood (Forêt de Villers Cotteret) until 2 o'clock in the afternoon. We may have to fight a rearguard action until a later hour if there is a block in the road. We are to retire upon Rond de la Reine.'

It was apparent that if the First Division took long over their luncheon we should be wiped out. By this time everyone had got their second wind, their feet were hard and they were cheerful . . .

It must have been about 7.30 when we went into the wood . . . The C.O.

said to me, 'I want you to gallop for me today so stick to me'. I lost him at once
in the woods behind No. 4 but swinging to my right found him at the
crossroads . . . I asked him what chance he thought we had of getting more
than half of us away. He said he thought a fairly good chance. Then he said to
me, 'How is your rest cure getting on now? There is very little that looks like
manoeuvres in the millennium about this, is there?' We talked about Ireland
and Home Rule, riding outside the wood. The grey damp mist had gone and
the day was beautiful.

Aubrey was sent with messages to different officers. As soon as he
returned he was sent off again. Although the British Expeditionary
Force was a small, highly professional army, it was exceedingly ill-
equipped. Despite the fact that the motor-car and radio were well
established in civilian life all military provisions and ammunition were
horse drawn and there were no field telephones or wireless. Orders were
carried by gallopers who were often killed before they could deliver their
messages.

I went off at a hard gallop, and had got halfway there, with the wood on my
left and open land on my right, when the Germans began shooting at about
three-quarters of a mile. Our men were firing at them from the wood, and I felt
annoyed at being between two fires and the only thing visible to amuse our
men and the Germans. I turned into the wood and, galloping down a sandy
way, found the road filled with refugees with haunted faces. We had seen
crowds of refugees for days, but I felt sorrier for these. I suppose it was that the
Germans were so very near them. I gave my message to Pereira, who advised
me to go back through the wood, but I knew the other way and thought I
should soon be past the German fire. I had not, however, counted on their
advancing so quickly. When I came to the edge of the wood they were firing
furiously – shrapnel, machine-gun and rifle fire. Our men had excellent cover
and were answering. I then tried to make my way through the wood, but it
was abominably rough. There were ferns and brambles waist high, and great
ditches; the wood was very beautiful with its tall trees, but that, at the
moment was irrelevant. Moonshine stood like a goat on the stump of a tree
that made an island among the ditches, and I turned back to take the way by
the open fields. When I got outside the fire had grown very bad. I raced for an
orchard that jutted out of the wood. Bullets hummed and buzzed. Coming to
it, I found that there was a wire round it. I then popped at full speed, like a
rabbit, into the wood again, through a thicket, down an enormous ditch, up
the other side, bang into some barbed wire, which cut my horse. It was like
diving on horseback. I turned round and galloped delicately out again, riding
full tilt round the orchard.
     I found the Colonel . . . It was, I suppose, now about 10.30. Desmond, the

Colonel and I rode back into the big, green wood. It was very peaceful. The sun was shining through the beech trees, and for a bit the whole thing seemed unreal. The C.O. talked to the men, telling them to reserve their fire until the Germans were close on them. 'Then you will kill them and they won't get up again.' That made them laugh. The German advance began very rapidly. The Coldstreamers must have begun falling back about this time. The Germans came up in front and on our left flank there was a tremendous fire. The leaves, branches, etc., rained upon one. One's face was constantly fanned by the wind from the bullets. This showed how bad their fire was. My regiment took cover very well, and after the first minute or two fired pretty carefully. Moonshine was startled to begin with by the fire, but afterwards remained very still and confidential . . . The Colonel then told me to gallop up to the Brigadier to say that the retreat was being effectively carried out . . . Eric [Gough] said to me 'The Germans seemed hardly to have an advance guard; it was an army rolling over us'. I returned to the Colonel . . . A galloper came up and, as far as I heard, said that we were to hang on and not retreat yet. This officer was, I think, killed immediately after giving this message . . . We were ordered to resume the position which Hubert had been told to leave. The Germans were by this time about 250 yards away, firing on us with machine guns and rifles. The noise was perfectly awful. In a lull the C.O. said to the men: 'Do you hear that? Do you know what they are doing that for? They are doing that to frighten you.' I said to him: 'If that's all, they might as well stop. As far as I am concerned, they have succeeded, two hours ago.'

The men were ordered to charge, but the order was not heard in the noise, and after we had held this position for some minutes a command was given to retreat. Another galloper brought it, who also, I think, was shot. Guernsey, whom I met with his company, asked me to gallop back and tell Valentine he must retire his platoon; he had not received the order. I found Valentine and got off my horse and walked him some yards down the road, the Germans following. He, like everybody else, was very pleased at the calm way the men were behaving.

I mounted and galloped after the Colonel, who said: 'If only we could get at them with the bayonet I believe one of our men is as good as three of theirs'. He started in the direction of the Brigadier. Men were now falling fast. I happened to see one man drop with a bayonet in his hands a few yards off, and reined in my horse to see if I could help him, but the C.O. called me and I followed him. The man whom I had seen was Hubert, though I did not know it at the time. The C.O. said: 'It is impossible now to rescue wounded men; we have all we can do'. He had a charmed life. He raced from one place to another through the wood, cheering the men and chaffing them, and talking to me; smoking cigarette after cigarette. Under ordinary conditions one would have thought it mad to ride at the ridiculous pace we did over the very broken ground, but the bullets made everything else irrelevant.

At about 1 o'clock we went up to the Brigadier at the corner of the road. The fighting there was pretty hot. One of the men told the Colonel that Hubert was killed. The Colonel said: 'Are you sure?' The man said: 'Well, I can't swear'. I was sent back to see. The man said he was about 600 yards away, and as I galloped as hard as I could, Guernsey called to me: 'To the right and then to the left'. As I raced through the wood there was a cessation of the firing, though a number of shots came from both sides. They snapped very close. I found Hubert in the road we had been holding. I jumped off my horse and put my hand on his shoulder and spoke to him. He must have been killed at once and looked absolutely peaceful. He cannot have suffered at all. I leant over to see if he had letters in his pocket, when I hard a whistle 25 or 30 yards behind me in the wood. I stood up and called: 'If that is an Englishman, get outside the wood and up to the corner like hell. You will be shot if you try and join the rest through the wood. The Germans are between us.' I bent over to pick up Hubert's bayonet, when again a whistle came and the sound of low voices, talking German. I then thought the sooner I was away the better. As I swung into the saddle a shot came from just behind me, missing me. I rode back as fast as Moonshine could go. The lull in the firing had ceased, and the Germans were all around us. One could see them in the wood and they were shooting quite close. The man who finally got me was about 15 to 20 yards away; his bullet must have passed through a tree or Bron's greatcoat, because it came into my side broken up. It was like a tremendous punch. I galloped straight to my regiment and told the Colonel that Hubert was dead. He said: 'I am sorry, and I am sorry you were hit. I am going to charge.' He had told me earlier he meant to if he got the chance.

I got off and asked them to take on my horse. Then I lay down on the ground and an R.A.M.C. man dressed me. The Red Cross men gave a loud whistle when they saw my wound, and said the bullet had gone through me. The fire was frightfully hot. The men who were helping me were crouching down, lying on the ground. While he was dressing me a horse – his, I suppose – was shot just behind us. I asked them to go, as they could do me no good and would only get killed or taken themselves. The doctor gave me some morphia, and I gave them my revolver. They put me on a stretcher, leaving another empty stretcher beside me. This was hit several times. Shots came from all directions, and the fire seemed to be lower than earlier in the day. The bullets were just above me and my stretcher. I lost consciousness for a bit; then I heard my regiment charging. There were loud cries and little spurts of spasmodic shooting; then everything was quiet and a deep peace fell upon the wood. It was very dreamlike.

The glades became resonant with loud raucous German commands and occasional cries from wounded men. After about an hour and a half, I suppose, a German with a red beard, with the sun shining on his helmet came up looking like an angel of death. He walked round from behind, and put his serrated bayonet on the empty stretcher. The stretcher broke and his bayonet poked me. I enquired in broken but polite German what he proposed to do next; after reading the English papers and seeing the way he was handling his bayonet, it seemed to me that there was going to be another atrocity. He was extraordinarily kind and polite. He put something under my head, offered me wine, water and cigarettes . . .

The Germans passed in crowds. They seemed like steel locusts. Every now and then I would hear: 'Here is an officer who talks German' and the crowd would swerve in like a steel eddy. Then 'Schnell Kinder' and they would be off. They gave a tremendous impression of lightness and iron. After some hours, when my wound was beginning to hurt, some carriers came up to take me to a collecting place for the wounded. These men were rather rough. They dropped me and my stretcher once, but were cursed by an officer. They then carried me some distance and took me off the stretcher leaving me on the ground. The Germans continued to pass in an uninterrupted stream. One motor cyclist, with a bayonet in his hand, was very unpleasant. He said: 'I would like to put this in your throat and turn it round and round' waving it down to my nose. That sort of thing happened more than once or twice but there were always more friends than enemies though as night fell the chance of being left without friends increased. As it grew dark I got rather cold. One of the Germans saw this, covered me with his coat and said: 'Wait a moment I will bring you something else'. He went off and I suppose stripped a dead Englishman and a dead German. The German jersey which he gave me had no holes in it, the Englishman's coat had two bayonet cuts.

The wounded began to cry dreadfully in the darkness. I found myself beside Robin [Innes Kerr] who was very badly wounded in the leg. The Germans gave me water when I asked for it but every time I drank it made me sick . . .

Late that night the wounded were moved to a makeshift hospital and Aubrey's wound was operated on and dressed. 'Then I was helped out to an outhouse and lay beside Robin. It was full of English and German wounded. They gave us one drink of water and then shut and locked the door and left us for the night. One man cried and cried for water until he died. It was a horrible night. The straw was covered with blood, and there was never a moment when men were not groaning and calling for help. In the morning the man next to Robin went off his head and became animal with pain . . .'

Later that day they were moved to Viviers where they found Valentine Castlerosse, who had had the point of his elbow shot away as he brushed a wasp off his nose. Here then, except for Tom Vesey, were Aubrey's companions in the railway carriage from Nine Elms. All three of them had experienced the same mixture of German brutality and German kindness. Unwisely Lord Castlerosse and Lord Robin had made use of their titles hoping to impress their captors, while Aubrey had emphasised his importance as a Member of Parliament. The Germans in dismay said, 'Surely you have not already mobilized both Houses of Parliament.' Later, as the French advanced and it became clear the hospital would have to be abandoned, the Germans decided that they would take with them these three very important prisoners. Hastily all three changed their tune. Aubrey said, 'I have only just been elected and have no influence', 'Mine is a very new creation, I am a nobody', said

Lord Castlerosse while Lord Robin earnestly explained, 'Mine is only a courtesy title, I don't count at all.' Fortunately the Germans were persuaded by this more realistic assessment of their importance and left them behind with the other wounded prisoners.

At the hospital they were well treated. Meanwhile news of the battle where they had all been wounded was saddening. Not only was Colonel Morris dead, but every single man of the seventy odd who had charged with him at the end had been killed.

The prison diary is depressing. Each day records at least one death. Aubrey, who had been in considerable pain, was cut open again and the bullet which was all in bits extracted. After this he felt much better. There is a curious entry in the diary for 10th September: 'They don't like giving us morphia. Luckily I have got my own medicine chest, which is a good thing for all of us, as I can give the others sleeping draughts.' Another entry the next day adds to the mystery. 'It is very trying lying here in bed. We have nothing to read except *The Rajah's Heir* which V[era] sent to me and which has become known as the treasure house of fun. It is a sort of mixture of *Hymns Ancient and Modern* and the *Fairchild Family*.' How can Aubrey have held on to a book and a medicine chest as he was galloping around the battlefield? How could he have possibly kept them with him on his stretcher? It is not explained.

In the last days of captivity the diary has hourly entries and at 3.10 p.m. on 11th September Aubrey reported: 'The French are here. They came in in fine style, like conquerors; one man first, riding, his hand on his hip. The German sentries who had been posted to protect us wounded walked down and surrendered their bayonets. The French infantry and cavalry came streaming through. Our wounded went out into the pouring rain to cheer them. They got water from our men, whose hands they kissed. The German guns are on the sky-line. The Germans are in full retreat, and said to be cut off by the English.'

Two days later Aubrey left the hospital on his homeward journey. It was a month to the day since he had landed in France. Back in England he received a characteristic letter from Raymond Asquith:

20.9.14

My Sweet Aubrey,

   I am more than a little pleased that you are safely back again: though from the moment I saw your name on the casualty list I had the strongest possible presentiment that it would all end happily.

   It was thoroughly characteristic of you to be shot and lost but equally characteristic to be found and healed. I would always put my last shilling on your luck in these little things . . .

Please have your quiver full of prose and verse. Though as a matter of fact I suppose a battle is far too much like a railway accident to be susceptible of description.

Au revoir

    Raymond

9

Anzac 1915

Aubrey's wound in his stomach healed without complications and after a week in London he was allowed to go down to Pixton for a period of convalescence. His hopes of a return to the battlefront were quickly dashed: red tape had caught up with his unorthodox entry into the British Expeditionary Force. The dismal facts of his appalling eyesight were exposed. It became clear that there was no chance of his returning to France as a combatant soldier. However, his knowledge of the East and Eastern languages remained. Intelligence work in the Eastern Mediterranean was the obvious field for his talents. Mark Sykes, who had scraped an acquaintance with Colonel Oswald FitzGerald, Kitchener's friend and military secretary, was happily hatching many schemes for his own and Aubrey's deployment. He wrote:

> FitzGerald told me he had sent my name with two others to Conkey Maxwell [C in C, Egypt] as possible special Service officers – but nothing else. I don't see where this blooming 'hist while I whisper in your ear' stunt comes in. Obviously George [Lloyd] and you were the other two. Pompey [Aubrey] and Crassus [Lloyd] both suitably disposed of, the way opens for conquering Caesar's [Sykes] mighty tread!! Crassus is with the Yeomanry. Pompey lies sick. Hullo! this won't do! The real Crassus got a regrettable incident in N. Mesopotamia. Wash out the simile and change the conversation. Antwerp* will put two pounds in Enver's scale and may tip the beam – it is a bad business . . . We shall rue our delay if we get into war with Turkey now – we have given the devils too long to prepare – and the Germans too long to intrigue. I suspect the Syrians have been got out of Syria, and damned hard-bitten Anatolians put in. I have been preparing pamphlets of a seditious kind for Syria. There is one confounded fly in the ointment of peroration. And therefore: 'O ye Arabs plump for Russia and France whom ye know are sweet even as honey, who never, never say boo to a Moslem goose'.
>
> You are either to shave your chestnut beard or else wear a turban round your head instead of your stomach now that you are convalescent . . . B.L. [Bonar Law] must be made Leader of the Progressive Party on the West Belfast Municipal Council. Asquith must be tried by Court Martial for breaking his word and acquitted for having risked his immortal soul for the good of the country . . .

Now I have babbled for our mutual amusement . . .
A brilliant letter upon my soul.
So now Aubrey au revoir
Yrs
MARK

Within days of this letter came the news that Turkey had indeed
entered the war on the side of Germany. Aubrey had hoped against hope
that Turkey might remain neutral. But the strong pro-German bias of
Enver, and Russia, the traditional enemy of Turkey, fighting on the
Allied side with undisguised war aims which included the annexation of
Constantinople, made Turkish entry into the war almost inevitable.
Nevertheless it was a blow to Aubrey and increased his reluctance to go
to Egypt. Mark Sykes had no such hesitations. In an unusually joke-free
letter he urged Aubrey to go to Egypt and peremptorily mapped out for
him what his aims should be. It is an interesting letter because it
foreshadows the later campaign of T. E. Lawrence, and shows that Mark
Sykes, sitting in London, had imagined, two years before the event, the
adventurous enterprise against the Turks in Arabia for which Lawrence
later became famous.

My Dear Aubrey
    I certainly consider it your duty to go to Egypt. And situated as you are there
is nothing to prevent you.
    Now the important people whom we should get over on our side are the Beni
Sadir – they are desert Bedawin and hate the Turks in their souls. However
they must come to us not we go to them. We should establish a base at Akaba
and an intelligence officer there with large powers. The various tribal people
will come in by degrees. They should first be done up to the nines and given
money and food – but no arms. Presently they will begin to talk. The intelligence officer should find out what their idea is – also whether the Beni Sadir
will make it up with the Druses. Then premiums might be offered for camels,
say an exorbitant price £50 or £60, then a price for telegraphic insulators, 2
francs each, then a price for interruption of Hejaz railway line, and a good
price for Turkish Mausers and a good price for deserters from the Turkish Army
– the Beni Sadir would run these thro'.
    Then try and establish relations with the Druses of the Hauran. Get some of
their people down to Akaba (preliminary to this of course peace between the
Beni Sadir and the Druses), if possible keep the whole of the Hejaz railway in a
ferment and destroy bridges. For this reliable agents would be required who
understood demolitions – Armenians for choice.
    Later on a spring rising of all the Shamiyili desert tribes could be looked for,
Anazill, Beni Sadir, Druses, Adwan. If the whole lot moved west along the

line, the Turks would be completely paralyzed, and with adequate encouragement, the nomads of the Jaziroli would come on too and make hay round Aleppo.

In these raids a great distinction must be made between government and fellah-hin and we should pay the Khoweli or Tax for Syrian fellahin to the Bedawin so that all crops and homesteads should be immune – stock and cattle however should all be lifted, as it is on this that the government depends for supplies and taxation.

With the railway broken and the stock raided and the local government smashed, the Turks will not be able to keep the field and the people will welcome our arrival on the coast say in June or July when Germany should be on her last legs.

With the letter was an accompanying map, roughly drawn, of the Hejaz railway. Tribes were marked along the route and suggested points of attack. Mark's letter was soon followed by an official request that Aubrey should travel forthwith to Egypt and report to the Arab Bureau in Cairo. Aubrey obeyed his instructions. Perhaps he took with him Mark's letter and map and showed them to Lawrence when they met in Egypt.

Aubrey and Lawrence eventually became close friends. On their first meeting however, they were each a little dismissive of the other. Aubrey, in his diary, commenting on his fellow members of the Arab Bureau on the Sinai side wrote, 'Newcombe, captain and head, a vain ambitious inarticulate man; Leonard Woolley, a good sort, archaeologist. Lawrence, an odd gnome, half cad – with a touch of genius'. It was a shrewd assessment. Lawrence for his part was a little in awe of Aubrey's reputation, but not overawed; he wrote in a letter home, 'Then there is Aubrey Herbert, who is a joke, but a very nice one: he is too shortsighted to read or recognise anyone: speaks Turkish well, Albanian, French, Italian, Arabic, German.' He then describes, inaccurately, Aubrey's career to date: 'He was for a time chairman of the Balkan League, of the Committee of Union and Progress, of the Albanian Revolution Committee. He fought through the Yemen wars, and the Balkan wars with the Turks and is friends with them all.'

Even at this early stage in their acquaintance Lawrence's tendency to romanticise Aubrey is evident. Aubrey was eight years older than Lawrence but he was still talked about at Oxford when Lawrence went up. Over the years many legends had grown up round his name. It took time before Lawrence learned to distinguish between the man and his myth, but with understanding came great affection, so that even twelve years after Aubrey's death Lawrence could write: 'Some friends of mine, in dying, have robbed me. Hogarth and Aubrey Herbert are two empty places which no one and nothing can ever fill.'

Aubrey and Lawrence had travelled out to Cairo by separate routes, Lawrence and Newcombe arriving on 14th December 1914, a few days before Aubrey, George Lloyd and Leonard Woolley. Two other passengers on board ship from Gibraltar soon became part of Aubrey's group, the architect Edwin Lutyens and the painter William Nicholson. Aubrey liked them both enormously. 'Nicholson is a wonderful man,' he wrote to Mary, 'I should like to get him to paint you.' While Lutyens he describes as 'a divine imp, sillier than anything I have ever dreamt of, quite futile and occasionally brilliant. He sits all day writing things like

> Shed no tears for Captain Talbot
> He has gone to heaven; – all but
> Captain Lloyd has died at Malta
> Perished on his honour's altar,
> Shed no bitter tears of salt, ha
> He might have perished at Gibraltar.

with very blasphemous and indecent caricatures. He is the kind of man who would deaden and deafen Raymond. His life on board is a simmering revel.' Aubrey spent most of his time working on his Arabic and playing chess. Lutyens's way of playing infuriated George Lloyd: 'When George makes a wrong move Lutyens takes out a match, lights it, and sticks it in the hole in the chess board of the square where it ought to have been put.'

The Intelligence Bureau in Cairo, usually known later as the Arab Bureau, was under the direction of Colonel Clayton, a fatherly and shrewd figure, whom all his officers liked and admired. However, Aubrey's immediate superior was Colonel Newcombe, whom Aubrey neither liked nor admired. The dislike was mutual.

Aubrey's first impression of General Maxwell recorded in his diary was favourable, 'I think he is a good man, and strong. None the weaker because he likes his port and pâté de foie gras. Mere ascetics are poor judges of men.' (Aubrey was not wholly consistent in this observation; later he was to criticise Sir Ian Hamilton for dining well on the *Arcadian* while the troops suffered at Gallipoli.) He was however a little shocked by the frivolity of Egypt; he wrote to his mother, 'This place is as grotesquely unreal with its Christmas trees and race meetings as the war was grotesquely real.' The social life was intense. 'The entire peerage and House of Commons is here,' he wrote with customary exaggeration to Elsie in February 1915. By this time Mary had joined him which meant that he could not avoid the coils of Cairo society.

Mary had been determined to come to Egypt from the moment Aubrey was posted there. And Aubrey was pleased that she should come. The war with its dangers and separations had intensified Aubrey's and Mary's need for each other. Aubrey wrote in a letter to Mary on his way to Egypt, 'I never realised that I was going to be so close to you.' It is an odd confession but he was expressing a genuine puzzlement. Like many men of this generation Aubrey's attitude to women was, though ardent, chiefly poetic and chivalrous. He had loved and admired Mary and had wooed and married her, but he had expected her to fill and beautify only one compartment in his life and not to permeate his whole existence. He had envisaged his life with his men friends, his life of action and adventure, and his life of thought and politics as things apart, outside his marriage and his home. Now, beset with the uncertainties of war and the spectre of death, he acknowledged something which he had not noticed before, but which had imperceptibly and gradually come about: the importance of Mary in every aspect of his life.

Mary, also, had been deeply influenced by Aubrey. Her independence of spirit, her abounding energy, her huge and loving heart were all sunk in him. Her children came a very poor second. Her former preoccupations with the vagaries of society and the canons of taste had dissolved long since. Now she was wholly wrapped up in Aubrey, and took to herself his hopes and his frustrations. And there were many frustrations at the Arab Bureau. Aubrey found his work uncongenial. His main task was the wretched business of questioning prisoners and deserters, Turks, Armenians, Albanians and Arabs. He ran round in circles uncovering futile plots in which neither he nor anyone else believed. At other times he sat at his desk composing propaganda leaflets to be distributed among the Turkish soldiery.

None of this satisfied Aubrey's desire for adventure or service. Mark Sykes's distant exhortations to go and blow up railways were far beyond the scope of his dreary office job. In February he wrote to Mark:

Shepheards
9 Feb 1915

Oh Mark,
   Here is to make a beginning. I left England in an historic gale. The ship rolled 37 degrees. She could only roll 44. We went down to the sea that was near as a lion behind his bars . . .
   I am glad we did not annex [Egypt]. Our policy has been clear and high in this war. We have not gone out for loot but to protect small people . . . Six years ago when there was a good deal of pro-Turkish feeling here an enterprising Syrian bought a thousand Turkish Grammars. He only sold 40. Now he has sold the other 960 at an enhanced price to the Effendis.

The last idea is that the Turks are to bring thousands of camels down to the Canal and then set alight to their hair. The camel, using its well known reasoning powers, will dash to the canal to put the fire out. When they have done this in sufficient quantities the Turks will march over them. As a matter of fact, bar rag, it seems the canal is absolutely impregnable . . .

Opinion is divided here as to what we ought to do or not to do in Syria. My own feeling is strongly this. We are here in a fortified arm chair. If we leave this position we go out to gather thorns for ourselves and others. We involve ourselves in new obligations, some foreseen, and others impossible to foresee. We land in Syria. The Syrians will rise like YEAST . . . to come to our rescue. Then the Turks will turn round and eat up the Syrians and it will be up to us to save them . . . Again the natives unless they are the simplest souls alive, which I believe they are not, would ask us a few little questions. To break the yoke of the Turks, they would say, is good but do you after intend to hand us over to the French, for if so you are not fighting for freedom. NO. Here we have the traditional and best frontiers of an empire, sand and sea, let us stick to that.

I suggested to Sir John Maxwell and General Birdwood that as a piece of IMPERIAL WIT they should make this answer to Turkey's declaration of a Holy War. They should announce that at the conclusion of the war every Moslem who desired should have the opportunity to go at the government's expense to Mecca, and the Shiahs to Kerbela. There's statemanship for you.

Our own little lot is the intelligence lot, a very nice fellow en chef, Col Clayton. My department is made up of engineers, MPs, archaeologists and MPs. All except the MPs are very keen on making up new policies. They seem to think that the WO and the FO not only work lucidly in a sort of millennium with each other but also that Russia and France are only sweetly reasonable. I began developing a policy which they tried to prevent by giving me the whole of the Turkish Army handbook to learn by heart and a great map of Turkey to do with the movements of all the Turkish troops. Thank God I had my servant Johnny Allan with me, he did the map. Poor George Lloyd is ill, ptomaine poisoning, but inshallah not bad.

Now having sent you this exquisite cameo I descend to breakfast.
Yours
      Aubrey.

Mark Sykes replied:

April 1 AD 2030
My Dear Pompey,
Please tell Crassus how sorry I am about his stomach ache – and that I shall probably take my legion into Belgia or Gaul next month . . .

I perceive by your letter that you are pro-Turk still. I got a summons from Field to attend a meeting of the Ottoman Society to which I never belonged . . . I immediately wired to McKenna [Home Secretary] and I have every hope that the whole crowd have been clapped into barbed wire – ha! ha! How furious this must make you ha! ha! again. Your Policy is wrong. Turkey must cease to be. Smyrna shall be Greek. Adalia Italian, Southern Taurus and North Syria French, Filistin (Palestine) British, Mesopotamia British and everything else Russian – including Constantinople, and Noel Buxton, and I shall sing a *Te Deum* in St Sophia and a *Nunc Dimittis* in the Mosque of Omar. We will sing it in Welsh, Polish, Keltic and Armenian in honour of all the gallant little nations. Then with Enver and Aubrey Pompey bound hand and foot we will proceed to make a throne of them while we sing 'Over the Asp and the Basilisk shalt thou triumph' in the Green Mosque at Brusa. The Turkish people would welcome this.

You have been an idle dog and not done as I told you. You ought to have an office at Akaba – and you ought to be flooding Syria with prophesies, acrostics, anagrams etc.

Here's a Prophesy

> When the Sultan with one arm sold his turban
> to the Pig with one arm then
> did the House of Osman fall.

> When a Jew and a pig eat the bread
> of Moslems out of one dish then were
> the Turks turned back.

What the deuce is the use of you, pray?

I urge all I know to attack and seize Constantinople – thence Vienna.

How do you fancy the great Servian Empire which must arise after this war stretching from the Adriatic to the confines of Roumania.

The war continues much as usual by land and sea.

The Russians certainly ought to have Alexandretta. We are going to be a great people after this war – not merely a fortuitous concurrence of atoms living on the off chance of the Tories winning a by-election every ten years.

Ireland has ceased to exist and Carson and the Serpent weep on each other's bosoms saying 'Damn these blashted English what a lovely war they've spoiled in Oireland all for the sake of Europe an' who t'inks av us now!'

I have no other news for you – only you must work – stir up mischief in Syria and you will get Germans massacred and the Turks ousted – keep worrying – never leave orientals alone too long. If you don't feel like fighting them send money and cartridges to the right people – Never give the Turks a moments peace.

Yours,
     Caesar

P.S. I disapprove of a Protectorate [for Egypt] – it only means trouble later on. Albanians and all black people want sound, strict, unbending government.

TO THE CENSOR

THIS IS A BRILLIANT LETTER FROM ONE GENIUS TO ANOTHER. MEN OF BASE CLAY CANNOT BE EXPECTED TO UNDERSTAND. PRAY PASS ON WITHOUT FEAR.

Mark Sykes Lt. Col. FRGS, MP, CC, JP.

Among the jokes and the exaggeration and the fantasy the censor would have been hard pressed to detect in this April Fool letter the clear outline of Sykes's convictions about the Middle East. Aubrey would have had no such difficulty and he cannot have relished the thought, if it occurred to him, that it was the ideas of Sykes, close to the seat of power in London, and not the ideas of Herbert, stuck in the Arab Bureau in Cairo, which were more likely to shape the future of the Middle East. For the seeds of the secret Sykes-Picot Agreement of 1916 which carved up the Middle East between British and French spheres of influence – and was anathema to Aubrey – were clearly to be discerned in Sykes's letter of the previous year.

On the question of the future of Syria, Aubrey and Lawrence saw eye to eye, and were both in violent disagreement with Mark Sykes. Aubrey wrote angrily, 'This is a war for liberty and small peoples not for French financiers' and in his diary he repeated, 'I want to see the French out of Syria; Syria independent; if she chooses to come to Egypt offering herself as a satrapy well and good. We should take Alexandretta; no more territory but just accumulate Gibraltars wherever we can.'

Aubrey was not the only frustrated and discontented member of the Arab Bureau. George Lloyd was also champing at the bit. He worked harder and harder but did not disguise his chagrin at the futility of his efforts. He shared Aubrey's dislike of Colonel Newcombe and wrote a memorandum on his shortcomings which by mistake got sent to Newcombe. It did not ease relations.

By the middle of February 1915 Colonel Newcombe was as anxious to get rid of Aubrey as Aubrey was to be rid of Newcombe. It was suggested that Aubrey should go on an intelligence-gathering mission with the battleship *Bacchante* which plied along the hostile, Turkish-controlled coast of the Eastern Mediterranean watching for Turkish troop movements. Aubrey was glad to exchange the squabbling office in Cairo for the wardroom of the battleship. Mary meanwhile stayed on in Cairo. With a friend, Margherita Howard de Walden, she rented a charming house, 8, ibn Zanki, from a sinister Austrian baroness.

The *Bacchante* sailed from Port Said on 12th February. Two days later, after visiting Haifa and Beyrout, she arrived at Alexandretta. 'This is the way that we are making war,' Aubrey wrote to Mary. 'We swim majestically into a harbour, we look at the town sombrely, and the town seems to wilt, and again slowly we sweep out. Not a camel moves, not a mine stirs. The towns look prosperous but dead with fright.'

By the time Aubrey left the *Bacchante* ten days later he was able to write with satisfaction in his diary: 'The whole ship's company is now Turkophile.' Aubrey was conscious of no impropriety in loving the Turks at the same time as being at war with them; nor apparently were these congenial sailors. It was an attitude fraught with complications but Aubrey maintained it throughout the forthcoming Gallipoli campaign, as did many other Turkophiles.

On 19th February, while Aubrey had been sitting outside Alexandretta on the *Bacchante*, the Navy, in an ill-considered and worse-executed attack on the fortifications of the Dardanelles, had been repulsed by the Turks. It was the untoward beginning of the luckless Gallipoli campaign. In London the War Cabinet belatedly agreed to use the Army. Whereas previously the idea had been for the Navy to clear the way for an army to reach Constantinople, now the plan was for the Army to clear the way for the Fleet to do so. The decision to land a force came too late. The bombardment of the Straits had already given the game away to the Turks. Before they had been unsure where the attack might come. Now they knew. The Germans sent the experienced General Von Sanders to take charge of Turkish preparations. In February there had been only two divisions on the Gallipoli peninsula. Had the Allies then attacked with a joint military and naval force they would undoubtedly have won their way to Constantinople. Now the Turks moved in another four divisions, built railways to bring up the heavy howitzer guns, dug trenches and laid barbed wire entanglements, while the Allies continued to waste precious time. Kitchener promised divisions, retracted his promise, promised again.

In Egypt General Birdwood, who commanded the Australian and New Zealand division, was informed that his men were destined for the Gallipoli expedition. Aubrey had made the acquaintance of both General Birdwood and his second-in-command, General Godley, formerly of the Irish Guards, who commanded the New Zealanders. General Godley suggested to Aubrey that he join his staff. Aubrey accepted the offer and was appointed Liaison Officer and Interpreter on the General's staff. His servant, Johnny Allan, who had accompanied him in Albania before the war, was enlisted as a sapper so that he could come too.

The last weeks in Egypt were enjoyable. Aubrey was at peace with himself. The weather was beautiful, Mary was by his side and there was an abundance of good company. Friends passed through continually. In March, the gallant Hood Battalion came, among them Oc Asquith, younger brother of Raymond and Beb, and Rupert Brooke. Brooke wrote to Oc's sister Violet Asquith, 'We had a delicious glimpse of Aubrey and Mary in – I forgot I mustn't say. And rode wildly on donkeys through black and white mysterious streets at midnight under a full moon.' Charles Lister and Patrick Shaw Stewart, other doomed members of the Hood Battalion, stayed in Port Said and reported that they were diligently practising their only sentence in Turkish: 'Do not kill me. I am a friend of Herbert Effendi.'

In March, Mervyn, too, arrived in Egypt. He had several times tried to volunteer for the army but the Foreign Office had refused to release him. He despised his civilian job, and his transfer to Egypt at least brought him closer to the war. In April Elsie arrived to join her sons. She was only just in time to see Aubrey. Three days after her arrival he set off, bound for the Greek island of Lemnos where the British Mediterranean Expeditionary Force was gathering for the Gallipoli invasion.

On 12th September 1914 Aubrey had left for France; now seven months to the day, on 12th April 1915, he again boarded ship to go on active service. His mood was very different on this occasion. In September he had gone an amateur to war, full of zest for the fight against an enemy he recognised. This time he went without enthusiasm to fight an enemy he liked in a campaign he judged ill-conceived.

At Lemnos, the troops and ships hung around in Mudros Bay making preparations for the landing. Aubrey wrote in his diary: 'The depression is profound. The general impression amongst the Intelligence is that we shall get a very bad knock . . . The Intelligence and Hamilton don't seem to be in touch . . . It seems incredible that we are not better informed . . .'

For two weeks they waited in Lemnos while the scale of the incompetence and ignorance in London and at General Headquarters became daily more apparent. Aubrey wrote in his diary: 'Winston's name fills everyone with rage. Roman emperors killed slaves to make themselves popular, he is killing free men to make himself famous. If he hadn't tried that coup [the naval bombardment of 19th February] but had co-operated with the Army, we might have got to Constantinople with very little loss.'

Aubrey's anger against Churchill reflected the general mood of the informed officers at Lemnos, but it was not altogether fair. Aubrey knew the situation in the Eastern Mediterranean but he did not know the situation in London. There, the general lack of direction, the placid composure of Asquith, the secretiveness and indecision of Kitchener, made it impossible for Churchill to carry a bold and decisive policy with the War Cabinet. Many in the Cabinet and Army and Admiralty believed

that no troops or effort or ammunition should be diverted from the
Western front. Others believed in other sideshows. Churchill believed in
breaking the impasse on the Western front by carrying the war into
Turkey, the backdoor to Austria. His policy was not at fault but his
impatience was catastrophic.

Aubrey's Lemnos diary, with its gloom and despondency, is not a true
guide to its author's mood. He was fully occupied in the sort of tasks he
enjoyed, hiring local brigands and haggling for mules. One of the former
brigands, Christos, became his devoted servant. After Johnny Allen was
wounded he became Aubrey's valet and stayed with him throughout the
campaign. Aubrey wrote to Mary, 'There have been Turkish vocabu
laries to write, scraps of intelligence to do, winds to meet and wine to
drink and Greeks to beat, so everything has conspired to make me
happy.'

On the eve of departure he wrote, 'Here we are off at last. Band
playing, troops cheering, the wind blowing and the sea shining. Well it'
the way to begin an odyssey, and I start upon it with a real thrill. I don'
feel as if it was real men and friends I was going to meet. The whole thing
is so incredibly unreal. We are like ghosts called upon to make a pagean
on the sea. Every way one turns, from the African savage on shore to the
Etonian fop, to the wooden horse of Troy or to the wily Greek of this
place, it is all a dream.'

The dream soon turned into a nightmare. Early on Sunday morning
25th April, the Allied troops landed, the British at Cape Helles and the
Australians and New Zealanders north of Gaba Tepe on a beach which
became known as Anzac Cove. The Navy had intended to land them a
Gaba Tepe but a combination of strong currents and general incompe
tence had resulted in the landing taking place a mile further north, in
more difficult country. This was extremely lucky. The Turks were
expecting them at Gaba Tepe and had they landed there they would
assuredly have been wiped out. As it was, towed in open boats, with no
protection from shell or shot, they floundered ashore safely, without loss
of life.

The initial success that had been gained by their improvised landing
did not last. The troops in their first rush had gained the heights of the
Sari Bair ridge, but the difficult terrain and the military genius of the
Turkish divisional commander Mustapha Kemal (later the ruler of
Turkey, Ataturk) defeated them. Slowly they were driven back down
the mountain slopes. Aubrey, on the beach, missed the fighting on the
ridges. He saw only the endless stream of dead and wounded as he was
sent hither and thither to interrogate non-existent Turkish prisoners
That evening 600 wounded were stowed on board the SS *Lutzow*, th

ship in which Aubrey had arrived, with a four-day voyage to hospitals in
Egypt in front of them, their only medical attendant a veterinary
surgeon.

Later that night General Birdwood sent a message, in General Godley's
writing, to Sir Ian Hamilton. He admitted defeat and suggested re-
embarkation. General Birdwood realised that once he had failed to carry
the heights, it was slow suicide to remain. His troops were exhausted
and demoralised. They had fought heroically but they had lost. Sir Ian
Hamilton, woken from his sleep aboard HMS *Queen Elizabeth*, sent
back a message telling them they 'must make a supreme effort to hold
their ground . . . You have got through a difficult business, now you
have only to dig, dig, dig until you are safe.'

Hamilton thought it better to die fighting on land, than to be
slaughtered fleeing on the sea like the Persians at Marathon. He was
probably right. Aubrey was not privy to Birdwood and Godley's confabu-
lations. He wrote, 'Most of us thought the Turks would get through and
that we should be dead or prisoners the next day.' He was against
digging, 'Here we can only succeed with a rush. Touch a spade and we
are done.' There was, however, no alternative.

So began the long months at Anzac Cove. They dug in on the slopes
and on the beach. Above them the Turks dug in also. Turkish snipers
picked them off as they moved about the slopes or beach, or swam and
washed in the sea. Nowhere was completely safe. Aubrey moved dugout
five times, each time his previous one was demolished by shells. Headquarters moved three times for the same reason. The Generals, Birdwood, Godley, Bridges and Walker won the admiration of all. They were
reckless of their own safety. Feeling against Hamilton, however, was
widespread. 'Ian Hamilton has been here twice, I think for a quarter of
an hour each time and has never been around the positions at all. GHQ
are loathed,' Aubrey wrote to Mary in June. In July he wrote, 'Hamilton
has the obstinacy of weak men. I have had one or two instances when I
have seen how he and his staff believe what they want to believe in the
face of all sense and evidence.' Before the Dardanelles campaign
Hamilton had been a popular general. An agreeable man of wide
culture, he was a good talker, and an able soldier. He had a reputation
for gallantry and as a military administrator but he had many faults as a
commander-in-chief, among which were a false optimism and an inabi-
lity to face facts. His relationship with Kitchener, to whom he was
intensely loyal and dangerously deferential, was a factor that influenced his conduct. Kitchener had ordained that the Gallipoli campaign
should be a sideshow. Hamilton therefore failed to press hard enough or
soon enough for the men and ammunition which alone could have saved

the situation, and his optimistic reports misled the politicians in London. Hamilton's other great failing was personal conceit. This is apparent in his diaries and was obvious to his men.

Hamilton's Gallipoli diaries are in marked contrast to Aubrey's. It is difficult, at times, to believe that both deal with the same campaign. Hamilton was remote from the tensions of being ceaselessly under fire day and night, or from the effects of the unrelenting din, or from the constant and disgusting smell of the rotting carcasses of both men and mules, or from the claustrophobia of being confined for months on end to a narrow strip of beach. His published diaries, instead, are full of the sparkle of the sea, the joys of good company, the exploits of heroes, and his ineffectual tussles with the War Cabinet.

The extracts from Aubrey's diaries which he chose for publication in *Mons, Anzac and Kut* give a different impression from the original, unexpurgated text. (Perhaps the same is true of Hamilton's diary.) In the published version Aubrey left out most of the horrors. To have published these, particularly the terrible details of the condition of the wounded or the occasional moments of broken morale among the men, would have caused great distress to the relatives of the dead. His letters, also, seldom dwell on the dark side of the campaign. They were written to reassure rather than alarm, and were filled with the exhilaration of the outdoor life, the elation and excitement of battle, pride and admiration at the courage both of the Anzac brigade and of the Turkish soldiers. He was able to write to Mary, 'I am curiously and completely happy.'

But there was another mood in his letters, a mood of angry resentment. Aubrey's poor opinion of the character and capacities of his Commander-in-Chief, Sir Ian Hamilton, has already been mentioned and, as the Gallipoli tragedy unfolded, was to grow in bitterness and intensity. He also shared the near universal hatred of the troops at Gallipoli for the politicians at home whose blunders they believed had caused their present miserable situation. Unlike the troops or the generals – with the exception of Hamilton – Aubrey had direct knowledge from his wife of the political chatter at London's dining tables, particularly the table at No. 10 Downing St, where Mary continued to be a frequent guest. He did not like what he heard. One letter in particular caused Aubrey to express himself in unbalanced terms. Mary wrote on 12th June shortly after Asquith had formed his coalition government and had, at the insistence of the Conservatives, removed Churchill from the Admiralty: 'Wednesday night I dined in Downing [St]; sat next to Winston. He was in a curious state, really rather dignified but so bitter. He and Clemmy look very broken. He told me that if he was Prime Minister for 20 years it wouldn't make up for this fall.' Aubrey replied,

'As for Winston, I would like him to die in some of the torments I have seen so many die in here. But his only "agony" you say is missing being P.M.'

Even the Prime Minister, of whom Aubrey and Mary had always been particularly fond, was not immune from Aubrey's censure. Aubrey wrote to Mary, 'I think the old man was pretty deep in this business. He always had a dilettante interest in this part of the world and has been very school-masterly about it. I think he knew what Winston was doing.' And in another letter, 'he has a mind of granite and the soul of a rather bad bridge party.'

Mary herself was as violent as Aubrey about the politicians and the older generation. She wrote in July 1915, 'Beb[Asquith] lisps all day long his hatred of politicians and I agree with him. I suppose they must go on, but you must abolish this mouldy old generation and their shibboleths of parliamentarianism, even [Lloyd] George and his steel shavings are better than this dry rot. Beb wants to bring back an army at the end of the war and string up his father and Bonar and all old men to lamp-posts and then have a great and glorious army to rule England and let every-one be democrats and soldiers together. I am inclined to think it will do short of that . . .'

Aubrey's anger was stoked by the daily sight of men dying slowly and squalidly on the beach, while medical officers on more than one occa-sion wrangled over petty, bureaucratic rules and regulations. He also suffered with and for the Turks. Their wounded moved him as deeply as his own. He wrote to Mary: 'I am pretty hardened now but they all go to my heart, our men and the Turks, you see very splendid things on both sides.' But he was not hardened and Mary knew it. She wrote, 'My darling I hope you are not having to see too many beastly things. Oh it's damnably hard for you. The only thing left to say is that it's not one nation hurting another but a whole raving universe . . .'

It was not only the politicians that Mary hated. She hated the fact that being a woman she had no active part to play in the war. She complained of drifting between 'the amazing, uncomprehending rowdy young things and the dried up old sticks of the older generation'.

The social sensations of the summer of 1915, while Aubrey suffered on the beach at Anzac, had been the engagements of Venetia Stanley and Violet Asquith. Venetia, a bridesmaid at Aubrey and Mary's wedding, had for some time ruled over the heart and imagination of the Prime Minister. Asquith, always susceptible to youth, beauty, breeding and intelligence, found all of these in Venetia. He had become besotted with her, writing her several letters a day, sometimes during cabinet meet-ings. Her engagement was a bitter blow to him. Meanwhile society was

shocked by her choice of spouse, Edwin Montagu, a liberal politician
and cabinet minister. Edwin Montagu was a Jew and Venetia renounced
Christianity to marry him. Mary felt sorry for her in the storm that arose
and wrote to Aubrey begging him to write to Venetia and give his
'blessing because Violet was being "so poisonous" about the engagement'.

Violet's own engagement, however, was not uncontroversial. She
selected her father's secretary, 'Bongie' Bonham-Carter, a Balliol friend
and contemporary of Aubrey's. What shocked in this case was not that
she had chosen someone outside the bounds of society but that she had
chosen, so unromantically, to marry an old friend. Aubrey found it more
difficult to write to Violet than to Venetia. 'How can one congratulate
on something that is tepid?' he asked Mary. But he did write and Violet
wrote back explaining her choice: 'He has known – understood and
endured everything that has ever happened to me – and is big enough to
hold it all and a lot more without cavilling or grudging. To him I need
never bowdlerize, or explain or translate. I feel him a foundation of rock
on which to build my life.'

In general Aubrey found it difficult to respond to the letters of gossip
and politics which arrived at his grim and bloody peninsula like missives
from outer space. He wrote chiefly to his family. Besides his regular
letters to Mary and Elsie he wrote often to Mervyn in Cairo, and to his
sister Vera in London, who sent him a weekly hamper from Fortnum and
Mason containing always among other things pâté de foie gras, caviar
and turtle soup. Only about one in three of the hampers arrived at their
destination. Aubrey's letters to Vera are mostly about nature. In May
1915 he wrote: 'The nightingale, a very brave bird, goes on singing in
spite of the cannon but the cuckoo has been terrorised into silence,
though one of them still sings but has changed his note through fright. I
don't blame the cuckoo really.'

He did however write one serious political letter to Lord Robert Cecil
who had become a minister at the Foreign Office in the new coalition. In
this letter Aubrey explored the possibility of peace with Turkey and
asked what machinery the government had on the spot, should there be
any overtures from the Turks. Lord Robert's reply was a disappointment.
He wrote, 'In this question we are absolutely bound to Russia . . .' and
he gave no encouragement to individual peace initiatives.

Meanwhile the campaign in the Dardanelles continued grimly. After
the landing in April there had been a brief lull while both sides dug in.
On 6th May Hamilton ordered an attack. At Krithia six hundred yards
were gained for the loss of 6,500 men, a cost of over ten men for every
yard. At Anzac, although many trenches were taken, they were later

retaken by the Turks, with huge losses on both sides.

The battle raged for three days. Aubrey reported in his diary:

May 6

The dead are unburied and the wounded crying for water between the trenches. I have got the doctors to talk to Birdwood about an Armistice. He thinks the Germans would not allow the Turks to accept an armistice . . . We attacked Achi Baba at 10 a.m. There was intermittent fire all night. This morning I went to the trenches with the General (Godley). Up by Walker's Ridge the view was beautiful. The plain covered with friendly olives . . .

May 7

A better night and morning. I have asked to be allowed to go and tell the Turks that if they surrender they will not be killed. The General doesn't want to say yes but has consented. I can get within twenty-five or thirty yards of them . . .

They have our exact range and are pounding in one shell after another . . . The dead mules that have been towed out return to us. 2 boats needed to take them away again. I have borrowed a megaphone from Commander Dix (wounded) . . . I am getting quite deaf from the shelling. This is the twelfth day. It doesn't seem possible not to have been hit. 3 cases of self-mutilation in N. Brigade . . .

1.30   I went up Monash Valley, which the men call the Valley of Death. I passed a stream of haggard, tragic figures, wounded and unwounded, coming down through the brilliant sunlight. I saw Monash at his H.Q. and General Godley with him. General G. said he wouldn't have me standing up shouting when I made my speech to the Turks. The shelling overhead was terrific, I don't know how many bursts a minute but the smoke made a shadow between us and the sun. It was like the continuous crashing of a train going over the sleepers of a railway bridge . . . Old Monash tried to speak on the telephone to say I was coming but it was a difficult business made worse by the noise. Finally I went up the slope to Quinn's Post, with an escort, running and taking cover, and panting up the very steep hill . . . I got into the trench and found Quinn, tall and open-faced, swearing like a trooper, much respected by his men. He sent for his officers but they slept . . . The trenches in Quinn's Post were narrow and low, full of exhausted men sleeping. I crawled over them and through tiny holes. There was the smell of death everywhere. I spoke in three places. In the first place my speech elicited a furious volley, part of which came through the sandbags, but after that, silence and amazement. I didn't lie down, it was no use doing that. I said: 'Comrades, keep your heads down, lest while I speak an accident should befall you. I am an English Officer and do not lie. If you want to surrender throw down your arms, hold up your hands, and come across in daylight. You will have good food and good water given you. This is a German business. Between us and you there is no quarrel.'

. . . The wounded have been left to die of thirst between the trenches. The Turkish wounded and ours too. It is a filthy shame and could be prevented.

Aubrey, later in the campaign, used the megaphone again on several occasions. A groan would go up from the trenches when the slight, myopic officer with the megaphone came stumbling along for the men knew that for the next few hours they would have to endure intense fire in retaliation. No Turks ever came over as a result of his efforts.

Next Aubrey turned his energies to the arrangement of a cease fire for the burial of the dead. He had raised the matter with Birdwood and got others to raise it also. The days passed; the Turks counter-attacked with great loss of life; and the sun beat relentlessly down on the thousands of corpses between the lines until the smell became insufferable. Hamilton, however, curtly refused Birdwood's request for authority to negotiate a truce. Aubrey asked leave to go on board the *Arcadian* and make the case to the Commander-in-Chief. Leave was granted and on 19th May Aubrey boarded the ship. The first person to greet him was Compton Mackenzie, who was at the time attached to Sir Ian Hamilton's staff. In *Gallipoli Memoirs* Mackenzie records his delight at encountering again the man

> whom I had last met near midnight in the top digs of a house in King Edward Street, Oxford, when on opening the window to a loud tap Aubrey Herbert came peering in, on his way back from Christ Church to Balliol by roofs, gutters, parapets, pipes and window-sills. Everybody who knew Aubrey will understand how one's heart would leap to see him come peering up the side of the *Arcadian* on that blue May day in 1915. I had the chance of a long gossip with him as we walked round and round the deck, in a series of rapid diagonals, for Aubrey was so short-sighted that he really could not see well enough to walk straight. I think he was holding forth passionately about the woes of the Turks and the beauty of their characters, gripping my arm from time to time and exclaiming 'My dear, we *must* do this' or 'My dear, we *must* do that'. As we zig-zagged along I suddenly became aware that a shape was following our course, though what that shape was I did not dare for a moment to look round and ascertain so acutely was I aware of a menace, an almost diabolical menace in its shadowing. At last I plucked up courage to turn my head. Imagine my dismay when I saw the Commander of the *Arcadian* stalking along the deck after us with the air of one who is tracking a pair of assassins. The faintness of despair came over me. His eyes protruding like a Bateman admiral's were fixed upon a meandering line of ink stains that stretched from one end of the deck to the other. I looked at Aubrey. Yes, there in the pocket of his service jacket, or rather fixed to the outside of it, was a fountain pen that was dripping with every step he took. I played a coward's part.
>
> 'Aubrey' I said 'I must run now. And by the way, I think your pen's leaking or something.'
>
> I cannot remember what steps were taken to restore the Commander of the

Arcadian to consciousness; but I do remember that those ink spots were still traceable when we went ashore ten days later.

Aubrey makes no mention of this encounter in his diary which is taken up with his conversations with Sir Ian Hamilton about the truce. These conversations marked the beginning of a personal antipathy between the two men. Aubrey despised Hamilton. He thought him an ass and a poseur. Hamilton for his part, although reasonably polite in his published diary, criticising Aubrey only as 'excessively unorthodox' clearly returned Aubrey's dislike. Compton Mackenzie on a later occasion, noting the coldness with which Hamilton spoke of Aubrey, remarked, 'It is difficult to believe that Aubrey ever irritated anybody; but I do not think it is an exaggeration to say that he irritated Sir Ian extremely.'

At their meeting Hamilton agreed in principle to an armistice for burying the dead. He wrote in his diary, 'Herbert is keen on meeting the Turks half way and I am quite with him *provided* Birdie [Birdwood] clearly understands that no Corps commander can fix up an armistice off his own bat, and *provided* it is clear we do not ask for the armistice but grant it to them – the suppliants.'

In fact this armistice was very much Aubrey's initiative. He somehow contrived to make the Turks think the English were seeking a truce while making the English think the Turks were the suitors. His diary sheds no light on this manoeuvre. Compton Mackenzie, however, was under no illusions; he wrote: 'It has never been perfectly clear who really did ask for this truce. Liman Von Sanders says we did; Sir Ian Hamilton says they did. My own opinion is that Aubrey Herbert alone was responsible for it.'

Although Sir Ian Hamilton did not give his permission outright that evening he was clearly in a mood to be persuaded. 'He said "I should like to do the decent thing". He looked very worried and asked me to tea which I refused', Aubrey reported in his diary. Aubrey spent the night on board as he was unable to get off the *Arcadian* that evening. By the next morning the situation had changed.

As I waited after breakfast Sir Ian Hamilton came up in a fussy rage and asked vehemently 'What do you think of it now?' I didn't know what he was talking about. He said, 'Last night the Turks put up a white flag and massed behind it in their trenches. They meant to rush us and used a ruse. If you had had your way our fellows on the beach would now all have had their throats cut or be swimming about in the sea. It was very difficult for me to say no to Birdwood after the very nice way in which he asked me'. I said I knew nothing of all this. That it wasn't a question of sentiment as he said but of sanitation, and that

even if the Turks were treacherous every day in the week it was no reason why
we should share Asiatic cholera with them. He repeated 'I am very glad I had
the strength of mind to refuse Birdwood'.

Aubrey left the *Arcadian* in anger. Back on Anzac beach he heard a
different story. There had indeed been an incident involving the Turks
and white flags, but it had not been the Turks who had been at fault.
What had happened (according to Aubrey's diary) was that while he
was away there had been a parley. The Turks had put up some white
flags in good faith. There had been some confusion and during this one
Red Crescent man had been shot by mistake. General Walker had then
gone out and talked to the Turks. A truce remained a possibility, though
both sides were nervous.

Meanwhile Hamilton, still in a fury, wrote a letter beginning, 'My
dear Birdwood, I am frankly horrified . . .' General Birdwood was not
intimidated. He finally obtained a reluctant consent from Hamilton and
told Aubrey to talk to the Turks at the first opportunity. On 22nd May,
only three days after he had boarded the *Arcadian* to tackle Hamilton,
Aubrey carrying a white flag and accompanied by Sam Butler (head of
Intelligence) crossed the wire entanglements at the far end of the beach
and continued along by the sea. Eventually they were met by a fierce
Arab officer and a Turkish lieutenant. They waited, sitting smoking in a
field of poppies until the commander, Kemal Bey Ohri arrived. Kemal
Bey went with Butler to arrange the truce with General Birdwood.
Kemal was blindfolded and carried over many non-existent wire
entanglements to dupe him into believing in extensive defences. Aubrey
was taken back to the Turkish lines as hostage for Kemal's safety. He was
a happy hostage. He too was blindfolded and then put on a horse and led
round in circles to confuse him. At last he was taken to a tent in a grove,
where the blindfold was removed and his host, Sahib Bey, said, 'This is
the beginning of a life-long friendship.'

They ate cheese and drank tea and coffee in the tent. Sahib Bey was
anxious to impress Aubrey with the Turks' well being. They talked
together for a few hours in slow, courteous, eastern fashion and parted
friends as Sahib had predicted. Kemal Bey's negotiations went smoothly
and the next day Hamilton received a letter in French from the German
commander, Liman von Sanders. Hamilton wrote in his diary: 'On my
return found a letter from the Turkish Commander-in-Chief giving his
"full consent" to the armistice he himself had asked for! A save-face
document no doubt.'

The Truce was arranged to take place on Whit Monday, 24th May. It
was to last eight hours. Aubrey's diary for 25th May gives an account.

We had the truce yesterday. I was afraid something might go wrong but it went off all right . . . At 7.30 we met the Turks. Izzedin, a Colonel, a pleasant sharp little man, Vassif, the son of Vassif Pasha, who gave me a card *Sculpteur et Peintre* and *Etudiant de Poésie*. I had a few words with Sahib but he did not come with us.

We walked from the sea and passed immediately up the hill, through a field of tall corn filled with poppies, then another cornfield, then the fearful smell of death began as we came across scattered corpses. We mounted over a plateau and down through gullies filled with thyme where there lay about 4,000 Turkish dead. It was indescribable. One was grateful for the rain and grey sky. The smell was appalling. A Turkish Red Crescent man came and gave me some antiseptic wool with scent on it, and this they renewed frequently. There were two wounded in all that multitude of silence, crying in the gullies. The Turks were very distressed and Skeen strained a point to let them send water to the first wounded man who must have been a sniper crawling home. I walked over to the second, who lay with a high circle of dead that made a mound round him, and gave him a drink from my water bottle, but Skeen called to me to come on and I had to leave the bottle. Later a Turk returned it to me. Nazim, the Turkish Captain with me, said: 'At this spectacle even the most gentle must feel savage and the most savage must weep'. No one made offensive remarks except Howse, the Australian doctor.

The dead fill acres of ground, mostly killed in one big attack, but some recently. One saw the result of machine-gun fire very clearly; entire companies annihilated – not wounded, but killed, their heads doubled under them with the impetus of their rush and both hands clasping their bayonets.

The line was not easy to settle . . . In one gully the dead had to be left unburied. It was impossible to bury them without one side seeing the position of the other . . .

Trouble occurred almost at once, but by that time I had made friends with a lot of the Turks, and when the Australian complained that they were making loop-holes, the Turks invited me to go and look. Then the Turks said that we were taking their rifles; this came from the dead land where we could not let them go. But they took my word for it when I had panted down and up and seen with my own eyes . . .

Much of this business was ghastly to the point of nightmare. I found a hardened old Albanian and got him to do anything I wanted. He was a sous officer. Then other Albanians came up, and I said 'Tunya tyeta'. I had met some of them in Janina. They all knew my name and began clapping me on the back and cheering, while half a dozen funeral services were going on all round over the remains of our poor fellows. It was unseemly and I stopped it. I asked them if they did not want an Imam for a service over their own dead but the old Albanian pagan roared with laughter and said their souls were all right.

I didn't see many signs of fanaticism; one huge savage-looking Anatolian refused cigarettes and looked curses at me. Greeks came up and tried to surrender to me, but were ordered back pretty roughly by the Turks. Considering the number of their men we had killed, they remained extraordinarily unmoved and polite. I might have been able to do the same vis-a-vis the Turks. I couldn't have to the Germans. Probably they couldn't have with the Russians . . .

Our men gave cigarettes to the Turks, and beyond the storm-centre at Quinn's Post, the feeling was all right . . . We sat down and sent men to look for Skeen. Vassif was nervous and almost rude. Then Skeen came. He asked me to go back as quick as possible to Quinn's Post, as I told him I was nervous at being away, and to retire the troops at 4 and the white flag men at 4.15. I said to Vassif: 'Everyone has behaved well, but we must take care that nobody loses his head. Your men won't shoot you and my men won't shoot me, so we must walk about, otherwise a gun will go off and everybody will get shot.' But Vassif faded away.

I discovered that the Turks time was 8 minutes ahead of ours and put on our watches. The Turks asked me to witness their taking the money from their dead as they had no officer there. They were worried by having no officer and asked me if anyone were coming. I, of course, had no idea, but I told them I would see they were all right. They were very patient . . .

The burying was finished some time before the end. There were certain tricks on both sides I think. One of the Padres got the communication trench which had bothered us so much filled in by burying the dead there. Both sides did a bit of spying . . .

At 4 o'clock the Turks came to me for orders. This couldn't happen anywhere else. I retired their troops and ours, walking along the line. At 4.07 I retired the white flag men, making them shake hands. Then I came to the upper end. About a dozen Turks came out. I chaffed them, and said that they would shoot me next day. They said, in a horrified chorus, 'God forbid!' The Albanians laughed and cheered and said, 'We will never shoot you'. Then the Australians began coming up and said 'Goodbye, old chap, good luck!' And the Turks said: 'Oghur, Ola gule gule gedejekseniz gule gule gedejekseniz' (smiling may you go and smiling come again). Then I told them all to get into their trenches, and unthinkingly went up to the Turkish trench and got a deep salaam from it. I told them that neither side would fire for twenty-five minutes after they had got into their trenches. A couple of rifles went off about 20 minutes before the end but Potts and I went hurriedly to and fro saying it was nothing. At last we dropped into our trenches glad that the strain was over.

I walked back with Temperly and got some whiskey for the infection in my throat and iodine where the barbed wire entanglements had cut my legs. I am glad that I worried about this truce though it would probably have come about anyhow. This morning all of us who were there still feel the infection in our throats and noses, and shall for some days . . .

The spirit of fraternity did not last long. The next day the *Triumph* was sunk by a submarine in full view of the beach. Aubrey wrote: 'Every picket boat dashed off to pick up the survivors. The Turks were good and never shelled them at all. There was fury, panic and impotent rage on the beach and on the hill. I heard Col. Bill, half off his head, like a wounded bird saying "You should kill all enemies. Give them cigarettes!!!" He shook his fist. Men were crying and cursing. Very different from last night when they were all wishing each other luck.'

The month of June passed with spasmodic fighting. Spirits were low and the casualty lists from France added to Aubrey's depression. He wrote in his diary 'One feels ashamed of being alive'. He also wrote to his old friend Reginald Farrer, who had been turned down for military service, and was now in the wilds of the Tibetan mountains, pursuing his rare plants but intermittently pursued by demons of guilt. The letter, via the British Legation in Peking, took a long time to reach Reginald and his reply took even longer to find Aubrey.

Lanchow

My dear Aubrey,

No words can express the relief and joy of being assured that you were still alive 6 weeks ago . . .

I had the hell of a time in the spring, sitting fat and idle up here till the end of March . . . In this mood I even wrote a melancholy note to Mary but she did not encourage morbidity by replying . . . Against your picture of 3000 rotting dead I only have that of twenty times that number of dancing purple poppies . . . So the summer went quite well but the telegrams grew steadily darker, lighted only and balefully by the news of Violet's very insipid engagement and Venetia's only too startling one . . .

I am on my way South, to a season of autumnal collecting on the Kanzu-Szechuan Border; but after I got here and ate a good dinner, I felt how little I deserved it, with so many of my betters taking their last dinner of all. Goodness knows what follies I might not have perpetuated had I not been stiffened in sense by a letter from a foolish female cousin of Gerard's [Collier] 'putting it to me straight' that I ought to come home and 'do my bit' instead of letting it be said I was shirking! *Shirking*, Dio mio! Let her and her likes come out and shirk in a Tibetan valley: it might brace 'em a bit . . . My dear, you'll never join them, will you? One feels so helpless, and at times, so miserable.

On 28th June, Johnny Allan, Aubrey's servant, was hit by a shrapnel bullet in the calf of his leg. He left on a hospital boat bound for Alexandria. Two days later Aubrey and a gallant Australian, Major Reynell, did what General Godley described in a letter to Mary as 'a V.C. action in reverse'. They rescued a wounded man from between the lines. The man was a Turk; had he been one of their own, they would certainly have been decorated for their action.

Towards the end of July there was a lull in the fighting. 'There is something almost awful about this calm' Aubrey reported in his diary. There was little to do on the beach and so it was with pleasure that Aubrey complied with an order to present himself at GHQ to prepare some intelligence work on the Islands. He wrote, 'My heart is very divided at going. Very glad to have space and water and carelessness. That is what men want, not safety. I feel half a holiday maker, and half a deserter.'

On Imbros, where Sir Ian Hamilton had his headquarters, Aubrey found the mood different from Anzac, where disease and death had brought in their wake a settled spirit of resigned depression. On Imbros there was less resignation and more anger. Many officers were openly disaffected and the large camp of war correspondents was harshly critical of Sir Ian Hamilton's handling of the campaign. Aubrey wrote in his diary on 24th July: 'Preparations being made for a landing. They say it will be down South. If so it looks like the sacrifice of more and more men, and Constantinople still unwon. Rochdale has gone home to make a row. He says he won't have any more of his men murdered. The whole tone of the officers about Ian Hamilton is almost beyond belief. The man who disobeys an order is not far off being a hero.'

Aubrey was instructed to go to Mytilene. He was to pretend to be on sick leave and make his way round the island, which had become a hot bed of German espionage and British counter-espionage. However Aubrey did not have to fake illness. He was immediately struck down by fever and had great difficulty in avoiding being sent to Egypt on a hospital ship. Instead he went to Tenedos, where a few relaxed days by the sea brought recovery. Then he went on to Mytilene, feeling well and refreshed.

There he found many old friends: Vedova, ex-chief of the Smyrna fire brigade, a figure of fantasy and farce, who claimed to be a poet and clairvoyant, a mesmerist and a masseur, a specialist in rheumatism and the science of detection. Vedova was the chief allied agent on the island. Controlling him, or rather failing to control him, was Compton Mackenzie. Vedova was at the quayside when Aubrey's boat docked. With many a melodramatic gesture and conspiratorial whisper Vedova brought Aubrey to his spy chief – Compton Mackenzie. Mackenzie was delighted to see Aubrey, although more than a little amazed at his appearance. He wrote later to Aubrey recalling their meeting:

How well I remember you, in the electric light of the gardens, which made more canary yellow than ever your canary yellow uniform. For luggage you had a typewriter, and you were wearing red Turkish slippers and the only thing that bothered you particularly was that you hadn't got a tie. I remember wondering why you should bother about a tie when you had only one button on your tunic. However next morning we went to look for a tie together and you pounced on one at the local hosier's which you thought was just the thing and you still thought it just the thing even when I pointed out that it was covered with purple lozenges, lustrous as amethysts . . .

Aubrey, though enormously enjoying his interlude on the islands, was anxious to get back to Anzac Cove. He was afraid of missing the attack which had been the cause of so much dissension on Imbros. At Tenedos he bade farewell to Mackenzie. 'I never saw him again on this earth,' wrote Mackenzie, 'He had of all the gallant gentlemen I have met the most endearing personality . . .'

Aubrey arrived back too late for the first attack which began on 6th August. While the Anzac forces attacked up the steep ravines and spurs of Sari Bair, the landings of the new divisions took place to the north of Suvla Bay. The secret had been well kept. Everyone, including the Turks, had presumed the landing would be in the south. At Suvla Bay the Turks were taken completely unaware. Unfortunately the British commander, the elderly General Sir Frederick Stopford, failed totally to take advantage of the surprise. He did not even go ashore until a day and a half after the landing. The soldiers bathed on the beach instead of taking the heights, and the Turks had time to bring up divisions and dig in. Four days and 25,000 casualties later, it was clear that the landings had failed.

At Anzac Cove things did not go much better. Here it was not cowardice or bad generalship that brought defeat but geography. Attacking uphill in thick scrub and over sheer rock, in blazing heat, with scant water, the physical conditions of the terrain proved too much. Aubrey, who reached Anzac on 7th August, the second day of the battle, was employed in questioning prisoners. There were two Germans from the *Breslau* and *Goeben*. Aubrey wrote, 'they were the first I had not treated gently and I got a lot of information out of them.' On 8th August Aubrey watched the second attack from an outpost near Anafarta: 'We saw our men in the growing light attack the Turks, it looked so cruel I could hardly bear to see it, for it was like a fight in fairyland: they went forward in parties in the beautiful light, with clouds crimsoning over them, sometimes a tiny gallant figure in front, then a puff would come and they would be lying still.' Outside the hospital Aubrey stumbled on an old school-fellow, Critchley Samuelson. 'He had been wounded about 3 a.m. the day before and had lain in the sun on the sand all the previous day. He recognised me, and asked me to help him, but was delirious. There were fifty-six others with him. Macaulay and I counted.

It was awful having to pass them. A lot of men called out – "We are being murdered". The smells were fearful. They had not been cleaned . . .'

The diary for the next few days is a woeful list of friends killed or wounded. Some died in his presence: 'I was sitting at breakfast listening to Col. Manders talking when suddenly Charlie Bentinck said 'By God he's killed'. He fell back quite dead with a bullet through his temple . . .'

Aubrey, who had no clear role in the battle, became more and more concerned about the wounded. Gradually he turned himself into an unofficial medical orderly:

August 10
At the hospital no one knew who was chief since poor Manders had been killed. The doctor on the beach said he could not keep the wounded there longer, he was losing them and his men from rifle fire. I called Bentinck. We got 200 men from the Canterbury reinforcements. They had been fighting without sleep since Sunday morning [8th August]. They evacuated about 300 wounded to below Walker's Ridge. They did not complain. The wounded Turks were left. They called to me pitifully in the night and at dawn. Later I went back and gave them drink and shifted them into the shade, when they all grew pathetically cheerful . . .
. . . The general (Birdwood) has not slept for three nights. The day went badly for us. We lost Chanuk Bair and without it we cannot win the battle . . . The Turks have fought very finely. Our own men were splendid. The N.Z. Infantry Brigade must have ceased to exist . . .
    The condition of the wounded is indescribable. They lie in the sand in rows upon rows, their faces caked with sand and blood; one murmur for water; no shelter from the sun; many of them in saps with men passing all the time, scattering more dust on them. There is hardly any possibility of transporting them.
    We all did what we could but amongst the many it was impossible. There was enough water for all, but wounded men without cover in that sun would have drunk a river dry. I did my best for the Turks . . . An order had come that they were not to be evacuated before all our own men had gone; this is natural but was of course an order of lingering death. However I kept them alive with water . . .
August 12
I told some Maoris to shift some Turks lying in the sun. They said 'Let them die' . . . The lines of wounded are creeping up to the cemetery like a tide, and the cemetery is coming to meet the wounded . . . On top of the ridge we heard a wounded man calling for water. I asked twice to be allowed to go, but the General refused which he had scarcely the right to do. Tempers have got very short.

On Friday 13th August Aubrey went down with fever. By the next day he was on his feet again, though weak. The attack was over, but the wounded remained. The Navy would only evacuate at night; the medical authorities clung to red tape. Two volunteer doctors told Aubrey how they had been made to spend their time seeing if the wounded waiting for evacuation had blue tickets or green tickets, work which a corporal could have done, and at a time when the shortage of doctors was desperate. An RAMC General refused to have his kitchen moved to make room for the wounded saying, 'Damn the wounded I am not a Quartermaster.' Eight bell tents which could have given many men protection from the sun were never erected. Aubrey felt bitter against the RAMC, as did many individual doctors who laboured devotedly sometimes disregarding orders. Aubrey wrote to Mary, 'I think there is going to be a great row one day about this last fight here.'

Mary, meanwhile, had returned to Egypt. At the end of July, she had left England with Lady Howard de Walden and a small band of trained nurses and a matron to open a hospital for wounded soldiers. She also brought with her to Egypt her cook, Mrs Alcard, but not her maid Carlotta, who as a German was unable to travel. In June Mary had been arrested in London for contravening the Aliens Act. Only the eloquence of her solicitor saved her. He pleaded that her anxieties about Aubrey made her careless; the magistrate dismissed the case as one of 'exceptional pathos'. Carlotta was left with Lady de Vesci to whom Mary wrote on her arrival in Egypt, 'Give my love to Carlotta and tell her to keep very calm and happy and do any work that comes her way and have no qualms about her place not being where it is – her being there is what I want most and she does no one any harm and could be of use to no one in Germany.'

Mary hoped that she might see Aubrey. By the end of August there was little fighting on the Gallipoli peninsula. Disease, weariness and flies were now the chief enemies. Although he longed for leave, and although there was no reason why he should not take it, pride and duty held him back. Soon, however, the matter was taken out of his hands. Ever since his bout of fever at the end of July he had been intermittently unwell. On 4th August he was ordered on board a hospital ship. Dysentery was diagnosed, and his protests carried little weight after he had fainted during his first interview with the doctors.

On arrival in Alexandria, Aubrey took a cab straight to Lady Howard de Walden's nursing home. His convalescence was a time of particular felicity. The contrast with his life on the peninsula was delicious with Mary, Elsie and Mervyn dancing a loving attendance. By the end of three weeks Aubrey felt restored in health and spirits. Colonel Clayton invited him to return to the Arab Bureau promising interesting and responsible work. Aubrey was tempted but loyalty to his General prevailed.

General Godley was popular with neither his men nor his officer and he clung to Aubrey as a friend to whom he could talk. Aubrey returned at the end of September, although officially he had another two months' sick leave.

The weather had changed; it was no longer oppressively hot. He wrote to Mary, 'There is a chill and a thrill in the air, and the valley is graciou with swallows. The great Arbutus berries are everywhere in the hills and the men wear them in their hats. At night the cliffs and hills twinkl with a dozen camp fires, and all day long in the big sap men go by talkin in very low voices.' But he was bored. He did not have enough to do. I the morning he accompanied the General on his rounds of the trenches The afternoons and evenings stretched long and empty. No offensiv was planned. The Turks sat on in their impregnable defences. Ther were no new prisoners to interrogate. On 4th October he wrote to Mary 'This is now a sinecure.' Aubrey wanted to leave but was still trouble about abandoning his General. His doubts were resolved for him. Hi health again broke down. On 12th October, exactly six months to th day that he had sailed from Egypt to join the Gallipoli expedition, h was evacuated in a hospital ship. Two days later, on 14th October, th Dardanelles Committee met in London and decided to recall Sir Ia Hamilton. The new commander, Sir Charles Monro, made up his min before leaving England that if a complete evacuation of the peninsul were practicable it should be carried out. On 19th and 20th Decembe the final evacuation of Anzac was completed and on 8th–9th Januar 1915 Cape Hellas was also evacuated. The campaign had cost the Allie over 250,000 in casualties and still more in prestige, always a mos valuable commodity in the East. Not an inch of territory had bee gained, scarcely a German soldier had been diverted from the Wester front. Hesitating Balkan neutrals drew their conclusions. In Novembe 1915 Bulgaria entered the war on the German side and kept 600,000 allie troops tied up in Salonika until 1918.

Aubrey, who had complained at the beginning of the campaign o being 'locked on the wrong side of a backdoor of a side show' wrote at th end, 'I never want to see again a mule or a monk, or a backdoor, or a sid show, or Winston or flies or bully beef.' Sooner or later he saw them al again.

10

≪≪◇≫≫

Kut 1916

The hospital ship put in at Alexandria on its way to England. Aubrey unobtrusively disembarked and hastened to Mary's hospital. There he found Mary immersed in work.

While in Cairo Aubrey went to see Colonel Clayton, his old chief. He found an air of uncharacteristic resolution in the dusty offices of the Arab Bureau. Colonel Clayton asked Aubrey to go and see Kitchener and Grey on his return to London to inform and persuade them of the policy of the bureau. On the basis of a letter written by Aubrey, and annotated by Clayton ('a little too strong' was a recurring comment), Aubrey was to draft a memorandum on the Arab question which it was hoped would be the foundation of British policy towards the Arab countries of the Ottoman Empire.

Aubrey wrote the memorandum at the end of October 1915 while on board the P & O boat *Karmala* on his way back to England with Mary. The main issues at stake were the precise extent of the territorial promises the British were prepared to make to the Arab leaders and in particular to the two sons of the Sherif of Mecca in return for their active support against the Turks, and how to square these concessions with known French aspirations in the area. The main obstacle to agreement was the Arab claim to the four Syrian towns, Damascus, Aleppo, Hama and Homs. The memorandum urged that these towns must be conceded to the Arabs. Aubrey knew the difficulties. He wrote: 'No one who knows Syria can fail to realise the bitter disappointment to French aspirations involved in the loss of Damascus and those terrains. The connection between France and parts of Syria has been very close, and the ambition to make that connection closer still is ages old. But this is not a time when dreams can outweigh strategy. It is after all only the partial sacrifice of a territory which is not yet hers that is asked of France.'

Aubrey suggested that the French might be reconciled 'by a) the promise of generous compensation elsewhere (Nigeria)? or b) by convincing them of the acute danger of this situation . . . or lastly c) by persuading them to accept a wider sphere of influence with a larger measure of autonomy for the inhabitants of that sphere. This alternative would mean a policy of British disinterestedness in Palestine in favour of France.'

Although his memorandum was couched in rational and diplomatic terms, Aubrey was riding an old hobby horse. Ten months ago, when he arrived in Egypt, he had written in his diary 'I want the French out of Syria' and now, reinforced by Clayton, he was saying the same thing in different language.

In London the memorandum was seen and approved at the highest level. Aubrey saw Sir Edward Grey, still Foreign Secretary. He found him very changed 'and infinitely weary'. Aubrey submitted his memorandum in early November. At the end of that month the French sent to England François Georges-Picot, a professional diplomat, to stake their claims. Picot announced that France would accept nothing less than all Syria and Palestine, except for the Holy Places. Mark Sykes, Aubrey's old friend, entered into negotiations with Picot which resulted in the secret Inter-Allied (Sykes-Picot) Agreement, the basis for the British Mandate in Palestine and for French post-war claims in Syria and the Lebanon. Aubrey's memorandum of November was consigned to the wastepaper basket. However, the earlier favourable reaction had been interpreted by the Arab Bureau in Egypt as approval and certain promises were made in January to the Sherif of Mecca which ran directly contrary to the Sykes-Picot agreement and which were to result in accusations of bad faith.

Aubrey was still far from well. The doctors in the Dardanelles had ordered three months' complete rest, which Aubrey had failed to take. By jumping ship in Alexandria and involving himself once again in the affairs of the Arab Bureau he had denied himself a quiet convalescence. On his return to England he found himself immediately enmeshed in meetings with high officials and politicians. He arrived in England on 2nd November; by 21st November he left England for Paris and Rome on a secret mission; in between he had shuttled between Grey, Curzon and Lansdowne. He managed to spend one weekend at Pixton. Cynthia Asquith who was staying at the time noted the changes in Aubrey. She found him 'chastened' by the war. He was 'thin and gaunt'. At Pixton, the autumnal beauty and beloved familiarity of the place soothed him. 'A great deal of feudalising went on all day. Pixton is a real stronghold', Lady Cynthia wrote, but later, on 14th December 1915, in London, she again commented in her diary on Aubrey's nerviness: 'Aubrey and Mary had been dining with Venetia [Montagu] at Coterie headquarters. He was in a state of frenzied resentment and irritation against Diana

[Manners] who rasps his war nerves. He is badly physically haunted by his experience.'

Indeed that same day Aubrey had received a letter from General Sir Charles Calwell, Director-General of Military Operations, the contents of which might well have brought on an increase in nervous emotion. He had, on his return from Rome on 8th December, visited the War Office and volunteered to return to Anzac. Plans for the Gallipoli evacuation were now being considered with urgency. It seemed inevitable that a small force would have to stay behind to cover the withdrawal. Aubrey volunteered to be part of this force. He knew that if he were taken prisoner he could be of great use to the other prisoners. He could talk to the Turks and see that both the wounded and unwounded were properly treated. He would also be in a position to explore unofficially through his friendship with many powerful Turks the strength of anti-German feeling and the possibility of Turkish withdrawal from the camp of the Central Powers. Sir Charles Calwell was attracted by the notion. He wrote to Aubrey: 'Yours is a very gallant offer. If I were in Birdwood's place I should accept it but he may think differently . . . Should you go you will carry with you the best wishes of all who know what you have in your mind.'

At the same time Calwell sent a wire to Birdwood, recommending the scheme. Birdwood replied to Calwell's wire in the negative. Events had moved with greater rapidity than the War Office anticipated. On 20th December, Birdwood successfully completed the evacuation of Anzac, getting all his troops off the peninsula with only one man slightly wounded. It was a glorious end to a dismal campaign. The success of the Anzac and Suvla evacuation led the military to hope the final withdrawal at Cape Hellas might be accomplished as easily. Birdwood wrote to Aubrey explaining his refusal: '. . . you could not possibly be in time, but please do not think for a moment that this in any way means I do not fully value and appreciate your very kind and noble offer to come out. I can only say that I consider it to be thoroughly characteristic of you, and there are very few men in the world who I think would have thought of such a thing, or been prepared to see it through, as I know you would have been . . .'

Birdwood's rejection was probably a relief to Aubrey. The Gallipoli campaign had drained him of more than just his physical health. Though proud to have been part of that gallant army, he had been shattered by the suffering he had seen. His offer to return was born of piety not preference. There were now much more attractive missions on the horizon, in particular the possibility of going to Albania.

It was in connection with Albania that Aubrey had visited Paris and

Rome in November. Albania had become the subject of earnest interest in Whitehall as a result of the terrible defeats recently suffered by Serbia, and Aubrey was the man of the hour.

In the autumn of 1914 Serbia had soundly beaten the Austrian invading armies, but at great cost to herself. In the summer of 1915 the Russian front in the Carpathians collapsed, freeing German-Austrian troops to deal with Serbia. Diplomacy and bribery failed to keep Bulgaria neutral. Thus by October 1915 Serbia faced alone the might of Germany, Austria and Bulgaria. She was, inevitably, crushingly defeated. Her starving bedraggled armies poured south into Albania towards the Adriatic. Before reaching Scutari thousands died on the way, of cold and hunger. In England guilt and concern was felt for the Serbs. It was agreed that food and supplies had to be despatched with haste and it was clear that the support and co-operation, or at least the neutrality, of Albania had to be assured.

So began again for Aubrey a series of high-level consultations with many of the same people he had been seeing days earlier on the Arab question. Aubrey wrote two memoranda on Albania in November. Apart from the difficulties of negotiating with a country without a central government (for since the departure of the Prince of Wied the country had been ruled by various self-constituted administrations, all practically independent) Aubrey pointed out that to prevent the Albanians throwing in their lot with the Bulgars and actually attacking the Serbian Army, some concrete promises of future security had to be made and some guarantees offered. Aubrey's tentative suggestion that the Italians should be induced to assume a Protectorate over an autonomous Albania won Foreign Office approval. Aubrey was hastily promoted to Lieutenant-Colonel, jumping the rank of Major, in order to give him more standing in negotiations with the Italians, and despatched to Rome from where he was supposed to go on to Albania.

Aubrey returned to England at the end of the first week of December without having been to Albania. He had failed in his negotiations with the Italians. His only practical achievement had been the despatch of two grain ships to the port of San Giovanni di Medua for the relief of the starving of Scutari, both Serbs and Albanians.

The new year of 1916 found Aubrey at Pixton, daily growing stronger and more restive. The Foreign Office had not entirely abandoned the idea of using him in Albania but Aubrey had become impatient of the indecisiveness in the halls of government. He had also become impatient of the government itself. He wrote in his diary, 'Asquith can't face any decision, K[itchener] is wrapped in pessimism. K and Grey and A[squith] ought all to go.' By the end of the year Kitchener was dead and Asquith and Grey had indeed gone. When the time came few people were to regret the departure of Asquith and Grey more than Aubrey. But in January 1916 he shared the almost universal exasperation with what seemed a near criminal lethargy and lack of direction in the government's prosecution of the war.

Aubrey was not prepared to kick his heels indefinitely in England while the Foreign Office studied the Albanian question. At the beginning of January he met in London Admiral Sir Rosslyn (Rosie) Wemyss, who had been second in command at the Dardanelles and had now succeeded de Robeck as naval commander in chief. The Admiral offered Aubrey a job in naval intelligence on his staff. Aubrey accepted but found his orders blocked at the War Office because of the Albanian business. He finally got clearance in late February. When his language qualifications (French, Italian, German, Turkish, Arabic, Greek, Albanian) were put before the Admiralty the only comment was 'this must be a very immoral man to know so many languages'.

The Admiral was based in Ismailia and Mary at once determined to come out to Alexandria and resume her hospital work. To her chagrin she found she was again pregnant, with what was to be her third daughter, Laura.

Aubrey left England on 25th February. Ten days later he joined Rosie Wemyss in Ismailia; 'he is an angel' wrote Aubrey 'everybody loves him.' Aubrey counted himself fortunate to be on his staff. He was also fortunate in the job, which exceeded his expectations. He had presumed that, reduced to Captain as he now again was, he would find himself once more working under some difficult Colonel of the Newcombe variety. Instead he found himself in charge of naval intelligence in Mesopotamia and the Persian Gulf. 'I am living in the highest circles,' he wrote, 'and developing a courtly manner.' He saw much of Colonel Clayton, who was despondent at the tatters to which their Arab policy had been reduced. Aubrey wrote to Mary: 'I am afraid that swine Monsieur P[icot] has let M.S. [Mark Sykes] badly down. I told him I thought it would happen. It is an awful pity both for the thing itself, and for M. and also because it is one up to the old early Victorians who are in a position to say "We told you so. This is what comes of disregarding the ABC of Diplomacy, and letting Amateurs have a shy at delicate and important negotiations".'

Also in Egypt were the Anzac Brigade and Aubrey saw again his generals, Birdwood and Godley. Their elation over their successful evacuation of Gallipoli had passed. They were disheartened and felt neglected. Aubrey wrote to Mary:

I had tea with Birdie, who was very sweet. Never you talk about the Simla manner. He is a dear narrow little man, frozen in hardness and melted in kindness. He was sad because he said they had got it in against him as an Indian Army man at the W.O. My General [Godley] touched me. He began by a sort of dance like a gigantic Japanese crane at sunset. He talked a lot about Gallipoli and what a dream it all was . . . He is one of the most heroic and selfish men I have ever met. After that he bullied all the generals at dinner, and smiled rather grimly when I ragged him about Ulster. I am glad to be able to whack back at him nonchalantly. But he goes to my heart when he says there is no one with whom he is able to talk over Gallipoli times, because we have all left him.

On 25th March Aubrey left Egypt in style. He boarded a special train for Ismailia with the Commander-in-Chief of Egypt, the Commander-in-Chief of the Mediterranean, the High Commissioner for Egypt, the Viceroy designate of India, the Prince of Wales and Ronald Storrs, the Oriental Secretary at the High Commission, referred to affectionately in Aubrey's diary as 'the Monster of the Levant'. Aubrey had not met the Prince of Wales before and described him to Mary as 'a good boy, with much more imagination than one would have suspected, I mean expected'. On board the Admiral's flag ship, the *Euryalus*, there was a mood of pleasurable expectancy. After months of idleness in Egypt the ship was bound for Mesopotamia. The Mesopotamian campaign which had been undertaken at the beginning of the war in an almost casual manner had now reached a critical stage.

In November 1914 the Government of India had sent a small force to occupy Basra in order to protect the oil fields and pipe lines of Khuzistan and to give reassurance to the sheikhs in the Persian Gulf under British protection. It was a cautious operation and orthodox tactics had been employed. The Indian Army Expeditionary Force had met with remarkable success and Basra was taken with little difficulty.

Mesopotamia felt no great loyalty to the Ottoman Empire. The Turkish Army was hampered by many Arab regiments and Arab officers of doubtful loyalty. With the capture of Nasirya in July 1915 the British were in possession of lower Mesopotamia. The original objectives of the campaign had been secured. The Turks had been driven back from Ahwaz and crushed on the Tigris. British prestige was restored in the Persian Gulf and the oil fields were safe. However, the humid summer heat, the disease-bearing flies, the thieving, murdering natives and the inefficiency and parsimony of the Government of India had all taken their toll. Rations were short, and sickness was rife. In these circumstances General Nixon, the commander of the Indian Expeditionary Force, would have been wise to consolidate his gains and halt his campaign. He did neither. Spurred on by success, and lacking clear instructions from India, he decided to advance to Baghdad. He relied, mistakenly, on promises from India of essential transport, food, medical supplies and reinforcements. In November 1915 the advance was halted at the bloody battle of Ctesiphon, sixteen miles outside Baghdad. The exhausted and depleted force under General Townshend fell back on Kut-al-Amara. Here another mistaken decision was made to stay and hold Kut against a Turkish siege.

By the time Aubrey was steaming down the Red Sea in the *Euryalus* at the end of March 1916, on his way to join the relief force in Meso-potamia, the situation at Kut already looked bleak. General Townshend had consistently misrepresented the real and considerable extent of his provisions, with the result that premature and ineffectual efforts were made to relieve him. Townshend's original estimate was that his food would only last till the end of January. Had he admitted at the outset that he had four months' supplies, the relief could have been properly co-ordinated and reinforced. But despite the setbacks which they had suffered, the military remained confident of ultimate success.

On 8th April the ship put into harbour at Bushire. Aubrey decided to leave his servant, Edward, behind there. Johnny Allan had not recovered from his Gallipoli wound, so Aubrey had brought in his stead a young Irish boy, Edward Murphy, from Abbeyleix. Edward had never travelled before and was suffering from the effects of the heat. Two days later Aubrey arrived at Basra, the same day that Townshend reduced rations in the besieged town of Kut to five ounces of meal a day for all ranks, British and Indian. Aubrey dined that evening with his old friend Gertrude Bell and the next day transferred to HMS *Snakefly* to go up river, where he began to hear the sombre tale of the Mesopotamian muddle. He was horrified by what he heard. After his Gallipoli experi-ence Aubrey thought himself an expert on bureaucratic incompetence. He found he was only a beginner. The Indian Government which mounted the Mesopotamian campaign had actually saved money in the last financial year, keeping the Indian Division in Mesopotamia short of food and without transport. Medical services were virtually non-existent, the armoury was ancient, the ammunition short. But morale was still amazingly high.

On 17th April Aubrey wrote Mary a long letter describing his life. He was living on HMS *Waterfly* and he wrote from Sanayat, three miles from the Turkish lines.

All our kit was left at Basra. I have only two shirts, both of which I wear at night on deck. We have had perfectly foul weather. It has looked as if

Townshend's last chance was being rained away . . .

Meanwhile there are a lot of Turkish prisoners here, and I am apparently the only officer either here or at GHQ who knows Turkish. The Admiral who is angelic is leaving this place for a bit and going down stream, and I hope to spend a few days in the trenches, as being completely away from fire when other people are under it is insufferable. We did get slightly bombed this morning but no one hurt . . .

The people here are very confident about Townshend. I am awfully glad to think I have been wrong. I always felt instinctively that he would not get out. It's been very fine. I am most awfully sorry for these people here. They have had to bring Indians to fight a Moslem people on a holy soil: far worse or at least as bad as asking our people to mop up Ulster men, for after all it is not the Indians' quarrel at all . . . They have had a filthy summer, and a cruel winter, and all the time they are starved, from bread to mails. They cannot get anything out of the Government of India. Everything here depends on Transport. You can't march up the river bank. They have not been given it. Everything here depends on observation. They have not been given balloons, because apparently Sir Joseph Meyer (of the dear old firm I suppose) wants to reduce the budget of India.

It is a beastly country. No thyme or rosemary like at Anzac; no trees, dragonflies as big as terriers and clouds of filthy little insects that almost blind one with their fecklessness. I have seen a good deal of Lake, the chief General, not much of Gorringe but he seems a pretty good man.

The fight before last on March 8 was an awful business. Sir I.H. [Ian Hamilton] over again. Our people seem constantly to lose their nerve and then go in for any kind of a gambler's throw to retrieve their reputation . . .

Four days later still at Sanayat Aubrey wrote to Mark Sykes, in much the same vein but more pessimistically:

Well the position here is absolutely bloody. There are first of all the floods. When you get a southwind the water banks up, and when it stops the damned river gives a sigh and spreads itself out all round. When a northwind comes, it drives huge tumults of yellow water across all this deplorable flatness . . .

Our men are very tired. The Turks are bringing up new troops, and the outlook seems to me extraordinarily doubtful. The soldiers are however confident.

We ought to have had a railway before we ever looked at this thing, or to have made a railway at least pari passu. Now we run quite a fair risk of becoming a second Kut ourselves. You must remember it only needs to have a few guns decently dug in and a couple of boats sunk to hold up traffic. Hallo that sounds like one of those mines. I am afraid you must have been having a beastly time with French P. [Georges Picot] . . .

By the next day, 22nd April, the outlook was no longer doubtful but hopeless. At 7.30 p.m. the defenders of Kut who had been waiting anxiously all day, hearing gun fire, received a telegram, 'Much regret that the attack on Sunnaiyat position this morning was repulsed.' Everyone in the relief force was haunted by a sense of time running out. For the starving men inside Kut every new day dawned in hope and darkened in disappointment. For the men outside, the burden of disappointment and responsibility hung heavy.

Townshend concluded that short of a miracle, Kut would not be relieved. By 26th April the meagre rations would be finally finished and the garrison would be dependent on supplies dropped from the air. Men were dying from scurvy, cholera and other diseases at an average rate of fifteen a day. One last valiant effort was made. On the night of 24th April the ship *Julnar* was loaded with 270 tons of food and, manned by a volunteer crew, attempted to run the naval blockade. Every single man from the naval flotilla volunteered for this suicidal mission. Aubrey, who had felt uncomfortably cosseted from danger throughout his time in Mesopotamia, was disappointed to be turned down by Admiral Wemyss. The little ship was soon spotted by the Turks. She was shelled all the way up river until she ran aground when the chain that the Turks had stretched across the river fouled the screw. The boat was captured with her precious stores, and her entire crew taken prisoner. The two officers were both killed and were awarded posthumous VCs.

All hope of saving Kut was lost with the *Julnar*. The air drops of food were unsuccessful, much falling outside the town or in the river. From 26th to 29th April the besieged men had lived on only four ounces of food a day, supplied from the air. Surrender was now inevitable. All that remained was to negotiate the terms. Aubrey's services as a negotiator were offered to General Townshend on instructions from the War Office on 26th April. The services of Captain T. E. Lawrence from the Arab Bureau were also offered. He had arrived a few days earlier but had been laid low with a fever so Aubrey had seen little of him.

Aubrey did not relish the task of negotiation. He believed that Townshend would get better terms if he personally conducted his own negotiations. The Turks honoured courage and the physical endurance displayed by his garrison had earned universal respect. The courtesy customarily accorded by a magnanimous victor to an honourably defeated foe should, Aubrey thought, be exploited to the full. On 25th April he wrote in his diary: 'We have no terms to offer the Turks except money, local or general peace, or the evacuation of territory. I don't think that the first will do the trick, we can't offer the second because of Russia, the third might be all right if it wasn't beyond Amarah.' The next day (26th April) Admiral Wemyss showed Aubrey two government telegrams which said that staying or retreating were not to be offered as part of the conditions. 'They are hopelessly optimistic about terms', Aubrey wrote.

Early that morning Townshend had opened negotiations with Khalil Pasha, the Turkish Commander, who was a nephew of Enver. Townshend had nothing to offer besides his obsolete guns, and money. The War Office authorised him to offer one million pounds for the safe parole of his force. No one at headquarters liked offering money. Sir Percy Cox, the Political Resident at Basra expressed forceful opposition. It was a last minute expedient, conceived by Townshend, and seized on by the War Office. Aubrey's objections to the use of bribery were practical rather than ethical. He did not think it would work.

By now, in fact, Townshend was cracking up under the strain. Some of his more unbalanced telegrams have never been published. Aubrey, however, saw them and noted them privately in his diary. 'He said that it was not his fault that he was there. He said that he was disgusted at the way he was treated and that it was not going to end there. He had had no word of praise through all this time. Eleven honours had been given for his battles, and forty-six to Gorringe for his "insignificant" fight at Kurna. He ended "show my telegrams to Admiral Wemyss".'

Aubrey told the Admiral the gist of the telegrams. Wemyss said that he would prefer not to see them. He was determined to protect Townshend from himself. And when Aubrey published his diary in 1919, in *Mons, Anzac and Kut*, he too protected Townshend's reputation. He deleted both the telegrams and his own comment: 'I am very sorry about his telegrams. The Turkish wireless may very well have caught them up, and the splendour of his defence be covered with shoddy jealousy, if the telegram is published in Berlin. But there can be no doubt his mind is touched . . .'

On 29th April, Townshend, having secured no concession from Khalil, destroyed his guns. At 1 p.m. the garrison wireless tapped out 'goodbye' and then there was silence. Meanwhile Aubrey, Lawrence and Colonel Beach, the head of intelligence at Force Headquarters, were in negotiation with the Turks, arranging the final details of the surrender. They set out early in the morning of 29th April. There had been no direct communication between the Turkish camp and Headquarters and it was uncertain whether the Turks would even agree to see them. Aubrey's diary takes up the tale:

> We three then went out to the trenches with a white flag, and walked a couple of hundred yards or so ahead where we waited, with all the battlefield smells round us. It was all a plain with a river to the north and the place

crawling with huge black beetles and singing flies, that have been feeding on the dead. After a time a couple of Turks came out. I said 'We have got a letter to Khalil'. This they wanted to take from us, but we refused to give it up, and they sent an orderly back to ask if we might come into the Turkish lines. Meanwhile we talked amiably. The Turks showed us their medals, and we were rather chagrined at not being able to match them.

Several hours passed. It was very hot. I was hungry having had no breakfast. Again they asked us to give up our letter. I said that our orders were to deliver it in person and, as soldiers, they knew what orders were, but that Colonel Beach would give the letter up if their C.O. would guarantee that we should see Khalil Pasha. This took a long time. The Turks sent for a tent . . .

After some time they agreed to Beach's proposal. We were blindfolded and we went in a string of hot hands to the trenches banging against men and corners, and sweating something cruel. Beyond the trenches we went for half an hour, while my handkerchief became a wet string across my eyes. Then we met Bekir Sami Bey.* He was a very fine man and very jolly, something between an athlete and Old King Cole. He lavished hospitality upon us, coffee and yoghurt, and begged us to say if there were anything more he could get us, while we sat and steamed with perspiration. He told us how he had loved England and still did. Then as we went I said that he had opened our eyes, putting my taut wet rag ostentatiously into my pocket. He shouted with laughter and said: 'No, no; you have chosen soldiering, a very hard profession. You have got to wear that for miles and you will have to ride across ditches.' Then he smacked us all on the back.

My eyes were bound, and I got on a horse that started bucking because of the torture of the flies. Lawrence had hurt his knee and could not ride. He got off and walked, a Turkish officer being left with him. Colonel Beach and I went on. Then our eyes were unbound, though as a matter of fact this was against the orders I had heard given.

At last we came to Khalil's camp, a single round tent, a few men on motor cycles coming and going, horses picketed here and there and the camp in process of shifting . . . Colonel Beach asked me to start talking. I said to Khalil, whose face I remembered, 'Where was it that I met your Excellency last?' And he said: 'At a dance at the British Embassy'. Khalil throughout the interview was polite. He was quite a young man for his position, I suppose about thirty-five, and a fine man to look at – lion-taming eyes, a square chin and a mouth like a steel trap . . . We began on minor points . . .

I went on to speak of the *Julnar*. He said there had been two killed on the *Julnar*. He was afraid it was the two captains. He was sorry. It made Beach and me very sad. I did hope they would have got through.

After that, I began talking of the treatment of the Arab population in Kut. I said that the Arabs with Townshend had done what weak people always do: they had trimmed their sails, and because they feared him they had given him their service. If they suffered Townshend would feel that he was responsible. Khalil said: 'There's no need to worry about Townshend. He's all right'. He added that the Arabs were Turkish subjects, not British, and that therefore their fate was irrelevant, but that their fate would depend on what they did in the future, not the past. I asked him to give some assurance that there would be no hangings or persecutions. He would not do this for the reasons he had already stated, but said it was not his intention to do anything to the Arabs.

We then discussed our sick and wounded. He said that he would send 500 of them down the river, but he required Turkish soldiers in exchange. Beach and I said he gained by having sound men instead of wounded. He agreed. He wanted us to send boats to fetch these men. He said that he was sending them drugs, doctors and food, and was doing what could be done. Beach asked for the exchange of all prisoners in Kut against the Ottomans that we had taken. He at first said that he would exchange English against Turk and Arab against Indian, because he had a poor opinion of the last two. I said some Arabs were splendid fellows, and very brave. He then pulled out a list of the Turkish prisoners of ours, and went through the list of Arab regiments swearing. He said: 'Perhaps one of our men in ten is weak or cowardly but it is only one in a hundred of the Arabs who is brave. Look these brutes have surrendered to you because they were a lot of cowards. What are you to do with men like that? You can send them back to me if you like, but I have already condemned them to death. I should like to have them to hang.' That ended that. We must see that Arabs are not sent by mistake.

He then said he would like us to send ships up to transport Townshend and his men to Baghdad; otherwise they would have to march which would be hard on them. He promised to let us have these ships back again. Colonel Beach said to me, not for translation, that this was impossible. We have already insufficient transport. He told me to say that he would refer this to General Lake. We then talked terms. Khalil said he would refer to Enver or Constantinople as to whether sound men at Kut could be exchanged against the Turkish prisoners in Cairo and India. He did not think it likely. He was going to give us the wounded in any case, at once. He would trust us to give their equivalent.

Guns. The guns had been destroyed. Khalil was angry and showed it . . .

Money. I said that the third condition we had offered was financial support for the civilians of Kut, I said we had offered one or two million. This he brushed aside and again returned to his proposal that we should send up boats to transport Townshend's sick and wounded to Baghdad. Beach whispered to me that we had not enough ships for ourselves at the present moment and no reserve supplies . . .

Khalil yawned, I thought more rudely than negligently, and I said the heat made us all sleepy. He apologised and said he had much work to do. He also said that he had seen Townshend that morning, and that he was all right, but had a slight fever.

Our final understanding with Khalil was that we were to notify him when we were sending up boats so that he might clear the river. He laughed and said that he had forgotten all about the mines; I laughed and said I had remembered them, but did not like to speak of them.

We ended with mutual compliments. Khalil called me aside, and said that he hoped we should be comfortable for the night, and that we were to ask for all we wanted. He was glad to continue an acquaintance that had begun at the Embassy at Constantinople on the occasion of a dance. We rode away, all the Turks saluting. I talked to Ali Jenab, who now seemed a fast friend, and said how angry the Germans would be to see us together. Before sunset we came to the Turkish camp. There the three of us sat down and, as far as we could for the flies, wrote reports. The Turks and I talked like old friends under the stars with camp fires round us. The Muezzins called from different places, and the sound of flutes and Turkish singing came through the dusk. They gave us their own beds, their tent and a most excellent dinner. Then Colonel Beach decided that I had better stay and go to Kut where I was to meet him and Lawrence, who would come up with the boats to take our prisoners away. I didn't believe that Khalil would accept this sort of liaison business. Beach wanted to go straight back. We pointed out that if he got shot in the dark by our people, it would upset everything.

I dictated a letter in French to Lawrence, asking [Khalil] for permission for me to stay and go across to Kut. How Lawrence wrote the letter I can't think. The whole place was one smother of small flies, attracted by the candle. They put it out three times. Beach and I kept them off Lawrence while he wrote. We got an answer at about two in the morning. Khalil said that it was not necessary.

All this happened on April 29th.

Aubrey was complacent about the terms he had negotiated. He wrote to Mary, 'We got the best terms we could, and were lucky to get any, since they held all the cards and we had none.' His complacency was ill-founded. He believed in the chivalry and honour of the Turks: he was wrong to do so. The Arab population of Kut, about whose fate Aubrey had felt deeply concerned, were treated with full Turkish savagery. Many were hanged, more tortured and all pillaged. The ordeal of the prisoners of war was worse. The failure to provide boats to transport them to Baghdad resulted in a march of particular horror and inhumanity. The prisoners were robbed, beaten and starved. Seventy per cent of the British taken prisoner at Kut died, either on the march to Baghdad or in captivity. Many of the atrocities were committed by the Arabs, but Turkish neglect, incompetence and indifference were the root cause. The full horror only gradually emerged, as for a long time rigid censorship prevented the story becoming known. Censorship also surrounded the unsuccessful attempt at bribery. However, the Central Powers made a propaganda field day out of it. Newspapers in Germany and Turkey carried banner headlines and cruel cartoons.

In happy oblivion of the fate of the defenders of Kut or the blow to British prestige that the revelation of the spurned bribe was soon to cause, Aubrey spent the next few days between the lines in negotiation with the Turks about minor details to do with the evacuation of the wounded. As the only Turkish speaker on the British side his services were much in demand. Most of the time he shuttled backwards and forwards between the lines with messages about boats which had been held up or blockages on the river or enquiries about missing men. He wrote in his diary, 'It was very curious and bitter sitting in the peaceful field with the friendly Turks between the lines; wild maize grew round us, the river murmured and above larks sang on every side; the stiff clay held the knee deep footholds of the Black Watch and others where they had charged across the field when it had been a trap and a bog.'

The Turks told Aubrey that they had hung some Arabs. 'I said that Khalil had said he had no intention of doing so. The Turks answered that these men were not natives but vagabonds. I felt Khalil meant to do it when I talked to him. It makes me angry.' How much angrier he would have felt had he known of the treatment of the prisoners of war now beginning their march to Baghdad.

Admiral Wemyss had gone to inspect the naval detachments on the Euphrates. Aubrey was left behind at the request of General Lake but would have preferred to depart with his admiral. 'Oh you foul land of Mesopotamia,' he wrote in his diary. There was some confusion about Aubrey's duties. He belonged to no particular chain of command and sometimes received four contradictory orders at once.

Although Aubrey got on well with General Lake he had revised his earlier favourable opinion of General Gorringe, whose aggressive and rough manner was widely resented. On 9th May Aubrey received a welcome summons from Admiral Wemyss to join him at Bushire. General Gorringe refused to release him. They had a stormy interview:

> I saw Gorringe after a 2 hours' wait. He began by telling me to look him in the face, which I did. He said I had been given to him. I said No that couldn't be, the Admiral was my chief. He roared like a bull. I gave him clearly to understand that it was a pleasure to serve Lake, but that it was only duty which made me serve him. I also said I meant to telegraph to the Admiral to explain why I was not carrying out orders. He couldn't prevent that, but said he must see the telegram. I telegraphed: 'Corps Commander says he cannot spare me until all the sick have left Kut. Much regret I cannot be with you. Herbert.' That again apparently made him furious. He is one of the worst cads I have ever met in my life, and it has been a real pleasure saying what others were not in a position to say to him . . . In the evening I said goodbye to Browne, and told him I didn't want ever to see his chief again as I had been accustomed to deal with gentlemen.

To Mary, Aubrey wrote describing the interview. 'I was very glad as I felt I was avenging a whole horde of poor devils that this swine has brow-beaten.' And indeed the next day Aubrey found himself the most popular man in the camp. There had been a witness to the roaring scene between him and the General who had reported it. Strangers came up to Aubrey and shook his hand. 'I was implored to stay and insult him once again,' wrote Aubrey on 10th May, but he was determined to join his Admiral and started down river the same day.

With him he brought a determination to do something for the forgotten army of Mesopotamia. In his last few days he had visited many regiments. The Devons were in the trenches and with them his friend John Kennaway and five men from Dulverton. On every side Aubrey heard, not just complaints, but almost incredible stories of incompetence and meanness on the part of the Government of India. At Basra Aubrey hoped to find General Lake and win his permission to send a telegram to Austen Chamberlain, Secretary of State for India. Aubrey had known Austen Chamberlain for years and though rather contemptuous of him ('he has his father's eye glass and the next man's mind') was in a position to appeal directly to him. The telegram was an outspoken attack on the Government of India and Aubrey knew perfectly well that he was breaching military regulations in despatching it. General Lake allowed the telegram to be sent but routed it via India. He wrote to Aubrey on 14th May, 'I should certainly, when it was censored in India as all our wires are, have been hauled over the coals for assenting to criticisms of the Government of India . . . Had I been able to see you and talk things over we might of course have arranged otherwise.' Although this letter is a little frosty, General Lake harboured no ill feelings towards Aubrey and in August mentioned him in a Despatch for 'gallant and distinguished services in the field'.

Before Lake's letter arrived Aubrey had already heard about the changed destination of his telegram. He was horrified as he was himself bound for India in the *Euryalus* which he had rejoined at Bushire. 'It is the worst practical joke I have ever had played on me,' Aubrey wrote in his diary. Admiral Wemyss, who was equally indignant about the sorry state of affairs in Mesopotamia, strongly supported the telegram when Aubrey showed him a copy. He considered sending one himself to Balfour on the same lines. After some discussion it was decided that Wemyss could be of most service by bearding the lion in his den, that is going to Simla personally and making strong representations to the Indian Government, while Aubrey would proceed to Cairo and agitate there. Both feared that the telegram would be muzzled in India.

Accordingly, when the *Euryalus* reached Bombay, Aubrey surreptitiously transferred ship and reappeared in Cairo a week later. While he made the rounds of important people in Cairo, who listened eagerly because the Indian Government had long been disliked in Egypt, the Admiral went to Simla. He wrote to Aubrey: 'I found them all in a great state of perturbation about your telegram. I think they had all hoped that you would accompany me as they would have liked to have had your blood, and I think it is as well for you that you went off when you did. The Viceroy told me that your telegram was looked upon as a political attack on the Financial Member of the Council, but I told him that he knew you quite well enough to be able to refute any such idea, and that even supposing you were wrong all through, there was one thing they could be certain of, and that was the purity of your motives . . .' In fact the Government of India pressed the War Office to punish Aubrey for his breach of military discipline by ordering a court martial. The War Office refused. Admiral Wemyss supported Aubrey throughout.

In Egypt Aubrey caught up with the home news. A garbled version of the Easter Rebellion in Dublin had filtered through to the Tigris and Aubrey had written presciently, in his diary, 'Let's hope it's the bursting of a boil. I am more afraid of the treatment than the disease.' Mary's letters waiting in Egypt were not reassuring. She wrote that the executions of the leaders of the rising 'added a new page of bitterness' to the Irish story, and on 10th May she wrote again, 'Do you know the P.M. actually offered Ireland to Edwin [Montagu]. It's almost too ghastly to think it a good moment for a Jew to conciliate the Priest. I wish they would stop the executions now . . .'

Aubrey arrived in England at the beginning of July 1916 determined to bring two men to book, Sir Beauchamp Duff, the Commander-in-Chief in India, and Sir William Meyer, the Financial Secretary. He wasted little time. Within days of his return, on 12th July, he asked in the House of Commons if the Prime Minister would give a day for the discussion of the conduct of the Mesopotamian campaign. Asquith replied with routine evasiveness. Aubrey, reinforced by Sir Edward Carson, persisted. 'The storm burst so unexpectedly', said The Times the next day 'that the Prime Minister was clearly taken aback by this straight hitting. He denied that there was a desire to keep anything back. Several members laughed at this and Mr Asquith shot an angry glance in their direction . . .' In the following days Aubrey spoke in the House on Mesopotamia four times, on 17th, 18th, 20th and 26th July. His tenacity was rewarded. Other members joined the attack. The Prime Minister yielded to the clamour and appointed a Royal Commission to enquire into the conduct of the Mesopotamia campaign.

There were people who were critical of Aubrey's singleminded vendetta. Maurice Hankey complained in his diary on 18th July 1916 of the sniping in the House of Commons. He described the snipers: 'a miserable crew, all out for some personal end, to whitewash themselves (like Churchill) or to get some general's head on a charger (like Aubrey Herbert). I see no sign of a sincere desire to help the war.'

By the end of that summer Aubrey's anger about Mesopotamia had burned itself out. He spent happy times with Mary at Pixton between visits to London. She had given birth on June 20th, before his return to England, to another daughter, Laura. Mary was bitterly disappointed. Aubrey was unconcerned. The summer was overshadowed by the lengthening list of casualties. The bitterest blow fell in September with the news of Raymond Asquith's death in the battle of the Somme. Aubrey wrote to Mervyn, 'A great bit of our life has gone with Raymond, the bit that was full of light.'

Aubrey awaited a posting with impatience, but not eagerness. He loathed being safe in England while his friends were dying on foreign fields, but he had lost all relish for war. Also, once the fire of his indignation over Mesopotamia had burned itself out, he had lost all relish for politics. He left England on 1st October, bound for Salonika. He crossed the Channel with his cousin Bron. They never saw each other again.

11

Balkan Soldiering
and Swiss Peacemaking

Of all the sideshows of the Great War perhaps the Salonika campaign was the most futile. Neither the British Government nor their military advisers ever had much faith in the usefulness of this front. At the insistence of the French, who felt a strong commitment to Serbia, British troops had been diverted from the Dardanelles and had taken part in Allied landings at Salonika on 5th October 1915. They had made no progress. Without the cooperation of Greece, whose King was a brother-in-law of the Kaiser and pro-German, hemmed in by impassable mountains, camped in malarial lowlands, the Allied forces had little chance of success. When Aubrey left the Dardanelles in October 1915 he had wanted to go to Salonika, writing in his diary, 'I should like to be in that show although it may be another page of Alice in Wonderland, covered with blood', but it was neither Wonderland, nor particularly bloody. The Central Powers had little motive for attempting to dislodge the Allies. It suited German purposes well enough that the Bulgarian army should keep a large force of Allied troops pinned down in the insalubrious plain round Salonika.

On 20th October 1916 Aubrey reported for duty to General Cunliffe-Owen. The General, an old but not cherished acquaintance, had no use for him. Then, at the beginning of November, he was given the job of liaison officer with the Italian army and his spirits rose. He wrote cheerfully to Mary that he had a good deal of office work 'at which I find I am all right as I am head of my own office'.

The Italian officers' mess was delightful and the Italian General, a giant of a man inappropriately named Pettiti, was a genial and agreeable master, a strict disciplinarian with a penchant for schoolboy jokes. Aubrey, with Edward Murphy again in attendance, was what he called 'bird happy'. He described his life to his sister Vera: 'I get down to Salonika once a fortnight, and sleep in a house for a couple of nights, and have a bath and catch a cold and beat some Greeks and for the rest of the time, I am either in camp here, or riding about.'

Aubrey's nerves, which had been raw after his return from both Gallipoli and Mesopotamia, were now steady and calm. In December 1916, however, news came of Bron Herbert's death. Bron, who had joined the Royal Flying Corps, had been missing since 3rd November, but it was not until the beginning of December that his death was confirmed. Mary wrote to Aubrey: 'I am so so unhappy for you and for all the others who loved him, even for myself for I loved him from a distance – but above all for you my own darling.' Her chief worry was that Aubrey might become reckless in his sorrow and she wrote: 'Life gets worse, but after all we are all in the hands of inexorable fate – no one should feel unjustified in being alive for you all went up together to lay your sacrifice of life many, many months ago and those that are left have just got to show their love to those who are gone by sticking to it and trying to keep the world, at least their little bit of it, as the others would have liked to see it.' She ended: 'It is your duty – not just to live – but to want to live.'

Mary was right to be anxious about Aubrey's reaction to the news. Throughout the autumn of 1916 the death toll of friends had been appalling. Each week brought news of another loss. Aubrey had borne each new death with stoical acceptance but Mary knew that Bron's might prove the breaking point. Bron was much more to Aubrey than a friend. He wrote to Bron's sister Nan a broken little note, 'Oh my dear I can't write. I am too selfishly sorry. I did love him so,' and to Mary an equally short note, 'Bron is more than I can bear, for him, this time as well as myself.'

Bron's death affected Aubrey profoundly. The change in his attitude to the war which became increasingly apparent can be traced to December 1916. He ceased to believe in a military victory; it was not that he doubted that the Allies could and would win (and with the entry of America into the war the following April this seemed assured), it was that he did not believe in a military solution. He could see no virtue in unconditional surrender and he passionately felt that the sacrifice of men should cease and the slaughter be halted. He wrote to Mervyn on December 16th, 'This damned war has gone on long enough.' He thought the people in England were 'blind and mad'. His mind turned towards a negotiated settlement and he spent many hours drawing up lists of minimum requirements and maximum concessions.

The death of Bron was the emotional impulse behind his change of attitude which, however, was also linked to the change of government in England. That same December, Asquith was manoeuvred out of office by Lloyd George and the Northcliffe press. The Conservatives were cajoled into supporting the Lloyd George coup by either a misunderstanding or a piece of sharp practice on the part of Bonar Law, Beaverbrook and Carson. Aubrey deeply distrusted Lloyd George. While Asquith had been in charge, Aubrey though critical and impatient of the phlegmatic conduct of the war, had trusted the broad statesmanship of Asquith to negotiate a fair peace when the time came. He had no such trust in the war aims of Lloyd George.

Mary writing to Aubrey from England on Monday, 4th December in the middle of the government crisis, took a snobbish rather than profound view of the change,

> I see Lloyd George has been doing coups d'état. I knew nothing of it. I saw the old boy [Asquith] dining at the D'Abernons Thursday night. He seemed a bit depressed as he always does now, but nothing out of the common. I avoided a drive home with him as he looked in a tiresome mood. I can't help thinking this coup d'état ghastly. I believe so firmly in him still as the only sane, and in a way, the only honest man possible. Not that he is as honest as some, but they are stupid, and the clever, with the exception of him, are not clever enough to be honest. And its awful to think that raving mountebank Carson and that beastly little Welshman having the whole of England in their hands with Bonar as a mascot. It is the end of the last pretence of gentlemen. For the P.M. whatever his lineage was in touch with the world and now the floodgate will be opened to Welsh, English, Scotch and Ulster bourgeois whose horizon is bounded by professional politics and who feel they have achieved a social success when they have dined in the House of Commons. How I loathe the bourgeois.

She did, however, end her letter, 'I apologise for filling a page with this empty nonsense.'

Mary's contemptuous opinion of Lloyd George, Carson and Bonar Law was inspired by her well-developed sense of worldly and intellectual superiority and not by political conviction. She believed that the small exclusive world to which she belonged encompassed the people who alone were fit to govern the country. Asquith and Balfour belonged inside this circle. Lloyd George, Carson and Bonar Law did not. What Mary did not expect and more importantly neither did Asquith was that Balfour and many other drawing-room Conservatives would throw in their lot with Lloyd George.

Asquith resigned on 5th December, the day after Mary had written to Aubrey, and Lloyd George formed a new government which was predominantly Conservative in its membership. None of the prominent Liberal ministers took office. Instead they followed Asquith into the wilderness. Within a week, Mary was writing calmly to Aubrey in a more accepting mood. Perhaps Balfour's post of Foreign Secretary in the

new government had influenced her. She had come round to the view
that the Conservatives had been right to join the new government. 'At
bottom the important thing is to give your services to the war.' But she
remained emotionally attached to the Asquith camp, 'One does love old
Father [Asquith] on these occasions. He's been very splendid through the
crisis.'

Toward the end of December the Italians moved their front and
Aubrey lost his job as liaison officer. He asked, and was refused, permission to go to Albania. 'The only alternative seemed to be going with
the 8th mounted brigade, and sitting on a peak with two ibex for the
winter', he wrote to Mervyn, 'so I asked to come back here [England] and
am really not sorry that I did so.'

In England Aubrey soon became immersed once more in the affairs of
Albania. That unhappy country had yet again become a battleground.
The South and South West were occupied separately and distinctly by
the French and the Italians while the North and part of Central Albania
were occupied by the Austrians and the Bulgarians. There were also
armed bands of Albanians and Greek royalists operating disruptively in
various occupied zones. Some Albanians joined the French forces, some
the Austrian and some the Italian, while Albanians outside Albania
struggled to keep the torch of nationalism burning and the cause of an
independent Albania alive.

Great Britain had entered the war in defence of Belgian neutrality and
had since then often publicly declared that she was fighting for the
rights of small nations. Yet she had signed the secret Treaty of London on
26th April 1915, by which Italy agreed to enter the war on the side of the
Allies. By doing this she had agreed to the possible eventual partition of
Albania. Italy regarded Valona and the island of Saseno as the key to the
Adriatic and vital to her national defence. It was a price of her participation in the war on the Allied side. The provisions about the partition
of the North and South were inserted on the insistence of Russia and
France who wished to further the influence of their protégés, Monte-
negro and Greece.

Aubrey was clearly unaware of the Albanian clauses in the Pact of
London. When later the Bolsheviks published the secret provisions at the
end of 1917, his reactions were predictable. He naturally rejected the
Allied plans to reduce Albania to a small Moslem state in Central
Albania, realising full well that this state was planned as nothing more
than a fiefdom for Essad Pasha. 'Essad's patriotism is to his purse. He is
the only Albanian beneficiary of the Pact of London.' Essad, in fact, in
all the confusing tangle of Albanian affairs, remains the only entirely
consistent figure. In Salonika, where he settled under French protection,

he posed as an ex-king, wore a uniform of his own design and decorated himself many times as the mood took him.

In the late winter and early spring of 1917 Aubrey, although still in ignorance of Allied designs for Albania, was very much aware that if the country was to emerge from the war as an independent nation there must be constant propaganda and her rights must be continually pressed upon the entente powers. For this purpose Mehmed Bey Konitza came to London as representative of Vatra, the organisation of American Albanians.

Mehmet Bey had started his career, when Albania was part of the Ottoman Empire, in the Turkish Foreign Service, and had served as Turkish consul in Roumania and Corfu. However, when Ismail Kemal had raised the flag of Skanderbeg in 1912 and declared Albanian independence, he had joined the Albanian cause and had been a delegate to the Ambassadors' Conference in 1913. His friendship with Aubrey had been cemented by their ride together across Albania that summer. Now with Aubrey's help and wide connections he worked indefatigably in London, pestering politicians and Foreign Office officials so that the cause of Albania should not go by default. Miss Durham, firing off letters to the newspapers, composing directives and pamphlets, holding meetings and discrediting opponents, worked alongside him with unflagging vigour.

Albanian affairs took up much but not all of Aubrey's time in the spring and early summer of 1917. He was also pursuing, under the sponsorship of General MacDonogh, the Director of Military Intelligence, plans for the furtherance of a separate peace with Turkey and, in his parliamentary life, he had once more become involved with the affairs of Ireland. Sir Henry Duke, the old West Country Unionist Member of Parliament who had been chairman of the Federalist group of MPs in the heady days of the parliamentary excitement over Home Rule in 1914, had after the Easter Rebellion been made Chief Secretary for Ireland. He invited Aubrey to be his parliamentary secretary. In the late spring of 1917, when Aubrey joined the Irish Office, Irish affairs were again of great interest. Another initiative was in the air. Lloyd George, in response to American pressure, and at the suggestion of General Smuts, announced that a Convention would be held at Dublin, where the Irish themselves from North and South would meet and strive to find their own solution. After the damage done by the 1916 Easter rising in Dublin, it proved to be Ireland's last chance of unity and seemed to come within a whisker of success. Aubrey, who was on friendly terms with most of the Irish Nationalists and with most of the Southern Unionists (and the positions of these two groups were not by that time far apart), was deeply involved in the setting up of the convention. His time was divided between the Irish Office in Old Queen Street, London, and the Chief Secretary's Lodge in Dublin.

An entry in his diary for this period gives the flavour of Aubrey in office:

June 3
Duke went over to Ireland, leaving me to do liaison with Lloyd George. The first thing that happened was a cypher telegram, for which I had no cypher, and the second thing, I had to open the sacred secret boxes that had no key. Broke them open with a chisel and hammer and the old clerk said: 'It's twenty-nine years I've been in this office, and never a day's work like this.'
June 18
The situation here [London] is getting more and more difficult with Lloyd George. I wonder how many people realised that in the change of government in December we had really a revolution. The cabinet is not sitting at all; the War Cabinet has no time to digest what it does, and Lloyd George acts independently of those under him . . . he queers the whole of the Irish policy without a thought.

A month later the situation in Ireland looked menacing. Another rising was gloomily forecast and the finer details of the convention had still not been agreed. Aubrey, meeting Arthur Balfour at dinner, told him that 'unless my chief got proper support from the Cabinet he would not be able to go on'. Arthur Balfour replied that at present he, Balfour, was 'fighting for the honour of holding a tiger by the tail'.

Nevertheless, the convention finally was convened. The Nationalists under Redmond, who had already turned down Lloyd George's first offer of immediate Home Rule for the Twenty-Six Counties with a final settlement after the war, needed the convention for political survival. Already they were losing support in the South with the Sinn Fein winning every by-election. Mary had written to Aubrey in October 1916, 'Sinn Fein seems less of a mad dream than a passionate certainty.' By July 1917 it was clear that unless the convention could produce a settlement, Redmond and the Irish Nationalists were finished as a political force. The Nationalists, therefore, came to the convention, which opened in August, with a real desire to settle, as indeed did the Southern Unionists. The Ulster Unionists were of a different mind. Lloyd George, to whom the convention's main value was as window dressing for the Americans and a means of buying time for himself, had privately assured Carson that nothing would be done without Ulster's consent, although promising Redmond to back the convention's proposals if there were 'substantial agreement'. In the end it was not the double dealing of

Lloyd George that wrecked the settlement but the foolish behaviour of
the Catholic Bishop of Raphoe, later Cardinal O'Donnell of Armagh. On
the trivial matter of customs levies and the even more trivial particular
of the dues to be paid by his flock in Donegal, the Bishop led the Catholic
episcopal delegates to combine with their historic enemies the Ulster
Unionists against the settlement proposals when they finally came to
the vote in April 1918: 47 voted in favour and 41 against. This could not
be described as 'substantial agreement', so Lloyd George's promise to
Redmond did not have to be put to the test. Aubrey, who had left the
Irish Office in the interval, was back with Duke for the final débâcle in
April 1918.

With the failure of the convention, Aubrey's intermittent job at the
Irish Office came to an end. In actual working days his post as Parliamentary Private Secretary was only of brief duration, but it represents
Aubrey's only government office during his parliamentary career. In
this same period from the spring of 1917 to spring 1918 Aubrey had also
found time for more amusing adventures. In July 1917 he had travelled
to neutral Switzerland on a secret mission to meet some Turks. The
mission got off to a bad start when his intentions were discovered by
Armenian and Zionist activists. A 'secret and confidential' report dated
16th June 1917 from William Ormsby-Gore to his brother-in-law Lord
Robert Cecil, by now deputy Foreign Secretary, records the opposition
which was stirred up by his mission:

> On arriving at the office I found Mr Malcolm [of the Armenian Committee]
> and Dr Weizmann, a Zionist leader, waiting for me. They informed me that
> they had come to see me about a matter which was to them of the first
> importance, namely the proposal of the British Government to allow Aubrey
> Herbert to get into touch with the Turks with a view to arranging a separate
> Peace between Turkey and the Allies . . . Both Mr Malcolm and Dr Weizmann
> were very much excited and very angry . . . Dr Weizmann thought the
> sending of Mr Aubrey Herbert who was notoriously pro-Turk, anti-Armenian
> and anti-Zionist, was a gross betrayal and quite incompatible with the
> encouragement he had received from responsible ministers of this country . . .
> Both stated they would do all they could to oppose Mr Aubrey Herbert and his
> designs, and that they intended to make as much trouble as possible.

Nevertheless Aubrey arrived in Berne on 16th July and over the next
week conducted a series of meetings with various Turks at Geneva,
Interlaken and Berne. In two long, secret memoranda for the War
Cabinet, Aubrey summarised these conversations. Tantalisingly, in
neither his memoranda nor in his diary does he name the chief Turkish
protagonist in his talks, although he names lesser figures. From later

allusions in Aubrey's diary it is possible but not certain that he was an influential Turk called Shefki Pasha.

During his first two days in Switzerland Aubrey made no move to see the Turks. He lived openly in his hotel and consorted with the Albanians Tourham Pasha and old Dr Tourtoulis. His notes on these conversations are absurdly mysterious: 'The red horses were terribly afraid of the roses. The white horses had increased the strength of the roses . . . The business of the dark horses had finished the red horses. The red horses would have no trouble killing the white horses, drown in a teacup said KMT,' etc. Aubrey knew that eventually he would be approached by the Turks and on his fourth day in Switzerland contact was made. From Aubrey's diary: 'At 3 "Mr Smith" walked through the room and I followed him out through a couple of streets to a car, and we went off to his flat. Nobody lived there as far as I could make out, and it was unfurnished except for one oriental picture. After a time my friend turned up. He said "How are you? I hope your wound is better. You must have had a filthy time with the Germans." '

Aubrey understood that his friend represented an influential anti-Enver group. They were not traitors to Turkey but they were anti-German. They were interested in forming an alternative government but they had no intention of overturning the government of Enver for the sake of Allies who might then proceed to partition Turkey. They desired guarantees from the Allies on this score. They saw no objection to semi-autonomous states in the outlying provinces of Armenia, Arabia, Mesopotamia, Syria and Palestine; indeed they welcomed the idea of a Turkey ringed by friendly Moslem states but they would not tolerate these provinces being parcelled out to the Allies.

Twenty minutes before leaving Switzerland by train for Paris, Aubrey was handed a memorandum in French. It contained, amidst much rhetoric, the peace proposals of the 'Nouveau Parti'. In his diary Aubrey wrote, 'I do not think that it is acceptable, but I think that it would form a base.' In Paris the Inter-Allied Conference was in progress. Balfour, attending as Britain's Foreign Secretary, sent for Aubrey. He was 'interested and excited' according to Aubrey's diary, but protested at Aubrey's choice of pseudonym for the unnamed Turk: 'Cadogan is such an honourable name', he said, and Aubrey obligingly used another. After the Foreign Secretary, Aubrey saw the Prime Minister. His diary for 25th July records: 'In the evening I had an hour with L.G. and Hankey. He sipped his tea and listened, while we sat on a balcony, and the crowd cheered in the Place de la Concorde. He took it all in well enough.'

In a memorandum* for the Foreign Office, he pleaded, 'If we get the luggage it does not matter very much if the Turks get the labels. When Lord Kitchener was all powerful in Egypt his secretary was wearing a fez. Mesopotamia and Palestine are worth a fez.'

Aubrey returned unobtrusively to London and his absence went unremarked. However, his outspokenness on every issue connected with peacemaking was making him very unpopular with his party. He was drawn increasingly toward the Labour pacifist members and supported Henderson's application to attend the Stockholm conference of all socialist parties to discuss the Russian Peace Programme. He wrote to Mervyn: 'Labour has come to stay here. The best thing that can happen is that it should be made responsible and to feel its responsibility quick. It was the irresponsible rich that brought us into disgrace. It is only responsible labour that is going to get us out of chaos.'

Mary, whose dislike of the Conservative party was ill-suppressed, did not object to Aubrey's political position but she was worried by his attitude to peace. Aubrey's voting record in the House of Commons had led him to be labelled in the unfriendly press as a pacifist. She believed that Aubrey, given a free hand, really could arrange a peace with Turkey, and she wisely saw that his increasingly pacifist course could only jeopardise such an outcome. She wrote to him:

> If you openly talk peace you make an expedition to Switzerland as impossible for yourself as for Morrell, Lees-Smith, Ponsonby and you know that if allowed to go you can be of more influence than any other envoy. I really think your usefulness lies in being quiet about general peace but clamourous about particular peace. And also darling, you have, for you, whose cunning I always worshipped, a curious naiveté about the simplicity and honesty of the stranger you meet. Why shouldn't they listen in silence and then calumniate you after. It's obvious human nature that at least 2 out of 10 are likely to do so. Well that's a heavy lecture.

The lecture was necessary. Aubrey had not yet drawn to himself the full odium that all patriotic people felt for declared pacifists. That honour was soon bestowed on Lord Lansdowne who at the end of November 1917 published his famous letter advocating an early peace in the *Daily Telegraph* (*The Times* having refused to take it). Lord Lansdowne wrote: 'We are not going to lose this war, but its prolongation will spell ruin for the civilized world, and an infinite addition to the load of human suffering which already weighs upon it.' This was exactly Aubrey's contention, but the popular press ran a campaign of vilification against the old statesman. He was branded a 'shirker' and a 'funk'. Photographs of Lansdowne House were published side by side with irrelevant pictures of slums and starving children.

Aubrey, in Italy at the time, was disgusted from a distance by the popular reaction. He wrote to Mary, 'I really feel after Lord Lansdowne's letter that politics are impossible.' Mary had described the violent anti-Lansdowne feeling in Yeovil. Aubrey wrote, 'Don't let the constituency bully you . . .' and he ended with a firm negative instruction, 'Don't let them [the Conservative party] canvass in the constituency. How do they know what I stand for?'

It was just as well that his constituents did not know. In Italy, Aubrey's attitude was understood among the military although he reported that the generals 'look at me out of the corner of their eyes'. There, his championship of Lansdowne could do him little harm but in England support for Lansdowne was political suicide. Aubrey's anger at the outcry was personal as well as political. Lord Lansdowne as Secretary of State for War had sought to heal Aubrey's injured pride, when Elsie had successfully pulled strings to stop him going out to the Boer War, and Aubrey had felt gratitude and respect ever since. Mary had known Lansdowne all her life as a close friend of her parents. During their married life, and throughout the war, Aubrey and Mary dined often at Lansdowne House. After one dinner in June 1917 Lansdowne sent Mary a verse, composed he claimed by another dinner guest but written in his own hand:

> Lady of the scornful smile,
> Spite of magisterial bile,
> Scorch on in your usual style
> Fast and furious mile on mile.
> But when passing down the street
> Should our glances chance to meet,
> Drop the scorn but keep the smile.

The reason why Aubrey was in Italy and unable to come to Lansdowne's defence (an omission he was to rectify later) was that once again he was engaged in Albanian affairs. In August 1917, shortly after Aubrey's return from Switzerland, there arrived at the office of General MacDonogh a suggestion from the Albanians of America that they should raise a brigade of three to four thousand fighting men, putting themselves under the command of Aubrey, in order to fight the Austrians in Albania. General MacDonogh was attracted to this idea. Aubrey, however, felt that the General's attitude was altogether too casual. In his diary on 3rd September he notes: 'The DMI's idea seems to be that he would put us down on a beach somewhere and say "God bless you" and leave us unprovided with food and equipment. He said to me "The

Albanians won't need much food." I said, "Well, I shall, at any rate", and he asked me to do a memorandum on it.'

All through the month of September Aubrey fitfully pursued the plan. Initially Balfour lent his support and finally on 28th September Aubrey left England for Italy to negotiate on the matter with the Italians. Once more he was promoted to Lieutenant Colonel. He wrote to Mary, 'Yesterday I became *di novo* a Lieutenant Colonel – a self made man. You are not to call me Captain Herbert now.' He had expected to carry with him to Rome a letter accrediting him with the task of negotiating with the Italians an Albanian Expeditionary Force. Instead, three days before he left he was warned that there had been a bad row about his mission in the Foreign Office and on the eve of his departure he received an official letter, not of support, but of repudiation: '. . . Mr Balfour desires however to make it clear that your visit to Italy has been author-ised on the understanding that you proceed in a private capacity only and that you are charged with no mission on the part of His Majesty's Government. He trusts also that you will bear in mind that His Majesty's Government would in any case be unable to commit themselves as to the provision of tonnage facilities for any Albanian volunteers whom it may be possible to obtain from the United States of America.'

Aubrey arrived in Rome on 6th October after a brief visit to Portofino. He saw at once that he had come at an inopportune moment. The Italian government was extremely unstable and Italy itself seemed on the verge of collapse. A few weeks later came the disaster of Caporetto, when the Austro-Hungarian army broke through, almost reaching Venice. Even before Caporetto morale was low in the capital. Accord-ing to Aubrey the government issued a decree that anyone who depressed anyone else should go to prison for ten years. Meanwhile the man appointed by the English to be head of their propaganda in Italy was a defrocked priest, and a home for soldiers opened in Rome by the English was situated in a non-conformist chapel. The Vatican was incensed. Aubrey wrote in his diary, 'Odd how we do things, there must be very few unfrocked priests in England, yet one can be found to send to Rome; there must be a very few non-conformist chapels in Rome, yet one can be found for a quasi propaganda centre.'

There seemed little point in staying in Italy. He arrived in England the same day that the sad news of Caporetto was published. It filled Aubrey with a desire to be with the Italians in their hour of need. 'I want to be in Italy', he wrote to Mary, 'though it will be like being in the room with a woman in travail.' London held few attractions for him. His diary appears generally disgruntled. At Pixton he felt more at home. There, the social changes wrought by the war had made little impression. It remained firmly feudal, although Aubrey riding round the farms remarked in his diary how funny it was to have his horse held by a farm boy, and at the same time to remember that the boy's brother held a commission in the army.

Aubrey returned to Italy at the beginning of November. He kept no diary and it is not clear what he was doing, but he was attached to the Italian army in some capacity and under the direct orders of General MacDonogh.

The year 1917 closed glumly in England. Old Asquith wrote to Mary on 27th December, 'It seems idle to talk of a happy New Year', but Aubrey, in Italy, had recovered from his earlier pessimism and wrote: 'As far as one can be privately and legitimately happy in these days, I am.'

12

Rebellious MP

By 1918 the spirit of high endeavour and dogged determination that had characterised the English response to war was not dead, but it was accompanied by a mental and moral fatigue that sometimes seemed to gain the ascendant. Both Aubrey and Mary, in their letters, displayed a growing weariness. Mary wrote: 'I cannot get myself into a frame of optimism. It is not that one's exactly pessimistic about the chances of this particular fight but the deeper pessimism of whether this battle won or lost is really going to relieve us from war or the sense of it all being a madness. I am afraid I see it as an interminable machine propelled by itself.'

It was not until mid-January 1918 that Aubrey returned to England. He had been present in Padua when the town was bombed and had helped carry crucifixes and madonnas from the Carmine while molten gold streamed down from the roof. 'I have never seen so beautiful a thing so brutally treated,' he wrote to Mary. Edward Murphy, who was with Aubrey, was unconcerned about the treasures of Padua but very nervous about his own safety. He was not an ideal servant for a soldier in war time. He was terrified of bombs, explosions and gunfire; 'one must admit', Aubrey wrote to Mary, 'he hasn't the natural courage of a lion.' After one air raid Edward lost his voice for three days. At first it was thought he was suffering from shock but it later transpired that he had resorted, in traditional Irish fashion, to the remedy of the bottle and had drunk his vocal chords into silence.

Three weeks after their return to England, Edward developed galloping consumption. Aubrey wrote to Mary: 'There is no chance for dear Edward. He does not know how bad he is. I was with him this morning. He is good and brave.' Within ten days he was dead. Aubrey stayed in London to be near him to the end. Edward was the last in a line of personal servants whom Aubrey loved. Kiazim, Johnny Allan and Edward Murphy had served him in strange places and circumstances. They had been companions and fellow adventurers as much as servants. There were to be no more servant-companions in Aubrey's life. He missed Edward sorely.

On Thursday, 17th January the day after Aubrey landed in England, the House of Commons held a secret session in which the Prime Minister explained the general position on all war fronts. Aubrey wrote in his diary: 'Lloyd George blackguarded the Italians talking in this sort of strain: "Yes they were all cowards. They ran away, but I sent men there and they stopped the rout." I interrupted him twice, to assert that it was not true, that the Italians had arrested the attack themselves. He was furious, and said that he had come to give, not to receive, information. So was the House. Unfortunately, without thinking, I was sitting in the place generally occupied by Mr Joseph King, amongst the pacifists.'

When Aubrey's leave was spent he did not return to Italy. A rekindled interest in politics delayed him. Thwarted from political suicide by his absence from England in November 1917, he was still determined to make the attempt and to speak in defence of Lord Lansdowne at the first opportunity. On his return to England he had called on the old states-man. Aubrey recorded in his diary, 'he did not talk much – he never does.' Lansdowne, Aubrey reported, was doubtful as to whether the Germans wanted peace now but he was optimistic about the influence of President Wilson who he was certain would bring pressure to bear in the direction of peace. Aubrey dissented, saying America was 'a big fat Cinderella' and that it was 'very rare that a lady who has got her ball-dress and arrived very late at the ball wants it to stop.'

On 17th February, at the end of a long and controversial speech, Aubrey paid his tribute to Lansdowne. He said that throughout the war he had felt a pride in his country but 'I am bound to say that at one moment I did not feel that pride, and that was when I saw the reception which was accorded to Lord Lansdowne's letter . . .' After recording Lansdowne's many public offices, Aubrey ended: 'and yet forty years of honourable service given to his country were not weighed for a moment by his countrymen in the balance against the hiccups of the *Daily Mail*.'

Lord Lansdowne wrote an elegant note of thanks:

My dear Aubrey,
     I must give myself the satisfaction of expressing to you the pleasure with which I read your speech – notably the concluding sentences – Such words as yours render one doubly indifferent to the abuse of the vulgar.

                                                                        Ys. ever
                                                                            L.

Aubrey himself soon had need to shelter behind the same mask of aristocratic indifference, for his few words in praise of Lansdowne brought down on him a torrent of abuse, both vulgar and refined. In his speech Aubrey had called for a response to Count Czernin's peace initiative and had declared himself as ready as ever to be killed 'for a cause but not for a query'. And more specifically he stated that he was not prepared to die for causes advocated by the Northcliffe press. He had been particularly angered by a leader which gloated on the eventual dismemberment of Austria: 'There may be some eccentrics who are ready to die for that leader in The Times. As far as I am concerned, it can shed its own ink.' In his constituency there were rumblings of discontent. Open rebellion came later, when Aubrey voted against the government in the only serious parliamentary challenge to its authority in the course of the war.

The Maurice Debate, which took place on 9th May 1918, was ostensibly about allegations made in a letter to The Times from General Sir Frederick Maurice. He accused Lloyd George and Bonar Law of lying to the House of Commons about the strength of the British Army in France at the beginning of 1918. By May this was no longer a live issue, but in writing the letter in breach of military discipline and etiquette General Maurice had sacrificed his military career. Lloyd George, who had indeed lied in the House of Commons, took the threat to his position extremely seriously. Later, when the crisis was over and his victory absolute, he was to prove singularly vindictive in the matter. He persecuted General Maurice and never forgave the ninety-eight Liberals who voted for an enquiry. For in the end, this was the size of the opposition, led by Asquith, together with six anti-war Labour members, one Irish Nationalist and one Unionist – Aubrey.

'What unique knowledge', a constituent asked, in an outraged letter, had led Aubrey to 'the invidious position of joining hands with the scum of English parliamentary life?' Aubrey had no unique knowledge. He had never met General Maurice. His first arrogant explanation to the bewildered and distressed Chairman of the Conservatives in his constituency was that 'on certain occasions, I choose to behave as a gentleman and not a politician'. Aubrey felt that when a man of the seniority and standing of General Maurice was prepared to sacrifice his whole career, he was entitled to a hearing. An enquiry seemed only elementary justice. The fact that Aubrey found himself the only Unionist voting for an enquiry was, from his point of view, irrelevant. He had told Asquith he could count on his support and he did not go back on his word. On the day of the Debate, Asquith made a poor speech, while Lloyd George produced a wonderful conjuring trick whereby he seemed to prove that the figures he had given the House had come from General Maurice himself.

The uproar in South Somerset over Aubrey's vote did not die down. The executive committee of the local party organisation summoned an extraordinary meeting to consider it. Aubrey was asked to attend. He declined and a few days later antagonised his constituency party still further by voting for Proportional Representation and again finding himself in the lobby with a number of pacifists. The chairman of the constituency party, with difficulty and misgiving, managed to prevent a vote of censure, but feeling remained high. Mary wrote to her cousin, Cynthia Asquith: 'I think Aubrey did right, but it had a curiously large effect, his whole constituency in arms, and people almost cutting him in the street, while I was railed at across the Ritz dining room. Bongie [Bonham-Carter] appears to have led the "Old Gang" into a mess again, ably assisted by Margot, who went up and down Bond Street like the Ancient Mariner clutching at mannequins, commissionaires, friends, taxi drivers, policemen, and whispering to them the good news of their [the Asquiths'] return to Downing Street.'

Margot Asquith was indeed in an emotional and irrational mood throughout the crisis. On hearing about the attacks on Aubrey in his local press, she sent a telegram to Pixton: 'Say nothing, explain nothing. Important letter follows. Asquith'. Since the Maurice vote, Aubrey was regarded even in Dulverton with grave suspicion. Such a telegram, which gained immediate currency in the town, was exceedingly unhelpful. The letter that followed was a dotty eleven-page pencilled scrawl in which Margot instructed Aubrey on how he should conduct his defence and urged him to further rebellion. A typical passage ran: 'I should be very plucky and tell your constituents plainly that you won't knuckle under to the press. *I should burn my boats.* You will be as famous as Dizzy or Randolph. It is useless for you to retreat. It will be suicide. If you don't burn your boats now you will never be heard of again – of this I am sure.'

By the time Margot's letter arrived, Aubrey had left England for Paris, en route for Rome and Albania. Mary, who opened the letter, was exceedingly angry. She had been left to do battle with the constituency and to bear the unpopularity which Aubrey's vote had caused. She was in no mood to accept Margot's unsolicited advice. Aubrey, when told of the contents of the letter, took a more detached and amused view: 'Tell Margot, whom I am not answering, that I did burn my boats but that only the oars took fire.'

Mary's rage on reading Margot's letter was compounded by the embarrassment she was already feeling as a result of an independent piece of blundering interference by her mother-in-law who had taken it on herself to ask Bongie and Violet Bonham-Carter, for Aubrey's sake, to put off a visit to Pixton they were due to make the following weekend. She considered that it would be most unwise for Mary to entertain any

Asquiths while local feeling was still high. The Bonham-Carters duly did as they were told and chucked. Mary was mortified and furious to learn that Lady Carnarvon was responsible. She wrote to Violet apologising for Elsie's behaviour. When she then received Margot's wild letter she assumed that Violet Bonham-Carter had been stirring the pot. She wrote again to Violet, this time in anger. Violet replied:

> 25th May, 1918
>
> Darling Mary – I had just written to you when your second letter arrived. I must say it surprised me very much – for you know me and you know Margot well enough to realize that I neither inspire nor control her pen – and am *always* (and in this case not less than in others) her victim and not her accomplice . . .
>
> Margot's letter sounds *outrageous* . . . I can hardly believe that even she – at her maddest – could accuse Aubrey of lack of hospitality or political courage!! his two most *glaring* characteristics.
>
> Still less can I believe that you seriously suspect me of lending even a 'spark' to such charges. You know that I *adore* Aubrey – have had more pure happiness from his and your hospitality than almost anyone's and have, I can truthfully say, a cleaner sheet of lip – as well as heart – loyalty to you both than to anyone I know.
>
> I am no more to be held accountable for Margot's actions than you for Lady Carnarvon's – (you will admit that of the two M. is the more frenetic and impossible to bridle.) Let us dismiss them both as a pair of (fundamentally benevolent) loonies – but do not for God's sake let them involve us in controversy or fiction – that would be giving them too much power . . .

Mary remained incensed with Margot and wrote her a stiff little note asking her to retract her remarks about Aubrey's courage. Margot replied by telegram: 'The last thing I intended darling. Everyone thinks Aubrey a hero Tory and Liberal alike. Love. Writing. Margot.'

The unfriendly ripples caused by Aubrey's February speech in support of Lansdowne became, after the Maurice Debate, fierce waves. Three weeks later, with the opening of the Billing trial at the Old Bailey, it seemed likely that Aubrey's political career in South Somerset would be finally submerged in a furious sea of distrust and disgust.

The Billing Trial arose from a criminal prosecution for obscene and defamatory libel. Mr Pemberton Billing, the defendant, was an independent MP for East Hertfordshire. He founded, in 1917, the Vigilante Society to promote 'purity' in public life and root out 'mysterious influences', and edited a paper called the *Vigilante* dedicated to the same ends. In earlier days he had been in turn an actor, inventor and air pioneer. The libel case arose from a passage in the *Vigilante* about the dancer Maud Allen. The piece headed *The Cult of the Clitoris* had been written by his assistant editor, Captain Harold Spencer.

It was through Harold Spencer that Aubrey became involved in the case. Spencer, an American, was a flamboyant eccentric who had in fact been discharged from the army in September 1917 for 'delusional insanity' although this did not emerge at the trial. Spencer had first come to England as a midshipman in the American navy in 1910. Since then he had lived in England, Rome and Albania. He claimed to have been an officer in the International Gendarmerie in Albania in 1913 and to have been personal ADC to Prince William of Wied during his brief reign. The first claim may have been true but the second was a total fabrication. He returned to England at the beginning of 1915 and was later that year commissioned a Captain in the Royal Irish Fusiliers. During the Serbian retreat in 1915 he was sent to Albania by Naval Intelligence. He remained there on and off until June 1917, when he returned to England under arrest and was discharged from the army as insane in September. Late in 1917 he met Mr Pemberton Billing and found in him a ready and credulous ear for all his fantasies most of which centred on an international conspiracy of German Jewish capitalists who were supposedly working for a German victory aided by corrupt men and women in high places in England. An earlier Spencer article had claimed the existence of a black book in German hands which listed 47,000 perverts in England, 'privy councillors, youths of the chorus, wives of cabinet ministers, dancing girls, even cabinet ministers themselves, while diplomats, poets, bankers, editors, newspaper proprietors and members of His Majesty's Household follow each other with no order of precedence.'

Aubrey had first met Spencer in October 1915, for sooner or later Aubrey came across everybody connected with Albania. Spencer had many stirring tales to tell of the internal fighting in 1914. They did not meet again until August 1917 when Spencer wrote to Aubrey saying he was in a convalescent home in London, being persecuted by the authorities. Aubrey, remembering him vaguely as an amusing and colourful figure, asked him to stay at Pixton in his usual indiscriminately hospitable way.

At the time Spencer, under semi-arrest in his convalescent home, was under the protection of Philip Kerr, the attractive, cranky, idealistic secretary and confidant of Lloyd George. Kerr, later Lord Lothian, was an old friend and distant cousin of Aubrey's and wrote the next day: 'I am glad that you have got Spencer staying with you for this weekend. I think it is up to us to help him out of the mess he has got into. So far as I can judge he has got obsessed as many others have been with the methods of the German Jew spy and intriguer, and sees evidence of his

handiwork everywhere. There is doubtless something in what he says
. . . He can't work with the M.I. people, and he is unbalanced in his own
conclusions . . . I'd like to see you about him next week – I'm finding out
the M.I. case against him.'

Meanwhile Samuel Hoare wrote to Kerr about Spencer, from Rome,
warning: '. . . he is a very dangerous person to have dealings with. He
has now written to the Military Attaché a letter on 10, Downing Street
paper, implying that you have taken up his case and that all future
correspondence with reference to it can be addressed to you at 10,
Downing Street . . .'

Spencer's letter to the military attaché in Rome on Downing Street
writing paper was one among many that he wrote. Later he wrote to
several people he regarded as his persecutors on Downing Street paper,
saying that Lloyd George was his creature, and more damagingly he
wrote to his bank saying Philip Kerr would guarantee his debts. Philip
Kerr, away in Scotland at the time, came back to find two bailiffs sitting
in No. 10 awaiting his return. Aubrey, calling round at Downing Street
during Kerr's absence, wrote in his diary on 4th September: 'P.K's lady
secretary was indignant. She said Spencer was not grateful when people
did things for him. I said that was his charm.'

For a few weeks after the weekend Aubrey saw a certain amount of
Spencer. By mid-September, however, Aubrey was surfeited with
Spencer stories and fast losing sympathy with his persecution mania. On
15th September Spencer called at Bruton Street while Aubrey and Mary
were having breakfast. Spencer used some bad language. Aubrey,
furious that he should swear in front of Mary, unceremoniously turned
him out of the house. Two days later, Spencer was finally discharged
from the army for insanity, and for a time faded from view, only to
re-emerge six months later as assistant editor of the *Vigilante*.

The Billing Trial, presided over by Mr Justice Darling, opened at the
Old Bailey to packed galleries on 29th May 1918. Billing elected to
conduct his own defence and pleaded justification.

The alleged libel against the dancer Maud Allen was contained in a
short notice on the front page of the *Vigilante*:

THE CULT OF THE CLITORIS

> To be a member of Maud Allen's private performance
> in Oscar Wilde's *Salome* one has to apply to a Miss
> Valetta of 9 Duke Street, Adelphi, W.C. If Scotland
> Yard were to seize the list of these members I have no
> doubt they would secure the names of several thousand
> of the first 47,000.

It was the second day when Billing's two star witnesses, Mrs Villiers Stuart and Spencer gave evidence, that the trial degenerated into farce. The Judge lost control of the proceedings, when he was himself named as one of the 47,000 perverts in the black book. After being named, Mr Justice Darling seemed almost anxious that others should share his fate. When Spencer came to take the stand he was closely questioned by Pemberton Billing about who else was privy to the black book. Spencer immediately named Sir Eric Drummond, Aubrey's unfortunate guest at the Hanover Restaurant when Spencer was also present, saying vaguely, 'They told me it would undermine the whole fabric of Government if it was made public'. The Judge intervened: 'Who told you that if it were made public it would undermine the whole fabric of the Government? Give me the names, you have given other names.'

Spencer replied with only one, 'Colonel Aubrey Herbert'. He went on to claim that at the weekend at Pixton, attended by various Intelligence officers and Captain Lane, he had been warned to be quiet. (Lane was Smutts' A.D.C. who by chance had been staying at Pixton at the same time. There had been no Intelligence officers. The other guests were Cynthia Asquith, Charles Whibley and Margot Howard de Walden.) When Spencer was asked if he had at any time been threatened, he replied: 'Yes . . . At the time I gave the Italian Ambassador certain information Colonel Aubrey Herbert said "They will have you shot in a fortnight".'

With this revelation Billing dramatically asked the Judge for police protection for his two witnesses. Further questioning about who the 'they' were, who would have him shot, revealed that Spencer took the 'they' to refer to 'Colonel Aubrey Herbert's intimate friends, the so called Camarilla or clique that, under German influence, were trying to restore Mr Asquith'.

In further questioning Spencer named as conspirators almost every British diplomat or intelligence officer in Rome in 1917. Counsel's objection was over-ruled by the Judge, on the grounds that 'So many people have been mentioned, a few more or less makes no difference.' By this time the Judge had given up any attempt to direct the case and Counsel had almost given up appealing to him. He made a last attempt. 'My Lord, assuming all this evidence to be true, what bearing has it?' to which the Judge made the astonishing reply: 'Do not ask me, Mr Hume Williams.'

His first day in court had been a triumph for Spencer. The whole of England was agog. Some of his victims, however, were prepared to fight back. As the third day of the trial opened to a packed court, some of the top legal names in the land were present to protect their clients. Most eminent of these was the renowned advocate Marshall Hall who rose first to state that he represented Lord Carnarvon and his brother, Colonel Aubrey Herbert, and to express their willingness to go into the witness box. The Judge agreed that it was very unpleasant for people but claimed, 'My difficulty is to see how it is relevant to allow them to come here'. Marshall Hall declared authoritatively: 'Statements should not be made without an opportunity being offered of contradiction.' The Judge replied, 'My view is that people who are mentioned in this way must simply put up with it.'

Marshall Hall was acting on instructions from Lord Carnarvon and not from Aubrey. Porchy was furious at being dragged into the affair. He had seen Spencer in Aubrey's company by pure chance for five minutes. Aubrey's position was different. He had, through his own fault, become embroiled with the lunatic Spencer. He was, however, by now abroad on what he considered an extremely important enterprise as head of the British Adriatic Mission. He was out of touch with the general hysteria brought on by the trial and saw it only as an absurd farce. He did not realise how seriously the public in general and his constituents in particular, took Spencer's allegations. The last thing he wished was to be forced to return to England to give evidence. He wrote to Mary on 4th June as soon as he heard of Marshall Hall's intervention, 'Marshall Hall MUST GO SLOW. I WON'T come home.'

The same day that Aubrey wrote to Mary the trial ended. The jurors were out for eighty-five minutes before they returned a verdict of 'not guilty'. The applause was deafening. Thousands in the street outside who had failed to get into court cheered Billing and Spencer as they left the Old Bailey in a huge demonstration of popular support. By acquitting Billing of the charge of libel, the jury were seen to have endorsed Spencer's allegations of perversion and treachery in high places. The jury accurately reflected the feeling of the people. Asquith and the old gang, indeed the whole ruling class, were traitors and perverts. (Aubrey, not to be outdone by the inventiveness of Billing and Spencer, wrote to Mary that F. E. Smith and Lady Diana Manners were behind the whole affair.)

The ruling class wanted revenge. The chiefs of Intelligence and the police were determined that Spencer should not get away with his impudence or his perjury. Spencer, however, flushed with victory, became more impudent than ever. He wrote on 14th June to Mary Herbert enclosing a letter for Aubrey. With the letter to Aubrey, an abusive ramble, he enclosed two dedications for a book. He wrote: 'I want to dedicate my book to you. Which dedication will you choose?' The alternative dedications were:

To
Col. the Hon. Aubrey Herbert, M.P.
In gratitude for his kindness and in appreciation of his
fight to uphold the traditions of England against the
subtle corruption of the German-Jew.

To
Col. the Hon. Aubrey Herbert, M.P.
In remembrance of his kindness and with regret that
this descendant of English Knights and Defenders of
the Cross should put a doubtful future material comfort for his family before his duty to his country's
ideals, and that he consented to stand by and see the
world plundered and betrayed by the Jews in order
that his erring and warring friends should receive
forty percent of the plunder for their silence.

Mary saw these as an attempt at crude blackmail and immediately
conveyed copies to Marshall Hall and the head of Military Intelligence,
General MacDonogh. Marshall Hall was clearly nervous. He wrote pusil-
lanimously: '. . . I am reluctant to put anything in writing when one is
dealing with or speaking of the man you mention in your letter . . .' He
advised her to seek the advice of a firm of solicitors and ended plain-
tively, 'I do wish Aubrey would not make friends with such strange
people.'

General MacDonogh was more robust. He was, in any case, determined to nail Spencer on some charge, and was delighted with this
opportunity. He advised suing for defamatory libel. Mary's solicitor,
Mr Higgins of Traherne & Higgins, did not agree with the Director of
Military Intelligence. He was not at all sure there was a libel although
he recognised a 'threat savouring of blackmail'. He put forward another
suggestion, that Spencer could be got into trouble with the military
authorities because his letter had been written on official paper. Meanwhile Higgins wrote a solicitor's letter to Spencer: 'We are instructed to
inform you that Mrs Herbert can only consider the letter in the light of a
threat to identify her husband with your work, of the nature of which
she is unaware, and that in her opinion any dedication of a book to him
without his approval and consent would be a most offensive and unwarrantable proceeding . . . Mrs Herbert also requests that you will in
future refrain from addressing her any communications of any kind
whatsoever.'

Spencer replied that his letter had only been a 'tease'. Mary now regarded the matter as closed. It was obvious that Spencer's dedications were indeed a tease, and in any case Aubrey, in Italy, and by now fully informed of the affair, was against any pursuit of Spencer. He did not share Mary's feelings of outrage and indignation, but he was concerned about her. 'Now I hope that you are alright my precious Scaramouche and not fretting or worrying or thin. Don't mind what all those black-guards say. Spencer's letter to me seems to my mind simply mad and not very malignant . . . He has had a great success and can afford to be impertinent, and is a natural cad.'

In Rome Aubrey was surrounded by others named by Spencer. Rodd, the ambassador, de Salis, Minister at the Vatican and many other lesser known people suddenly made notorious. It was easy for him to be lighthearted. In July he sent Mary a letter describing his 'razzle dazzle' life in Rome; but while Aubrey was enjoying himself, Mary was doing battle in the constituency. In an unusually dispirited letter, she des-cribed the situation: 'I don't mind responsibilities but these are a bit too heavy. It's amazing in the constituency. The following is seriously believed: 1. You are a pacifist. 2. You are ratting to the old gang. 3. You believe in Free Love. 4. You are in German pay. 5. You are a sexual pervert.' She found that even those who continued to support Aubrey, believed implicitly all the allegations in the Billing Case. Others now questioned his war record. How, it was asked, had he managed to escape after being taken prisoner by the Germans in 1914? The answer, of course, was the Hidden Hand.

Aubrey's initial reaction to this news of constituency disaffection was one of angry disgust. He wrote to Mary: 'I repeat and repeat, but you won't believe it, it isn't worth fighting about. You can't argue with the snout of a hog, and the picture of you talking to those cads and fools makes me see red.' He answered further appeals from Mary in his most detached fashion: 'Don't worry. That's all. Spencer and all things will pass. I shall lose my constituency one day or it will lose me. The only thing that matters is that we are not together.'

When he at last realised the gravity of the situation, he wrote Mary a more considered letter:

Now about Politics. You go absolutely straight to my heart, and I can't bear to think of you, my Proud Spirit, left alone to argue with people . . . I have constantly during this war felt I could not carry on with politics if I lived through it, but that I should like to be in the next parliament. Sometimes I have felt I couldn't even face that, but that it was more difficult to face running away, when my own people would say I had let them down. Now make it perfectly plain that if they want another candidate, not only will I not stand in his way but that he shall have my support. I am not going in for any electoral tricks. The people who trust me now are the best people, and I am not going to lose or alter the quality of their trust, to get thin applause from a majority. It is no good Hayter's wanting me to support publicly this Gov. It's kind of him to wish it, but I would much rather be out of politics than be one of those people. When they do decent things I do support them but not over things like [Lloyd] George's turning the House into a jury, and asking it to condemn the man in the dock without a hearing . . . In the end people know what men really do mean well by them apart from politics. That's what made [Lloyd] George, because in the past he did mean well by the people, old age pensions etc. Well there. Now I love you with my whole heart. My life with you is more dear than I can say. It's sad enough for us with all the good people that have gone, if one is going to worry about what beastly people say, existence would be intolerable.

Mary did not like the note of defeatism in his letter. Her temporary attack of dejection had passed and she answered in fighting spirit:

I disagree with you that things aren't worth fighting. It's no good pretending that we live in the 14th century. We accept democracy and therefore the only remnant of feudalism left to us is to try and lead and inform it. It's duty not pleasure. If you take an independent line, and bow before the storm it raises, it's as subservient as taking the orthodox line. The days when resignation meant stamping the impress of your opinions is passed. There are too many people pressing around for it to make its impression. The only thing to do is to do as you did, take your independent line, stick to it, fight them on it, and conquer or fall.

Meanwhile Aubrey was absorbed in his new life in Italy and Albania. 'It's a big job the DMI has given me', he had written gleefully to Mary on 22nd May as he left for Paris. The 'big job' was the British Adriatic Mission, of which Aubrey was given charge. It was not very big, in size or importance but, for Aubrey, being his own master was bliss. It was based in Valona, the Albanian port coveted and presently occupied by the Italians. General MacDonogh's purpose when he established the British Adriatic Mission was threefold. First he wanted accurate military intelligence of Austrian and Bulgarian troop movements and strength in Albania and Macedonia because the Anglo-French-Serbian army in Salonika was again planning an offensive. He needed someone who knew Albania, could speak Albanian and Greek, and was able to select and run local agents. Secondly he needed a man who could speak Italian and work harmoniously with the Italians, for another purpose of the mission was to observe and influence Italian activities in Albania. For these purposes Aubrey was ideally suited. The third objective of the mission was to establish a British presence in the area and to liaise

between the Italians and the Allied troops in Salonika. Aubrey's rather
unusual qualifications seemed tailor-made for the task and indeed
General MacDonogh had created the post and the mission with Aubrey
in mind. He had, too, another reason for sending Aubrey to Albania. The
old idea of raising an Albanian regiment in America was having its
annual airing. This time the American government, which had author-
ised other ethnic regiments, was in favour of the scheme and the Italian
government was cautiously friendly.

In Rome in June Aubrey continued his negotiations with the Italian
authorities, while in America the Albanian community, on the verge of
achieving all, split into two warring factions. Vatra (the hearth) was
the largest organisation of Albanians and it was Vatra that sent
Mehmed Konitza to England to represent Albanian interests with the
Allied Governments in Europe and to counter the propaganda of Essad
Pasha. However Mr and Mrs Dako of Jamaica Plain, Massachusetts split
from Vatra through a distrust of Mehmed whom they wrongly suspected
of selling South Albania to Greek interests. They formed another party
called the Albanian National Party and nominated old Ismail Kemal in
Paris to represent Albanian interests with the allies. Both Vatra and the
Dakos appealed to Aubrey. Miss Durham who was uncompromisingly
behind Mehmed and Vatra wrote imperiously to Aubrey, 'Go and see
Ismail. Get out of him what is at the bottom of this mess. Get Dako
himself as a delegate. Frighten them into union.' Aubrey did his best. He
wrote to Ismail, he wrote to the Dakos and received a blast from
Mehmed for his pains. Mehmed rebuked him in French for being in
communication with 'an ambitious neuropath' (Dako) but it was his
dealing with Ismail Kemal that he found hardest to forgive. 'You are in
sympathy with him. I can't blame you for it, for Saint Antony loved the
pig, but the conciliatory letter you sent him encouraged him in his
intrigues . . . As the Albanians love you greatly and place the strongest
confidence in you, your letter did not fail to make trouble.'

Aubrey was in sympathy with Ismail in a general way. He wrote to
Mary, 'Old Dismal (Ismail Kemal) may have sold everybody and everything but he has more statesmanship in one finger than all the rest of
them.' But Aubrey was also loyal to Vatra and Mehmed and his only
desire had been to promote unity.

Another complication was that Vatra had become unrestrainedly
anti-Italian and regularly passed resolutions condemning Italian intentions in Albania. This, not unnaturally, made the Italian government
suspicious of the proposed regiment. Meanwhile Vatra, encouraged by
the American government, went ahead with plans for its formation. On
17th July 1918 in Boston 'amidst indescribable enthusiasm', according to

the official bulletin, the proposal of 'an Albanian regiment under the command of Colonel Aubrey Herbert' was formally approved. 'Albanians will be proud to fight on the side of the Allies under the Albanian flag on the Albanian front as a unit of the British Army.' A month later the Italian Consulta accepted the Albanian regiment scheme under the command of Aubrey but as a unit of the Italian Army. Fortunately the end of the war came before this major discrepancy had to be resolved.

Aubrey gathered round himself a strange assortment of officers and agents in Valona. His pre-war secretary, Henry Sealy, became his right-hand man. Sam Hoare, in Rome, to whom all the mission's intelligence reports were addressed, wrote to Mark Sykes, 'Aubrey has now gone off into the wilds with a typewriter, a tent and a strange man who, dressed as an officer, was apparently once his private secretary.' Aubrey wrote to Mary, 'Sealy is terribly exalted over it all. The East has heard him calling, or he has heard it with a vengeance. He can't speak above a whisper about anything.' Sealy spent much time writing Aubrey formal notes, beginning 'Sir' which discussed with precision and clarity the relative merits of invisible inks, carrier pigeons and coded messages. Also on Aubrey's staff was a charming, unmilitary, scholarly man named Captain Goad. He refused to kill flies on the grounds that they were more perfectly made than he was. The flies, however, did not respect him as much as he did them and he was perpetually laid low with fly-borne infections. Then there was an orderly, once of Mappin and Webb, whom Aubrey described to his mother: 'An excellent man. He writes shorthand though he has never done it before, and cooks though he has never done it before, and talks Albanian although he has never done it before.' Added to these, as part of the permanent strength were: the two Yussufs, father and son, Albanians and scoundrels both; Mr Eden, an old consular hand; and an Italo-Serbian officer of shadowy background.

For three months, June, July and August 1918, Aubrey lived in Valona, paying visits to Salonika, Rome and the Albanian interior. He did not go behind the Austrian lines, although his agents did so with impunity. Valona was a revelation to Aubrey. The Italians had built roads and schools, erected monuments, cleaned slums, brought order and justice. 'It is curious', Aubrey wrote to his mother, 'that it has needed a world drenched in blood to bring peace to these parts.' The credit for this wonderful transformation rested solely with the remarkable Italian Commander-in-Chief, General Ferrero. On 3rd June, before Aubrey's arrival in Valona, General Ferrero published a proclamation which was read at Argyrocrastro before an assembly of Albanian notables. The proclamation promised free government, army and courts of justice. It declared: 'Come, all of you, under the flags of Albania and Italy, and pledge yourselves to Albania, which is today proclaimed independent, in the name of the Italian Government and under its friendly protection.'

General Ferrero sincerely believed in his proclamation. It was not a political manoeuvre to gain the support of the people. In Italy the government read it with alarm. The General had exceeded his brief. Consequently the General's days as Commander-in-Chief in Albania were numbered, though neither he, nor Aubrey, basking in his company, were aware of it. Relations between the British Adriatic Mission and Italian Headquarters could not have been more cordial.

In September Aubrey came home for leave. On 9th October he left England to return to Albania, saying goodbye to Mary who was leaving for Ireland. In Paris Aubrey heard the news that the Irish Mail boat, the *Leinster*, had been torpedoed by the Germans with all hands lost. Aubrey thought that Mary might have been on board and was beside himself with worry and misery. Within hours he received a telegram. She had crossed twelve hours before, on the ship's last crossing.

Aubrey left Paris like a reprieved man. The sinking of the *Leinster* had been to him the most frightening incident of the war. In Rome he found all was not well with the Adriatic Mission. He wrote to Mervyn: 'My show went wrong . . . My head Albanian (Bilal Arif), furnished with much fine gold by me, went off and shot two cousins of a man who had threatened to seduce his wife a year ago. I think he might have overlooked this in the world catastrophe. The Mission quarrelled hopelessly and a captain with a record for courage fled from Valona when Rome refused to send him out a special messenger with twelve tins of Sanitas. So I have to go back (to Albania).'

Aubrey's heart was no longer in the job. Like everybody else he could now only think of peace, for events had moved with startling rapidity. In June the stalemate had seemed eternal. Then the Germans had launched an offensive against the French, which failed. It proved the last and in August and September there were successful English and French offensives but no victories. Then came Allenby's victory over the Turks at Meggido, which shook the Bulgarians. Always weathercocks, the Bulgarians, rather than face the expected Salonika offensive, signed an armistice on 29th September, leaving the way open for the Allies to break into Central Europe. Ludendorff, the German commander, had no troops to close this backdoor. He lost his nerve and told the German government they must seek an armistice immediately. It was all very sudden.

Aubrey in the same letter to Mervyn, dated 14th October, wrote:

'Well, well, well, who could have foreseen all this. It really does look as if the War against the Germans is nearly over, and well over too. They seem to have accepted Wilson's fourteen points. It only now remains for Northcliffe to do the same. I like Wilson's aims and policy but I wish he wasn't such a Don in Sawdust. I believe Clemenceau said, God had only ten commandments, what does Wilson want with fourteen.'

Nine days later the Germans formally accepted the fourteen points and peace was definitely assured. By this time Aubrey was in Albania and sadly cut off from these momentous events. He found the British Mission in Valona in a sorry state. The small mishaps of September were soon overtaken by a much more serious calamity. General Ferrero after one year and one day, was relieved of his command, and sent north. He was replaced by a General Piacentini, who refused to meet Aubrey and demanded that he present fresh credentials. The few officers who remained of the old General Staff were miserably embarrassed and ashamed. A shift in Italian policy became evident, a more acquisitive and imperial attitude towards Albania, and a step backwards from General Ferrero's encouragement of nationalist aspirations. Aubrey was deeply sorry, not for himself or the Mission, which in any case was due for disbandment, but for Italy and Albania. He loved both countries, had rejoiced in Italy's benefactions under General Ferrero and had looked forward with real pleasure to Albania achieving her independent nationhood under the benign protection of Italy. Now he saw it all going wrong. He felt sad and discouraged although he wrote flippantly to Mary: 'A Pharoah has arisen who knows not Joseph, and shows no inclination to know him. To put it crudely I have struck a bad snag. My only fault in this is the fault of existing. Otherwise I am blameless. But the new regime refuses to recognise the works of the Old Regime . . . I had a great burst of rage over it, but in solitude . . . But I shall be glad to get away from this place. It was alright while my friends were here, but I am as lonely now as McKenna would be at Criccieth [Lloyd George's house in Wales].'

Aubrey left Albania on 7th November. He went to Rome and then Portofino. When the Armistice was signed on 11th November he was in Paris on his way to England. He wrote in his diary: 'It's like Death being dead. I cannot think of it, apart from the Millennium, and there is no sign of that.' He met three English friends in the Rue Royale. They walked glumly while the crowd surged and yelled around them. Aubrey felt a great thankfulness but he could not rejoice.

Mary, too, in England felt unable to rejoice and she was sickened by her friends gloating over victory. She wrote to Aubrey: 'Lunched at Adele's [Countess of Essex] where they all talked gluttonously of what they were going to do with Germany. Everywhere there was twinkling eyes and bombast and I felt soulsick and as if the last 4 years were like a weight around my neck, hating our Hunnishness.'

Her cousin Cynthia Asquith writing to Aubrey echoed the same feeling:

> I am beginning to gasp and rub my eyes at the prospect of Peace. It is more difficult to conceive than war was four years ago. It will be like coming round from an anaesthetic and a painful process. One doesn't realise how giddy one is until one stops spinning round. Reconstruction of one's personal life will take great courage and one will have to face long vistas again instead of blind corners. Sub-sub-sub-consciously I believe one feels as though the dead were dead for the duration of the war and one postpones one's final stocktaking.
>
> For God's sake no peace 'celebrations'.

13

Gloom and Peace

Before Aubrey left Albania on his homeward journey, he received a letter from Belloc. 'Do not accept the crown of Albania,' it said. 'Be content with a cellar of wine and the society of those who love you; and remember the man in my (unpublished) novel. Those pleasures which were beyond the reach of his immense wealth he sought in the consolation of religion.'

The warning was unnecessary. The crown was not at that time on offer although later, when it was, Aubrey was once again approached. But the admonition also was superfluous. Aubrey had no chance to seek contentment in his cellar of wine or in the society of his friends or even in the consolation of religion. He returned to find a bare cellar, a large overdraft, his friends mostly dead or scattered and the immediate and unwelcome prospect of a General Election and a disaffected constituency.

The election, which was completed by the end of December 1918, became known as the Coupon Election. Lloyd George and Bonar Law together issued coupons or endorsed the candidature of Unionists and Liberal MPs who were judged loyal to the coalition. Mary had sounded the alarm in October. 'There is a ramp on to make every MP sell his soul to Lloyd George and the Tories for good, but I think we can wiggle enough to get you elected as a very temporary coalition candidate.' Mary wiggled so effectively that Aubrey received the coupon although he only promised to support the coalition until the Peace Treaty was signed. He would have preferred to have been able to dispense with the coupon altogether as his friend Lord Robert Cecil did, but he needed government endorsement in order to be able to silence the critics in his constituency. Coalition coupon candidates swept the country. Asquith and all his ministers lost their seats and only twenty-six independent Liberals were returned to Parliament. The party never recovered. The Labour party, which increased its number of seats from 39 to 59, did better, with only the leading pacifists losing their seats. Aubrey's majority was comfortable, just under 3,000.

Many people were surprised that Aubrey's candidature had been endorsed. The vote on the Maurice Debate had been generally regarded as a test of loyalty and Aubrey had voted against the Government. The coupon in fact came to Aubrey through the good offices of the neighbouring Member of Parliament for Bridgwater, Colonel Peter Sanders, who happened to be a Unionist whip. Later Peter Sanders felt Aubrey had ill returned his help. An entry in Aubrey's diary in November 1920 gives Aubrey's attitude to the coupon.

> I said to Peter [Sanders]: 'I didn't ask for the coupon, but I will plead guilty. I have incurred a debt to you which I haven't paid. Call it £10. But now you ask for payment in the form of exaggerated usury – £100, for me to put my conscience in your pocket.' He said 'You have let me down. I had to fight for you with Lloyd George and the coupon did make a great difference to you.' I told him that I was very grateful, but that I had been perfectly clear that I would not undertake to support the Government beyond the conclusion of peace, and that even until then, if I wanted to be, I should be independent.

On the whole it was a sorry election, with candidates pandering to the basest emotions of the electorate, vying with each other in vindictiveness and greed. Miss Durham wrote to Aubrey to complain of the candidate in her constituency, 'The coalition candidate here sent out the most disgraceful programme demanding BLOOD – SORROW and the FRUITS OF VICTORY. I wrote and told him he had better stand for the Cannibal Islands or Dahomey.'

Certainly Aubrey found little to gladden his heart in the composition of the new Parliament. Gone were the familiar faces of the Liberal front bench and returned were a new breed of businessmen, demagogues and nonentities. Mary wrote to Violet Bonham-Carter to condole about her father's defeat in East Fife. Violet replied with some bitterness:

> I feel quite heartbroken. East Fife is only an incident in what has happened – and tho' sentimentally one might mind it after 31 years – that loss is swallowed up and lost in the great tragedy of seeing all one has loved and believed in disappearing in this vast landslide – and every landmark of loyalty, decency and independence submerged.
>
> I don't know how to bear it – from the public as well as from the personal point of view. One's heygate belief in things like democracy and one's country seem so outraged . . . Aubrey's re-election is one of the few bright spots.
>
> I dare not think of Father. The only thing that helps is to feel, seeing him as I do now, that he is the only figure in English public life at this moment I wouldn't be ashamed to be – he is as you know, constitutionally unaware of his own 'position' and indifferent to it – but he minds terribly seeing all who have followed him go under and that thanks to the defection and desertion of men he has erected (how glad that pioneer in desertion Montagu must be feeling today – that he ratted when he did!) . . .

In the general distress felt by people of Aubrey's world at the election results, his success was greeted with relief. Another survivor was Aubrey's old friend Mark Sykes, who was triumphantly returned with a huge majority in his constituency of Hull Central. Mark Sykes was not in England for the General Election but in the Middle East on a last mission attempting to patch up Anglo-Zionist and French-Arab differences. By the end of January he was in Paris attending the Peace Conference, overtired and dispirited, with his credit and influence both at a low ebb. There he fell victim to the terrible influenza which swept across the world after the war, killing more people than had been killed in the four years of hostilities. Sykes, already weakened by overwork, died within a week on 16th February 1919. Aubrey, on hearing of Mark's death, immediately travelled to Paris where he too was struck down by the influenza. For a fortnight he was extremely ill. After his recovery, feeling both physically and mentally exhausted, he decided to retire with Mary to Portofino, there to gather strength and come quietly to terms with their new, bereft, post-war world. He felt no enthusiasm for English life or the House of Commons. He wrote that with the death of Alex Thynne, who had been killed in the last months of the war, and Mark Sykes, 'The House of Commons lost all attraction for me.' Later, after Aubrey's own death, Mary wrote to Mark Sykes's widow about how desolate Aubrey had been at the time of Mark's death; how it had been 'the end, very end, of all that remained of Aubrey's early conception of life' and the beginning of 'his loss of faith in the happiness of this world'.

Portofino slowly worked its magic. Mary, anxiously watching over Aubrey, felt only profound gratitude for his deliverance. Her cousin Cynthia Asquith had remarked towards the end of the war how extraordinary it was that they, before they were thirty, should know more dead than living people. Mary had her thirtieth birthday that year in Portofino and as she looked at the ruin of the lives of so many of her friends, and compared her own good fortune with their desolation, she was frightened by her luck.

At the end of May Aubrey and Mary, refreshed and recovered, left Portofino. Aubrey returned to find his constituency once again in revolt. This time the cause of the trouble was his prolonged absence abroad. Aubrey's inappropriate response to these complaints was once more to take up the cause of Albania which he had neglected, along with the electors of South Somerset, during his Portofino hibernation.

At the outbreak of peace, as soon as the Armistice was signed, Mehmed Bey Konitza had travelled to Albania and gathered together a group of patriots. On Christmas Day 1918 the National Assembly met at

Durazzo. A cabinet was formed, headed by the ancient exile Turkhan Pasha, with Mehmed as Foreign Secretary. The cabinet appointed five of their number, including Mehmed, as delegates to the Peace Conference.

In Paris the delegation was swelled by two representatives from Vatra. In January the president of Vatra had written to Aubrey asking him to be their official delegate at the Peace Conference. Harold Nicolson wrote from Paris on 15th January:

> My dear Aubrey, I am extremely glad to hear you have been designated by Vatra as their honorary representative at the Conference and I hope that you will not find too much difficulty in securing some measure of recognition. I daresay however that you will meet with some obstacles in getting to Paris, although you will doubtless be able to overcome these with your accustomed energy. I should like to tell you for your private ear that you will find considerable difficulty in regard to Konitza . . . [The letter continued in a discouraging, detailed vein, ending] As I warned you in London I am all for the Greeks recovering up to the Voiussa and none of your arguments will move me from that attitude . . . As regards Ipek and Djakova there is more hope.

However, after the death of Mark Sykes in February, Aubrey, ill and dispirited had declined the Vatra nomination, writing, 'I think I can be of more use unofficially than officially'. Now in June he prepared to give his help. He found the Albanian delegation sunk in gloom. They had been denied representation at the Conference and the most they were permitted was to state their case to Committees dealing with territorial questions. Albania was occupied by the Allied powers and Italy, forgetting her earlier espousal of the Nationalist cause, showed every sign of desiring to make that occupation permanent.

The frustrations of the Albanian mission, coupled with the sinister presence in Paris of the scheming Essad Pasha, who was still peddling his dream of a small Moslem state of Central Albania, proved too much for the Albanian delegation. Their dissensions and disunity gravely damaged their already weak bargaining position. Mary, writing to Mervyn in July, claimed, not wholly accurately, that Aubrey's Albanian fervour was on the wane. She wrote, 'You know the quarrels of the Albanians in Paris gave him I think a pretty good sickener and he doesn't feel them paramount now.' Exasperated with the Albanians Aubrey had certainly become, but he never wavered in his efforts to get them a fair hearing. He did not however have much influence. The Foreign Office under Eyre Crowe, an old enemy of Aubrey's, was unsympathetic and the only official who was consistently helpful in Paris was Harold Nicolson. Aubrey reported in his diary of April 1921, 'He [Harold Nicolson] said Crowe hated me implacably. If I took up the question of

Ireland or Luxembourg Crowe would destroy both countries.'

Aubrey, like many others, was depressed and disillusioned by the whole circus of the Peace Conference. Looking back over 1919, he wrote in his diary, which he resumed in January 1920, 'Paris, as far as I could make out, was run mainly by Eyre Crowe. Wilson was simply bamboozled. Lloyd George does not know what a compass is in morals or politics. Clemenceau was out, quite frankly for "revanche" and we got tied to the tail of all this continental hate.'

Albanian affairs did not completely monopolise Aubrey's time during these visits to Paris. Middle Eastern friends and concerns also played their part. Gertrude Bell had written to him in April: 'O my dear they are making such a horrible muddle of the Near East. I confidently anticipate that it will be much worse than it was before the war – except Mesopotamia which we may manage to hold up out of the general chaos. It's like a nightmare in which you foresee all the horrible things which are going to happen and can't stretch out your hand to prevent them.'

Aubrey missed Gertrude Bell in Paris but he found Lawrence and his protégé, Emir Faisal, the ablest of the four sons of the Sherif of Mecca, and spent much time in their company. Lawrence had become very unpopular with the English in Paris because of his singleminded determination to make the Peace Conference honour the promises he had made on behalf of the British Government to the Sherif of Mecca, promises which were incompatible with the agreement reached by Sykes and Picot which formed the basis of the Middle East settlement endorsed by the Peace Conference. Aubrey was wholly on Lawrence's side in this dispute and they dined together often in Paris, abusing and deriding their fellow peacemakers, particularly the Director of Military Intelligence, of whom Lawrence, like Aubrey, had fallen foul. One day Lawrence went flying with Faisal over Paris. Faisal said, 'How dreadful, to have no bombs to throw upon these people. Never mind, here are some cushions.' And overboard the cushions went. Bombing Paris with cushions appealed to Aubrey, as did Lawrence's devotion to his cause. It was in Paris in 1919 that the friendship begun in Egypt in 1915, and continued at Kut in 1917, was cemented. Mary, however, who had formed no particular view of Lawrence in Egypt, met him again in Paris on a visit with Aubrey and took a firm dislike to him.

From the deliberations of the Peace Conference it was difficult for Aubrey to derive pleasure. The invention of aphorisms was, however, almost an industry and one of his main sources of amusement. Aubrey sent a batch to Mervyn: 'It was Cambon who said that the peace had got in it the seeds of a just and durable war, and I believe Lady Wemyss* said that, as the war had been a war to end war, so was this a peace to end

peace, I confined myself to saying that while President Wilson had
talked like our Lord, he had behaved like Lloyd George.'

These facile phrases disguised the tragedy which the Peace Conference represented for many of those whose fate depended on its deliberations. Neutral states like Albania found it impossible to obtain a hearing;
the Arabs who had thrown in their lot with the Allies found the promises
they had believed in broken and discarded; but the real victims of the
Peace Conference were the belligerent, defeated nations of the Central
Powers. Among these Turkey perhaps suffered most. When Lloyd George
handed Smyrna to the Greeks (although he had originally promised it to
the Italians) in April 1919 at Versailles, the Sultan's government had
weakly acquiesced. There followed the Greek landings at Smyrna and
Greek massacring and pillaging. The Nationalist movement in Turkey,
in that moment, ripened from flower to fruit; Mustafa Kemal resigned
from the army, and assumed its leadership. He was perhaps the most
remarkable leader to emerge from the First World War. Kemal belonged
to the new breed of Turk. He lacked the courtesy of the old Ottoman.
Meanwhile Aubrey's old courteous friend Damad Ferid who had been
appointed Grand Vizier after the war, was gradually outwitted by
Kemal. He had written to Aubrey in February 1919 trying to excuse the
terrible excesses of the Turks during the war: 'We have been the victims
of a secret revolutionary Committee . . . I would also like to explain
that all the massacres of the Armenians and the bad treatment of the
Greeks and that inflicted on the prisoners of war of which the shame falls
on us and of which the entire humanity is ashamed, that too is the work
of the same blackguards . . .'

In September, one of the blackguards, Talaat Pasha, the ex Grand
Vizier, wrote to Aubrey from a false address in Copenhagen, also, but
less convincingly protesting his innocence of the Armenian massacres.
Talaat wrote in French. His letter began, 'A mon ancien ami'. 'Je suis
dans les massacres armeniennes tout a fait innocent', he protested, and
promised proof in his forthcoming memoirs. He begged Aubrey to meet
him in some neutral country, and asked Aubrey to write to him at a
secret address in Berlin under the name of Sahid Bey. He had no desire,
he claimed, to further any personal interests, only to help Turkey, but he
begged Aubrey, in the case of a refusal, to keep his address secret.

Aubrey, though well accustomed to Balkan atrocities, had been horrified and disgusted by the Armenian massacres. One third of the two
million Armenians in Turkey had been murdered. He drafted a reply to
Talaat: 'I need hardly tell you that all those who have known you in the
past will welcome most cordially the proofs of which you speak, which
show that you were innocent of the responsibility for the Armenian

massacres. There have been many horrible things done in the war but, to my mind, that was the most horrible of all.

'. . . I do not, however, think that a useful purpose will be served by my coming abroad to see you. Meanwhile it is not necessary for me to say that I shall of course respect your confidence.' But he never sent the letter.

It was not like Aubrey to desert a friend in distress. And Aubrey, in general, had kept faith with the Turks, and had never reviled them when crude patriotism had dictated condemnation. However, Talaat was another matter. He was deeply implicated in the Armenian massacres. He was a public enemy of England. Aubrey felt he could not meet him clandestinely without the approval of the British Government and this would not have been forthcoming. Later in 1921 he was to be charged with exactly such a mission, but in 1919 Aubrey felt little personal inclination to see Talaat. He felt, however, a deep commitment to Turkey and spoke often and forcibly in the House of Commons on Turkey's woes. Porchy Carnarvon thought Aubrey was making altogether too much fuss about Turkish affairs. He wrote: 'You must not only see through Turkish glasses. Remember they have not behaved well to England and that you are an Englishman first and as far as I know with no drop of Turkish blood.'

Aubrey did not see only through Turkish glasses. Mary insisted that he should also from time to time wear Irish glasses. Sometimes she insisted too much. In September 1919 Aubrey rebuked her in a letter, 'I am ready in my own way and in my own time to raise Cain over Ireland.' He had, in fact, already in an impromptu speech in the House in July, attacked Carson in terms which should have satisfied even Mary's violent partisanship. Carson had referred to the Third Home Rule Bill, on the statute book since 1914, as a 'putrescent corpse' which had angered Aubrey into making an ungentlemanly jibe about Carson's ignorance of the smells of a battlefield. In Aubrey's attack he also drew attention to the very different response to the war shown by the Nationalist leader John Redmond and his brother Major Willie Redmond. He praised the Redmonds and damned Carson whose Ulster Volunteers he called 'the uncle of Sinn Fein and the step-mother of trouble all over the Empire from Egypt to India.' One passage in Aubrey's speech caused a great deal of bother later. He had said, 'During this war, misers have given their money, widows their only sons, pacifists their blood; but Sir Edward Carson will give nothing, and this is in the name of loyalty to the Empire. It is the loyalty of Shylock.' This passage was misreported in the Belfast papers as 'Ulster had given nothing'. An immense flock of anonymous letters followed, generally headed 'swine', 'traitor', 'Judas'; also a

long correspondence with his old friend Freddie Dufferin that threatened, at one moment, to end in pistols and coffee in France. Aubrey was
not altogether proud of his outburst. He wrote to Mervyn the day after: 'I
have refrained from going to a dance of Walter Guinness because I made
an extraordinarily caddish speech about Carson. Such that I can hardly
look any public school man in the face again. All men are cads sometimes or other and I expect I shall forget it quick.'

In the autumn Aubrey spent a good deal of time in the constituency,
successfully patching up relations with his supporters. He found he had
a new constituent. Lord Curzon, who in October had become Foreign
Secretary, that year moved into Montacute House, which fell within the
boundaries of the South Somerset constituency. Aubrey, calling to see
Lady Desborough who was staying, found Curzon in. 'I wanted to talk to
him about the East', Aubrey wrote to his mother, 'but he went off after
tea to buy an abbey, as another man goes off to buy a bun. Lady Curzon
promised to make an appointment, and I went back to see him next
morning. I met him on the doorstep at half-past ten. He thought that I
had slept in the house unbeknownst, but was urbane and vice-regal. He
said he wanted to turn the Turks out of Constantinople, but to give them
back Smyrna.'

At the end of 1919 Aubrey's war diaries were published under the title
of *Mons, Anzac and Kut*. Porchy wrote, in his usual forthright way, 'I
don't like the title. Why call Gallipoli, Anzac?' There was considerably
less interest in the book than there would have been had Aubrey
appended his own name. It came out simply as 'by an M.P.'. The
reviews, on the whole, were friendly but lukewarm. Aubrey's own
friends admired the book extravagantly. T. E. Lawrence wrote 'it is the
best book on the war hitherto' while Compton Mackenzie wrote later in
Gallipoli Memoirs, 'from some incomprehensible dullness of perception
Mons, Anzac and Kut has never been acclaimed as one of the very best
books about the war in any language.' Ettie Desborough, who had lost
two sons in the war, wrote emotionally:

'Aubrey, my dearest, this letter is perhaps one of those best not
written, but you don't know how subtly you helped me, it was partly
you yourself and partly reading *Mons* and I do want to put my grateful-
ness into your exchequer . . . *Mons* gave the *scale* again and with that in
mind nothing is unendurable. As a document I don't believe you have
any idea how good it is, holding the tingle of life itself – the strange,
dynamic force, the sense of fate actually manipulating the hours visibly
that possessed those days . . .'

Many others from that circle of Souls and Slips recognised in *Mons,
Anzac and Kut* the authentic voice of their vanished world. A more

surprising admirer was an American literateur, Owen Wister, who wrote a sonnet in the *Atlantic Monthly* entitled 'On reading Mons Anzac & Kut' somewhat in the manner of Keats's 'On first looking into Chapman's Homer'. Nevertheless the book's commercial and critical failure was a disappointment to Aubrey.

Reginald Farrer also wrote a book about the war called *The Void of War*. Like Aubrey's it was unsuccessful. Reginald had stayed in the East. He wrote to Aubrey from Upper Burma in October 1919, 'I'm glad you've done a war book: send it to me. And I am glad you liked mine. It was but a poor thing and nobody read it.' Reginald was at pains to assure Aubrey of his contentment in the Far East. He resisted all importunities to come back:

> I am really doing the thing that suits me best in the world (next to sitting with you over a bottle) . . . In plain fact I can't very well go on living at Ingleborough while the Family rule and I haven't means or will to live anywhere else in England. Unless you want a lodgekeeper? . . . I do not see that I can do better than make plant-collecting my business in life, and be only too thankful for the miraculous mercy that turns one's greatest pleasure in living into a possible livelihood. So I propose to be out here another year and then come back to England via Peking, early in 1921.

Aubrey replied on 24th November 1919.

> . . . Now, if I were you, quite seriously, I should not wait until 1921 to return to this country. You've been away too long anyhow and people here are like leaves in Vallombrosa. I can give you no picture of the way in which things are changing. The war seemed to me, on the whole, to produce less violent changes than the peace is doing. One hears stories every day of statesmen suddenly talking nonsense in the middle of a conversation, and being led off to lunatic asylums, and other people having fits, so you had better return while some of your old friends still remain in possession of their sober senses. My yearning now is to get out of politics and go and travel, and if I don't share the fate of the others and become gaga in the night, I hope that it may be possible to do so within a couple of years . . . But the world is gradually closing round me. I can't go to Ulster, nor to Greece, nor to Albania and I expect I shall be in trouble if I go to Turkey.
>
> . . . I am going to stay at the Wharf* next Saturday. Many people think that Old Father will come back again to power but I doubt it. We are governed by a terrible lot of rapscallions now . . .

Reginald did not take Aubrey's advice. He never returned to England. In November 1920 he died in the East. Four months before he had written to Aubrey from his camp at Nyitadi in Upper Burma, 'There's no post, no mails, no white man within a month's journey, nothing whatever to remind me of that distressful insane world of the West.' He was happy but had, ironically, at last decided to come home and face the realities of life in England.

> Do come out and meet me, and go home with me. We are moving on together you and I as it is. Lord help but I *cannot* realize I am 40! I don't believe I have ever felt a day older than 25, nor ever shall . . . On one thing I am determined, when I come home, for which I shall earnestly beg the enlightened help and good offices of Mary and yourself. For I am resolved, now at last, to do my duty and get wed: Find me a fair one please, not particular about looks; and assist my diffidence in the matter . . . Against all evidence, I *hope* by now, that I am a trifle more seasoned and less selfish and silly than I've always been . . . Dear Mary, I know, is romantic, and says she will only help if a definite object is shown her. But you must make her see better: how *can* I have a specific object, after 7 years of wandering. No I am ready to make one now: but at my time of life I can't afford to waste any more years in mincing and mewing about and pretending grand passions. *My* grand passion, I've always known, will come after matrimony, not before it . . . but I do want preliminary help and meeting halfway. When it comes to the point, I'm so horribly distrustful of myself and my power and even my wishes . . . Don't think all this cold blooded and businesslike, or let Mary think so: to want to marry is very proper and usual . . . Anyhow there it is: a serious intention and a definite request. And I mustn't feel as if I were writing to the stores to choose me a soap!

The letter arrived only a few weeks before the news of Reginald's sudden death, making the improbable search for a bride unnecessary. Reginald was one of the last survivors of Aubrey's youthful friendships, and dying as he did, when the season for dying was closed, must have made his loss all the more bitter for Aubrey. For by the end of 1919 Aubrey had brought himself back to a mood of acceptance and faint hope. The revolution that everyone feared, had not happened. The survivors of his generation had begun their lives anew. At the end of December, Aubrey wrote to his Uncle Esmé, now ambassador in Spain: 'Sometime ago, an accidental truth fell from the lips of Lloyd George, when he said that all the world had got shell-shock . . . Shell-shock as you know, is generally both mental and physical, and there often comes a stage when the doctor can say that the patient is going to recover, but when he cannot prophesy the exact extent of the recovery . . . Well, I think that's about our stage. It's quite clear that we are going to recover . . .'

Although Aubrey was able to explain away post-war England as a case of shell-shock, although he could write with hope for the future, he remained profoundly unhappy and out of place in the world of 1919. The old assumptions by which he had lived, the easy and open friendliness that had guided his relations, the reliance on jokes, the trust in his fellow man – all these things were shaken in the rude, callous and profiteering atmosphere of post-war England.

Others in his diminished circle felt the same alienation. Gertrude Bell, at the end of an immensely long, pessimistic letter about the Middle East, wrote: 'I am writing to you of nothing but of nations and politics which is rather a waste because you're one of the few people (because you're one of the most understanding) to whom I might write of all the other things; the human things; of the growing sense of isolation, of having outlived the world to which I belonged, of having come to the end of the vitality which created a new one. Nevertheless you belong, as far as I'm concerned, to the old world . . .'

14

'The dear journey's end'

The new post-war world, disowned by Gertrude Bell, was not entirely devoid of attraction for Aubrey. Politics, at home and abroad, were keenly exciting while the affairs of Albania continued to command his crusading attention. On the home political front Aubrey's energies were fully stretched in an attempt to form a new, fourth party. By 1920, although still receiving the Conservative whip, Aubrey considered himself an Independent. In November that year he formally crossed the floor of the House in a gesture against the government's Irish policy and thereafter sat where he felt inclined.

The group of disaffected Conservative members who made up the new party looked to Lord Robert Cecil for leadership. He was, however, a most reluctant leader. The task was hardly onerous. The group was small. Besides Lord Robert and his brother Hugh Cecil, the nucleus of the party consisted of Aubrey, Lord Henry Cavendish-Bentinck, Godfrey Locker Lampson and a newcomer, the youngest MP in the new parliament, Oswald Mosley. Other MPs who at various times were loosely attached to the group included Walter Guinness (later Lord Moyne), Billy Ormsby Gore (later Lord Harlech), Sam Hoare (later Lord Templewood) and Edward Wood (later Lord Halifax).

Apart from the Cecil brothers and Bentinck, who were older, and Mosley, who was younger, the rest of the group were roughly of an age, had been at Eton or university together and were old friends and political allies. Aubrey's first mention of Mosley, the newcomer, in his diary of 1920 records a disparaging comment by the young David Cecil, nephew of Lord Robert: 'David Cecil said that Oswald Mosley had got hair that was too new and an unused face.' Lord David was eighteen at the time and Mosley twenty-four.

Mosley's vitality and eagerness, and the ferocity of his attacks on the government soon gained him a powerful place within the little group. It is not surprising that he sought admission. They were an attractive circle, combining high mindedness with wit, and polemics with laughter. In his autobiography Mosley wrote, 'These men were intermediate between me and an older generation and their attitude was strikingly irreverent' and he describes Aubrey 'with his subtle blend of charm and vagueness in manner which covered a very acute intelligence'. Aubrey's intelligence was evident in his own assessment of Mosley, written in November 1920 while the Mosleys were staying at Pixton. 'I think', Aubrey wrote in his diary, 'Mosley has the elements of great success in him but he will be a lost leader one day.' Aubrey did not live to see Mosley's metamorphosis from Independent Conservative to Labour to Fascist to lost leader but by 1922 as the fourth party began to crack up Aubrey sensed that Mosley had already lost his way. 'Tom Mosley', he wrote in his diary, 'is a fox who has lost his tail and wants the rest of us to do the same.'

It was their common detestation of Lloyd George's policies that really gave the group cohesion. Time and again Aubrey, Mosley and Bentinck spoke in the House against Lloyd George's licensing of terrorism in Ireland and the operations of the Black and Tans. Aubrey generally favoured conciliation in Irish matters. During the long hunger strike of Terence McSwiney, Mayor of Cork, Aubrey wrote a letter to *The Times* urging clemency and another to his friend Philip Kerr who, even after the war, had continued to work in Lloyd George's private secretariat at Downing Street, known as the Garden Suburb. It was a formal letter ending, 'I therefore wish to associate myself with those who asked the Prime Minister to release the Lord Mayor of Cork as an act of clemency. He [the P.M.] is on much safer ground when he is making peers than when he is making martyrs.'

The new party was not only opposed to the government's Irish policy, it was also critical of Lloyd George's Balkan adventures. This was particularly Aubrey's hobby horse. The licensing of terrorism in Ireland was something many Englishmen were aware of and rejected but the licensing of Greek imperialism against Turkey aroused less interest or indignation. The government's hostility towards Ataturk's Nationalist movement in Turkey was generally shared by the House of Commons. Aubrey's was a lone voice of dissent although other members of his group were sometimes prevailed upon to make speeches in Turkey's interest. Venizelos, the venerable prime minister of Greece who exerted over Lloyd George an enormous influence, was an old acquaintance of Aubrey's. On a visit to London Venizelos rebuked Aubrey for his anti-Greek speeches in the House, but as always, they parted friends, Venizelos saying: 'We must both do what we think best for our different countries'. Aubrey writing to George Lloyd commented: 'He is a most remarkable and attractive man – no wonder he walked round those apes in Paris, who were all busy scratching their own fleas.'

The third major policy plank in the platform of the new party was support for the League of Nations. Aubrey was a passionate believer in the League and stumped the country making speeches at League meetings.

However, these three issues were hardly enough to warrant a new political movement; nor was the composition of the group, so exclusively aristocratic, widely enough based to form the foundations of a party. But the real failure was one of leadership. Lord Robert was neither ambitious nor decisive. Another grave disability, possessed in varying degrees not only by Lord Robert but by all the Cecil clan ('the Great House of Tarquin', as Aubrey called them), was a set of fanatical and idiosyncratic Anglican convictions. Aubrey, who liked and admired Lord Robert, was driven to exasperation by the frequent manifestations of this mania. He records in his diary in March 1920, after a conversation between the group about the divorce laws, 'Walter [Guinness] and I looked at each other. They might have been monks in 1250. Bob would resign the whole world to flames to save the rubric of his precious Church. God destroy his politico-theology.' With the Cecils preoccupied with theology, Aubrey obsessed by Turkey, Mosley and Bentinck often diverted by wild schemes, the party stood little chance of success. By November 1922 Aubrey sadly noted that the experiment was over. 'Dined with Bob on Wednesday. It was obvious that we were broken up. T. Mosley had been opposed by a Conservative, Bob by a bitter Labour man. Bob had gone more "Conservative" than the rest of us . . . I admire Bob and understand his difficult circumstances, but his failing to lead is a loss, however few MPs he led. He stood for a great deal. I think he still does, but he has a diminished brightness.' Following that election Lord Robert took office in the first Baldwin administration and thus ended the attempt at a fourth party.

But if the formation of a new party was just another minor 'if' of English political history, there was another 'if' of a more exotic nature in which Aubrey was more centrally involved: a renewed offer of the crown of Albania. There was a longstanding tendency, among Aubrey's friends, to jest about Aubrey's likely translation to the throne of Albania Thus in April 1920 T. E. Lawrence had written, 'Albania seems to be revolting in several ways at once, and he [Aubrey] will probably assume its crown for a few weeks.' Lawrence was referring to a little unrest which culminated in a small armed revolt by the Essad Pasha faction. The revolt was easily subdued and in June Essad was murdered in Paris by an Albanian patriot. (Arni Rustem, the assassin, was treated as a hero when he returned to Albania but was himself murdered in 1924.)

Essad died unregretted by his countrymen and with his death came the promise of a new stability. Already the Albanians had felt confident enough to press for a withdrawal of the Italian occupation of Valona and its surrounding country. On 29th May 1920 the Albanian government, in which Mehmed Konitza was Minister for Foreign Affairs, sent an ultimatum to the Italian commander, demanding a return of the administration of Italian occupied territories. The Italian commander was still Piacentini, the unpleasant general who had refused to recognise Aubrey's Adriatic Mission in the last months of the war. His undiplomatic response to the Albanian ultimatum was gunfire. The Albanians responded in kind. The Italian army, weakened by malaria and communist propaganda, was routed, and on 2nd September the last Italian troops left Valona.

That same September the Albanian government authorised Mehmed Konitza to approach Aubrey and sound out his reactions to their desire to have him as their Mpret (prince). It was not a unanimous decision. There were a few who remained loyal to the house of Wied but it was realised that in the climate of post-war international opinion it was not politic to attempt to restore a German monarch.

On 6th September Aubrey wrote in a postcript to a letter to Mervyn, 'The A's (private) have invited me to be No. 1 big man.' Mervyn, serving under his Uncle Esmé Howard at the British Embassy in Madrid, replied excitedly:

I was so idiotic that to begin with I couldn't think who A's was. Of course it is obvious – it is a wonderful thing to happen – full of interest and in some ways I think it would be just the thing you would *like for a time* – but it is a thing which in itself is bound to be full of bitterness and disappointment unless you get really sincere promises of support – in the first place I imagine from ourselves and I trust the F.O. less as I see them more – less than ever if as I imagine will happen [Eyre] Crowe becomes head . . . I am awfully glad they have asked you and it was only right that they should. It is a thrilling thing – a romance which one doesn't think of as possible nowadays. Do write and tell me what you think of doing . . .

Aubrey wrote again on 22nd September: 'I have kept it v. dark here. I saw 2 people in London. Their eyes popped out of their heads. One said "Go to Alabaster" [Curzon], the other said "Go to L.G." But I did nothing. If it comes, it comes, and with guarantees, I will do my best. If not I am very happy here or at Porto and would welcome quiet. I am very fond of the particular people and said I was touched and honoured. It was so prettily put. Meanwhile I have broke a ligament in my leg which is a bore . . .'

The two people in London in whom Aubrey confided were Philip Kerr and Maurice Hankey. In his diary he gives an account of both interviews.

Kerr was one of those whose eyes had popped out of his head, and it was he who recommended seeing Curzon. The diary continues: 'I said no, I didn't want to. Then he said I had better make it a fait accompli, go to Albania, get myself proclaimed. I said I did not want to have the Rupert of Hentzau business – it was too like D'Annunzio. He then said I had better see Eric Drummond and go out under the League of Nations. I partly agreed but said there was more glamour about being a highland chieftain than Eric Drummond's butler.' Eric Drummond, later Lord Perth, was an old Foreign Office friend of Aubrey's. He had become the first Secretary General of the League of Nations.

In fact, despite Aubrey's disclaimer, this was just the solution that Aubrey had proposed to Mehmed. Mehmed had demurred saying the Albanians wanted a King and not a League of Nations Commissioner but he did not totally rule out the notion. He was worried however that if the Albanians approached the League of Nations the matter would be taken out of their hands and the League might appoint someone other than Aubrey. Eric Drummond, when Aubrey talked to him, confirmed Mehmed's fears. '. . . Eric said that . . . if the Albanians invoked the League of Nations they would probably have some American who knew nothing about it put over them. That, he said, was far and away the best plan . . .'

Meanwhile Hankey had been more encouraging. In his diary for 11th September Aubrey gives an account of the conversation: 'I asked if I could talk to him as Maurice Hankey and not as secretary of the Committee. He said yes. When I told him about Albania, he said he thought it the best solution, because I knew the Albanians well and got on with the Italians and Venizelos and as far as I had seen him, the Crown Prince of Serbia. He wanted to act as intermediary with Lloyd George, but I said no, not until I gave the word. He said I could not expect financial or physical support; we had too many commitments, Ireland, Mesopotamia, etc.'

Later in November Aubrey had a further discussion with Hankey.

November 26
I went to see Hankey and we had about an hour's talk. Hankey wanted to know if I expected guarantees. I said no; of course, if I could get it, help, but I would ask for English financial advisers etc., and if I could not get those, neutrals – Danes or someone like that. He asked me, if I got into trouble, should I expect help? I said no, it was a Maximilian sort of business. He asked me how much I had said to the Albanians. I said I had told them that I had told him and Philip Kerr, pledging both to secrecy. He said 'I am rather proud of that. Philip Kerr and I are the alter ego of each other and we have not told each other.' I said, 'Well, do tell each other now, but not Lloyd George.' I

asked him if he thought I would be justified in accepting, when really it ought to belong to another man – Wied. He said there was no chance of Wied coming back, or his people, as far as he could see. I said I wanted him to understand one thing. I disliked the Government and Lloyd George's policy and, as far as I was concerned, crowns and thrones might perish before I asked a personal favour of Lloyd George. He said he quite understood that, and undertook to get me the Albanian Treaty of 1913.

From this diary entry it can be seen how close Aubrey was to accepting some sort of responsibility for Albania, though in what form was still to be determined. Meanwhile, on the advice of Eric Drummond, Aubrey had got the Albanians to apply for entry to the League of Nations. It was for this that he needed a copy of the 1913 treaty.

The Albanian treaty of 1913 did not exist. Albania's application to the League of Nations was unencumbered with documentation. The Albanians themselves were faint-hearted and would have given up the attempt but for Aubrey's constant pressure. All through November and December he bullied, lobbied and wheedled. Fortunately he had a powerful ally in Lord Robert Cecil who was in Geneva at the time as South African delegate to the League of Nations nominated by General Smuts. In December as a result of Lord Robert's public advocacy and Aubrey's private machinations the battle was won. Albania became a member of the League and her nationhood was assured.

Meanwhile in Albania there was a change of government. Mehmed Konitza lost his job as Foreign Minister and with his departure Aubrey's candidature to the throne gradually lapsed. J. Swire in his authoritative history of Albania, *The Rise of a Kingdom*, thus records the stories surrounding the crown of Albania:

Ludicrous reports appeared to the effect that Albania was seeking, and even advertising for a king! And it was alleged that the throne had been offered to all manner of people. It is said that Colonel Aubrey Herbert, who was largely responsible for the existence of Albania and had worked indefatigably in the cause of Albanian independence, was asked quite unofficially, whether if the throne were offered to him, he would accept it; but certainly it was offered to no one else, except perhaps by propagandists wishing to discredit Albania or by journalists as a practical joke.

An adventurer named Barnes offered it at a later date to the Duke of Atholl, but the crown was not in Barnes's gift. Atholl consulted Aubrey who advised against involvement. Aubrey continued working for Albania but there were few services left for him to perform after admission into the League of Nations had been secured. His old friends, the founding fathers, as it were, of the national state, sank into gradual eclipse, while the star of Ahmed Zogu rose. Faik Konitza, Mehmed's brother, wrote bitterly to Aubrey from America in 1922 about his work reorganising Vatra.

> It was meant as a society for the independence of Albania. Now I would like to turn it into a society for the political education of the Albanian people. This is hard enough, because I have no more my first faith. I am somewhat in the position of a monk who believes no more in God or the Church but continues to wear the frock for fear of wounding the feelings of his pupils, followers and friends. The Albanian people has some very fine qualities and the peasantry has given of late splendid proofs of endurance, patience, love of progress and order. But a gang of crooks, grafters, spies and upstarts has managed to occupy all the leading strategic positions in the body politic and it is more than useless to try and get rid of them. Under such conditions, I don't think there is much hope for the salvation of the country.

Faik did not even spare his brother Mehmed from his condemnation. His letter continues in tones of harsh and in the main unjust criticism: 'My brother, two years ago, was the most popular man in Albania, and he could have succeeded in making any reform he liked. He, however, preferred to gossip in the lobbies of the Paris hotels, instead of going to Albania, and so gave a chance to the lower elements who captured the strongholds.' Faik's disillusion was not shared by Aubrey, but as new stars rose in the Albanian firmament and old stars flickered and failed, his interest in Albanian affairs became more distant. Sometimes, like Faik, he would weary of what he called 'the bed sitting rooms of stuffy Balkan politics'. His love of Albania had been born of open-air travels and adventures, but his service to Albania was now confined to sorting out squabbles in smoke-filled rooms.

His love of Turkey brought more amusing tasks. In February 1921, at the request of Sir Basil Thomson of Scotland Yard's Special Branch, he travelled out to Germany for a secret meeting with Talaat. Lord Robert Cecil, when Aubrey confided to him his mission, was shocked. 'Good Heavens! Who on earth runs our Foreign Policy? Scotland Yard?' he said in outraged tones.

Talaat, whom Aubrey met in Hamm, had changed. 'He had grown thinner, and his good looks were sinister; his black hair was turning grey; his eyes were very bright. The urbanity of his manners remained the same. He was neat and well dressed, but obviously poor.'

Disliking Hamm, Aubrey persuaded Talaat to move. Together they boarded a train for Dusseldorf. In his diary Aubrey described an encounter on the journey.

We took an empty second class compartment, but as we left the station a German engineer entered our carriage. Talaat said, in Turkish, to me, 'We cannot talk French in Germany; it is too unpopular, and I do not know English. We had therefore better talk Turkish.' [Talaat's French in any case was far from good. Maurice Baring told Aubrey he had once heard Talaat say, very loudly, at a concert 'Elle chante comme un canard'; he had meant to say 'She sings like a nightingale'.]

The German engineer, who was intelligent and bloodthirsty, interrupted politely, 'Was fur eine Sprache sprechen Sie?' (What language are you talking?) 'Turkish', said Talaat, and for some time we all three talked bad German, which he occasionally translated, for my benefit, into Turkish.

Then Talaat said to me, speaking in Turkish: 'A curious thing has happened. This German believes that you also are a Turk, as he hears you talk Turkish to me. Now, for the first time, you are going to hear the whole truth about the Allies and your own country.' I said to Talaat, 'Please do not lead him on, for if he attacks my country I shall answer him.' Talaat's reply was 'This conversation is going to be extremely interesting for me, and it will be a very good test for your temper.'

The German, answering Talaat's skilful questions, said that he believed . . . that England and Germany could come to terms without difficulty, for, although they were rivals, they had many common interests. It was a different matter when he spoke of the French. He spoke of France with unmeasured and immeasurable bitterness. 'Fighting, conquering and being beaten Germans understand,' said he, 'we would be hypocrites to pretend anything else. We have been beaten, and we accept our defeat. Essen was the pride of our country; it made guns, it was the strength of Germany; now we must make sewing machines instead of machine-guns. What we do not understand is all this sanctimonious talk to which we are being subjected in our humiliation. Let conquerors dictate their terms as conquerors; do not let them pretend that there is civilisation or Christianity behind them when they inflict such terms upon us . . .'

The German engineer had been to Russia. 'Petrograd is a very sad place now', said he. 'It always was a sad place,' replied Talaat. 'The Russian is a kind man; he is a brute when he is in a crowd. Bolshevism is the essence of the Russian crowd.'

At Essen the German engineer got out, with cordial farewells to his Turkish ally, mixed with a great blast of invective against the French. 'We are beaten, utterly beaten', said he; 'but you cannot keep a nation such as ours down for ever. We will never forget the French insults, and the black troops, and the time will come when our children, or our grandchildren, will march into France, and we will finish with the French once and for all. I shall not see it, but I am happy in the knowledge that it will come to pass.

During the two days they spent together, Aubrey and Talaat had managed to cover every subject of interest to Sir Basil Thomson and much more beside. They got on easily and well together. They enjoyed the same jokes. After their last dinner, Talaat summoned the head waiter and asked him where he had served during the war. The waiter revealed that he had been in Turkey. Talaat was delighted. 'Then you were with us,' he said. It was a trick that always pleased Talaat – to associate himself with Aubrey. 'You saw what a nice people we are.' 'Yes', said the head waiter, expecting a tip. 'And', said Talaat, 'did you ever know Talaat Pasha?' 'No,' said the waiter, 'did you ever know minnenwerfur?' which made both Aubrey and Talaat laugh.

The next day they parted. Aubrey returned to London and Talaat returned to Berlin. There on 15th March 1921, three weeks later, he was assassinated by a Persian Armenian. The obituaries in the English press were savage. Aubrey in an article for *Blackwood's* magazine, wrote more generously: 'He died hated, indeed execrated as few men have been in their generation. He may have been all that he was painted – I cannot say. I know that he had a rare power and attraction. I do not know whether he was responsible or not for the Armenian massacres. All I know is that he was fearless; and anyone who, like myself, only knew him superficially, found him to be kindly and with a singular charm.'

Later that year, in the summer, when Aubrey revisited Germany, untrammelled by old friendships or secret missions, on his way to Constantinople, he found the country more prosperous and the people less bitter. The state of Austria, however, he found deeply shocking. 'It really makes one sick with rage to talk to the poor people,' he wrote to Mary. In his diary he wrote, 'Vienna is like a starving lady or a broken violin, and the lady will have to go on starving and the violin remain broken until an end comes to all this silly hatred.'

Czechoslovakia ('a ridiculous cubist name' according to Aubrey) which he visited on his way to Austria, interested him. He had a long talk with Edward Benes, the Foreign Minister, and described him in his diary, 'a young man, about 37, small, like his country. He is the end of the west, not the beginning of the east: quiet, not impatient.'

In Hungary, Aubrey called on the Regent, Admiral Miklos Horthy. Aubrey described him as a 'short, dark man with a good deal of magnetism, and a great presence'. Horthy spoke what Aubrey described as 'capital English'; his favourite adjective of abuse was 'caddish'. Many people and nations were thus censored. Horthy's conversation was almost exclusively sporting. 'He knows nothing of politics,' Aubrey wrote.

In Belgrade, the capital of the new Yugoslavia, Aubrey had no friends and made no calls. He was briefly detained in a police station after his

landlady had denounced him as a Turk. Aubrey had never liked the
Serbs. He liked them no better after this little incident.

Leaving Belgrade by train he discovered that the Bulgarian Prime
Minister, Stambolisky was a fellow passenger. Aubrey had met him the
year before when Stambolisky had visited England, and described him
then in his diary: 'he looked like a brigand, moving through a blackberry
bush'.

Stambolisky, when approached by Aubrey on the train, at first had no
recollection of him, but gradually memory returned and with it a genial
welcome. Aubrey stayed some time in the Bulgarian compartment and
then repaired to bed.

At Sofia there was a great reception for Stambolisky. 'I was hauled
into it', Aubrey wrote, 'and stood by him rather sheepishly. Then I was
given a motor and a detective and sent off to the Union Palace Hotel.'
Aubrey called on the young King Boris (his father Ferdinand had abdi-
cated at the end of the war). Aubrey liked Boris, ('a charmer'). Another
day he went to see Malinoff ('a very smart man'). Malinoff had a grasp
of European politics beyond the limits of King Boris or Stambolisky. 'If
Stambolisky is Cleon,' Aubrey wrote in his diary, 'Malinoff is Pericles or
if Stambolisky is a rustic Ll.G, he is Asquith.' Stambolisky was murdered
in 1923. By that time his idealism had become clouded by his irrational
and violent hatred of urban dwellers, whom he persecuted in what
became known as the Green Terror.

Three weeks after he had left England Aubrey arrived in Constantinople, penniless through improvidence. He was shocked by the condition of his beloved city. He wrote to his mother, 'the town is a disgrace.
There is robbery and no morals anywhere. Nothing like it would have
been allowed in the old Turkish days.' The first person Aubrey met was
his old friend Rifat. Rifat had written the year before that he awaited
Aubrey's arrival 'as manna'. After they had embraced each other
Aubrey said to Rifat: 'I must have money.' 'What do you want?' asked
Rifat. 'Fifteen hundred,' said Aubrey. 'Tomorrow morning, my dear,'
said Rifat, 'I can't do it now.' 'Alright,' said Aubrey, 'I will get it from
the porter.' 'I thought you meant pounds not piastres,' said Rifat.

Rifat put himself in charge of Aubrey. This involved a great number of
formal calls. 'They have been after me like a pack of very kind wolves,'
Aubrey wrote to Mary. 'A little more and I should go mad.' The first day
Aubrey saw Marshal Izzet, the Foreign Minister, 'a nice fat jolly man'.
The same day he saw Ali Riza, Minister of the Interior, and his old friend
Tewfik, who was now Grand Vizier. Later he paid formal calls on the
Sultan, Mohammed V, and the Heir Apparent, Abdul Mejed.

Kiazim turned up on Aubrey's second day in Constantinople and overwhelmed Aubrey with his welcome. Although Kiazim had a job and one with which he was well pleased, working for 'many Lords' as he boasted to Aubrey, he immediately returned to his duties with his old master. He loftily explained that his new Lords, the Intelligence, would give him all necessary leave to protect Aubrey as his life was so much more important than they or their work. Kiazim did not know that his Lords, British Military Intelligence, regarded Aubrey suspiciously and had already put him under surveillance. What was more absurd was that the officer in charge of keeping Aubrey under surveillance was his nephew, Henry Porchester. Porchester, whom Aubrey found an endearing and amusing lad, at once confided in his uncle his mission. Aubrey had been aware that he was being shadowed from his first day in Constantinople and was unconcerned. He knew that both British and Greek Intelligence were watching him but he was confident he could always lose any shadows in Constantinople. He amiably demonstrated to Porchester his prowess, using the simple expedient of entering by the front of a shop and leaving by the back.

Kiazim, who was probably the only man who could have successfully shadowed Aubrey, meanwhile briefly re-entered his service. Although very boastful about his present position, he was a little reticent about how he had fared in the intervening years. During the war he had been exiled as a British spy. On his return he had started a café but it had been ill patronised and soon closed. Then he had felt it necessary to kill a man and had spent a year in prison. Aubrey describing these misadventures to Mary wrote, 'Poor K'. Poor K. however was in jubilant form. It was not his way to dwell on the past and the present was rosy. So confident did he feel that he suggested that Aubrey should chaperone him to Albania, where he longed to return but was uncertain of his welcome. Aubrey, however, had no intention of visiting Albania, where his presence would have given rise to many complications. The place he wished to visit was Angora (Ankara), the seat of the Nationalist Government.

In England, Aubrey had been approached several times by Turkish intermediaries, suggesting that he should meet Mustafa Kemal (Ataturk). For although Aubrey was on friendly terms with the puppet government in Constantinople he had made no secret of his sympathetic leaning towards the Nationalist cause or his conviction that the Allies could and should come to terms with Angora. He had come out to Turkey with the clear intention of meeting Kemal but he was thwarted in his desire by the British Ambassador, Sir Horace Rumbold, who appealed to Aubrey, on a personal basis, not to go. Rumbold was in an embarrassing position. Three months earlier, the French government had despatched Franklin-Bouillon, President of the Senate Committee on Foreign Affairs, on a semi-official and semi-informal mission to Turkey. Franklin-Bouillon was still in Turkey, but in Konia, not Constantinople. He had been to Angora and although the British did not yet know the substance of his talks with the Nationalists, they were deeply suspicious. Rumbold had protested vehemently and suspected a military convention between France and the Kemalist forces. He felt that his protests at French behaviour would be weakened and made absurd if Aubrey were now to follow Franklin-Bouillon hotfoot to Angora for unofficial talks. Aubrey had no wish to embarrass Rumbold and saw the point of his argument. It was only later in October when the Franklin-Bouillon pact was published that the full significance of that visit was realised. The French had entered into a separate treaty with Turkey and broken any semblance of Allied unity over the occupation of Turkey.

So Aubrey left Turkey without visiting Angora, or Albania. He wrote in his diary on his penultimate day in Constantinople: 'I told Kiazim this morning that we must go by different boats; that we could not go to Albania for a lot of reasons. He looked very old and frail, but only said, "As you order". Ten minutes later I felt that I had been beastly to him and went and asked him if he was unhappy. He said, no, but he had thought we were never going to have any talk at all, and it was years since we had met, and he wanted to know about everybody, Mary, Maman, and all the family. I felt I had been a brute and we went off and had a long talk . . .'

By the end of their talk Kiazim had recovered his spirits enough to censure Aubrey for eating fruit in the street. Kiazim saw him off disconsolately though neither knew that they would never meet again. Aubrey was able to render one last service for his old servant. In September 1922 Aubrey received a letter from Ahmed Zogu, later better known as King Zog of Albania, then Minister of the Interior, assuring him that 'Kiazim Kokeli has already been employed'. The letter does not specify the employment but it must have been government service. In old age, therefore, Kiazim was able to return to his native land in peace and honour through Aubrey's intervention.

Meanwhile, within Aubrey's family circle there were some changes. In June 1921, before his Turkish visit, he had, with Mary, gone out to Madrid, for Mervyn's marriage to the daughter of the American Ambassador. Elizabeth Willard, the bride, was a tall, graceful American girl, a considerable heiress, to whom Mervyn had long paid court. Mervyn's wife was not the only addition to the family circle in these years. On 25 April 1922 Mary gave birth to a son. The boy was christened Auberon Mark Henry Yvo Molyneux; Auberon for Bron Herbert, Mark for Mark Sykes, Henry for Henry Bentinck, his godfather, Yvo for Mary's father Yvo de Vesci and Molyneux because it was the family name of the original owners of Teversal. Mary was overjoyed at producing a son after three daughters. Aubrey affected indifference, writing to Mervyn, 'I am glad it is a boy for Mary's sake, but I like girls better than boys.' Aubrey was indeed by now devoted to his girls, although the eldest, Gabriel, a wayward and original child, had captured the lion's share of his affections. The only clouds on his domestic horizon were financial.

From the end of the war it had been clear that Aubrey's books did not balance. For some time he refused to take the matter seriously. By January 1920, however, a reckoning could no longer be delayed. Elsie Carnarvon, as always, came to the rescue. She gave an immediate gift of £4,000, but on examining the accounts, discovered that a more radical approach was necessary. With considerable self-sacrifice she arranged to sell some of the farms of the Teversal estate. Aubrey felt sad and ashamed, noting in his diary that 'Teversal land never passed before for money'. In return Elsie demanded certain economies. Mary found these demands irksome and bridled under her mother-in-law's charges of mismanagement. Aubrey wrote, 'I am sorry about Maman. She gives everything but demands irrelevant and agonizing inquisitions' and, 'Criticism is nothing but a habit, desire to help is a passion.'

In the end the economies were not onerous. Pixton and Portofino were maintained at full strength and only the London house in Bruton Street was sacrificed and let for a large rent. Since Aubrey and Mary still needed a London base, Margot Howard de Walden lent them the top floor of Seaford House in Belgrave Square. Aubrey wrote in his diary: 'The results of poverty are very ironical. We have taken the Howard de Walden's top storey, and live in magnificence above a staircase of onyx and jasper. When Evan [Charteris] lunched, he destroyed his cufflinks, which were of onyx, because he said it was unworthy to wear what another man walked on.'

There was no reduction of entertaining at either Pixton or Portofino. Indeed in the darkest days of financial crisis, the Visitors' Book at Pixton was more than usually replete. There are some bizarre entries. In January 1921, King Faisal, the son of the Sherif of Mecca with whom Aubrey had made friends in Paris during the Peace Conference, came to stay with his ADC General Haddad and T. E. Lawrence. Faisal's fortunes were at a low ebb. Deposed by the French from the throne of Syria, he lived in London, while his friends busied themselves trying to find him another throne. 'He bears his misfortunes grandly,' Aubrey wrote. In London they played many games of chess together; Aubrey was usually the loser. Mary, however, had never met Faisal before he came to stay at

Pixton and wrote a description to her mother: 'The Emir – with great dignity and good looks and perfect English clothes, instead of the usual green flannel and yellow boot compromise of the oriental. Then, General Haddad very large, cunning and English – and little Lawrence, attractive but walking in his own halo. In the evening bridge and chess . . . Very odd tower of Babel mealtimes. He could talk a bit of French but vastly preferred talking about us in Arabic. Turkish talks with Aubrey. Quite good food. His own coffee and coffee cups . . .'

Whatever language Faisal talked at meals his comments were always delivered in the form of proverbs. One he produced at lunch 'everybody thinks their own lice gazelles' made the company sit up. Later in London Aubrey noted how discontented Faisal was becoming. He wrote in his diary: 'I was sorry for Faisal. He is always an eagle in prison. Now he is becoming an irritable eagle.' However his time of trial and waiting was nearly at an end. On 7th April Faisal left London. The day before he left he came to say goodbye to Aubrey. 'He said that the future was dark before him, that he would probably be ruler of Mesopotamia, that he was grateful to his English friends and hoped never to lose them.' Four months later Faisal became King of Iraq.

Lawrence, who had fought hard for Faisal, was pleased with the fruits of his labour; but his success did nothing to help exorcise his own private demons. In November 1922, after the General Election that brought to an end the Lloyd George coalition, he wrote to Aubrey:

The pretext of this letter is your re-election by your usual absurd majority which you would get if you declared yourself a Bolshevik or a Wee Free or a Prohibitionist, or a Mormon. It's a personal tribute and as such rather a jolly thing though in your place I'd be a bit sick of getting it so often!

But the real reason of the letter was a paragraph a while ago that your eyes were getting worse – that you might lose their sight entirely. I hope it isn't true or that if true you have accustomed yourself by now to it. It wouldn't be tactful for me to say that it seems to me a horror: and anyway you are sure to find a laugh somewhere in it: but I want to say that I'm more sorry than I can ever tell you about it and that if I didn't write earlier it was because I had hoped to see you and put it less coldly than by ink and paper.

However I can't come: because I went off some months ago and enlisted as the surest and cheapest way out of politics. You can ask for the Chiltern Hundreds: I can only get out of sight in the ranks and under another name. It's a quaint life for me, but so quaint as to seem unreal and therefore by no means harsh. Please keep the fact of it to yourself. I quote it only to explain why I've never called and why I can't call in the near future.

The paragraph about Aubrey's eyes, that Lawrence had seen in a newspaper, was unhappily all too true. Four months earlier, in July

1922, Aubrey in the middle of a speech, was visited by a spell of total blindness. He did not at first realise the gravity of what had happened. In his diary he wrote: 'I took an overdose of quinine, or rather a number of them. I went off to speak, seeing very darkly, to the Eastern Association, and when I got up, it may have been nerves, but utter darkness followed and I could neither see the audience nor my notes. This made my speech more violent than it would have been and it is a disconcerting thing to happen.' Oculists when consulted advised rest. What had happened was the beginning of the detachment of the retina of his right eye. This had been the one dread drawback that Elsie had weighed against the advantages of the operation for the division of the lens all those years ago at Wiesbaden. Mary and Aubrey obstinately clung to the belief that all that was wrong was a temporary side effect of an overdose of quinine.

Mary wrote to Mervyn, 'I don't quite know what to tell you about Aubrey's eyes. They don't seem much better yet, but if it is quinine it apparently takes a long time to clear off . . . I somehow feel confident myself but the other is so awful to contemplate. Aubrey is marvellously good about it. He gets every now and then quite clear sight but he compares it to the wrong end of a telescope.' For most of the time, however, Aubrey could see only dimly and depended on the blurred use of his very short-sighted left eye. Sometimes the right eye would suffer a total eclipse.

In August Aubrey began to realise or admit to himself the full implications of what had happened. Until then he had still struggled to lead a normal life, visiting the House of Commons ('I find, now that I can't see, it is very useful having the gift of distinguishing voices'). By the middle of August, however, on his oculist's advice, he took to his bed. He lay blindfolded in a darkened room with cushions and sandbags round his head. In his diary, which he continued to dictate most days, he wrote: 'I have been in a cruel temper the last week for which I pardon myself as if you lose your sight you are subject to a strain.'

Moreover it was a cruel time for him to be incapacitated. In Turkey, the nationalists finally lost patience with the Allies, attacked the Greeks and drove them from Smyrna. The victorious Turkish army swept on to the straits and reached Chanak where it threatened the small British force that held the neutral zone. Lloyd George, who had not abandoned his philhellenism with the fall of Venizelos saw the opportunity of restoring his flagging popularity with some foreign fireworks. He needed an external threat to bring back some unity and dynamism to his tired and failing coalition. In March 1922 Aubrey had written to Mary, 'I think it is near the end, the weary end of a dreary pantomime with the paint falling off the chief clown', but he was anticipating the fall of Lloyd George by seven months. That fall, for which Aubrey had yearned and worked was fittingly in the end encompassed by Lloyd George's Turkish policy. Although the Chanak crisis was defused by the English general on the spot, the confidence of the people, and more importantly of the Tory party, had been shaken. The country had been recklessly taken to the brink of war in an unnecessary and irrelevant quarrel. However, Lloyd George, Churchill and Birkenhead, all aroused and exhilarated by what they saw as their victorious stand against Turkish aggression, believed that the moment was ideal to call a General Election. It was to be a sort of khaki election, called in the wake of a war fever they alone had felt. In the cabinet, only Stanley Baldwin dissented. The Conservatives re-emerged as an independent party with Bonar Law as leader. Aubrey did not campaign in the election that followed. Mr Asquith sent him a riddle that he said always went down well at election meetings:

Q   What must a man do to bathe safely among sharks?
A   Have tattooed on his back 'Lloyd George won the war'. No shark could swallow that.

But Aubrey held no meetings. He had written to his constituency association offering to resign, explaining about his eyes and for the first time acknowledging that he might remain blind. They had unanimously asked him to continue, blind or not. Aubrey travelled down for the count. As Lawrence wrote, he had been re-elected by his usual 'absurd majority'. Elsewhere, Labour made huge gains while the National Liberals, under Lloyd George, suffered huge losses. The Conservatives were returned to power.

For Aubrey, these changes were now of secondary interest. His whole being was bent on the struggle to save his sight. The loss of hope of recovery came slowly. In December 1922, four months after the first premonitory eclipse, Aubrey travelled out to Germany to see Pagenstecker. Before he left he had seen every leading eye man in England inside and outside the profession. Some held out hope, others advised the immediate removal of the right eye to give the left eye a better chance. Lord Grey of Falloden, now almost completely blind himself, wrote touchingly, 'Indeed I feel for you', and dwelt on the comfort of braille, offering to help Aubrey with it.

Aubrey trusted Pagenstecker totally so when the old man shook his head as he looked at the right eye, hope was at last extinguished. Pagenstecker held out some hope for improving the sight of the left eye. Aubrey wrote to his mother, 'He thinks he can so improve the sight of the

242 THE MAN WHO WAS GREENMANTLE

left eye that I shall be able to shoot off the left shoulder. That would be a very great deal to attain.'

It was never attained. Aubrey remained blind for the nine months of his life that remained. At extremely close quarters, his long nose touching the paper, he could read and write using his left eye. There are handwritten letters from him of this period and they are not noticeably more ill-written than his usual scrawls. He could not see a yard across a room but he had, through years of bad sight and a boyhood of near blindness, developed his other sensitory gifts. In April 1923, after visiting yet another oculist in Paris with the usual results, he allowed his English oculist, Elliot, to remove the right eye. His daughter Bridget wrote to him in round childish hand, 'I hope you are well and happy', but for some reason she scratched out the word happy.

Aubrey did not have much to be happy about. A fortnight earlier his half-brother Porchy Carnarvon had died. Aubrey wrote in his diary, 'one never knows how much one cares for a person until it is too late.' Porchy died in a blaze of publicity. For many years he had financed the excavations of Howard Carter in the Valley of the Kings in Luxor. In the *Dictionary of National Biography* Porchy appears under the label Egyptologist but in truth he was no scholar. He was a gambler and the gamble of a lifetime came off when Howard Carter discovered the tomb of Tutankhamun. Porchy had travelled out to Egypt for the opening of the tomb. He wrote to Aubrey on 6th March 1923:

I have had a somewhat unpleasant time out here. The papers have been quite poisonous but that I don't mind. What at the present is fussing me is the state of Egypt. The whole business has been allowed to drift and the only thing to do is to get rid of Allenby. That is the first step and one that ought to be taken at once. He has been very weak, is badly advised, and I am sorry to say drinks. The last statement is confidential, but one day is sure to come out as I am not the only person who has seen him in that state. I am sorry for him, he is very straight, but slow and rather stupid. Nothing good will happen until King Faud has been definitely told that he must behave or go and Allenby cannot do this . . .

This typically cantankerous letter from Porchy was to be his last communication to Aubrey. Soon after he was bitten by a mosquito on the cheek. Blood poisoning set in, followed by pneumonia. He died in the early hours of 5th April 1923. It was ironic that having won such a gambler's throw, he should lose all through a mosquito bite. There were many who saw his death as more than ironic. The curse of the boy king Tutankhamun was popularly invoked as the cause of Porchy's death; a myth which persists to this day.

Soon after Porchy's death Aubrey left England with Mary and the children to spend a month at Portofino. There he worked on a travel book (*Ben Kendim*), compiled from diaries of old adventures. T. E. Lawrence to whom he had sent some extracts in February, wrote:

> I don't know what to liken it to – perhaps an Egyptian necklace of figured beads, whose string has snapped: – it's beautiful stuff, (Persian Gulf and Riza better than Yemen) the best material for a book that ever was, but it's not a book yet.
>
> In your place I'd retire to a solitary place and have the stuff read to me by a slave, again and again. Then I'd dismiss the slave and dream over those times until all the adventures came together. Then I'd dictate a slow story of my progress: avoiding so far as possible, what is here put: then I'd use this as the bag of plums and sift them slowly into the new cake, and stir them together with a third version, which would be a book of books.
>
> This advice is presumptuous, from me to you: but it is so very good that I long to see you make more of it. Can't you give up politics for a year or two and write something as good as you clearly can? Circs make it trebly hard for you but it's worth trying surely.

In Portofino Aubrey took Lawrence's advice and, tranquilly and nostalgically, listened to his diaries as they were read to him, and then dictated to his secretary. There were interruptions. In May he was visited by Bonar Law, who had not yet resigned the premiership but was stricken, though he did not know it, with a fatal throat cancer. Aubrey wrote an account of their meeting in his diary.

> I was shocked to meet Bonar: he seemed a broken man, quite different to what I had ever seen him before. He treated me like a long lost brother. After talking about my eye, he said, 'You know, it's no good. I shall have to give it up unless I get my voice back in the next ten days. They say there's nothing wrong with my voice. It is because I am so run down.' I said, 'Do give up for two months and have a complete rest. People didn't like L.G.'s doing that because it is unconstitutional and he did it for fun, but this is a matter of health.' He said he wouldn't do it; whom did I think the best man to follow him? I said 'Stanley Baldwin in the House.' He said, 'He's a good man and has improved a lot. They like him.' I said, 'He is like you, very straightforward and never sells the future for the present.' 'I think that's true', he said. 'What about Curzon?' I said half England spent their time making up stories about him: no man had more talent and less judgement. 'Yes,' he said. Derby, he thought, had no qualifications in the way of mind. I said, 'Whatever happens, you have put us on our feet again.' 'I have been an interim', he said, 'I think it has done good. How changed Ll.G's position is.' . . . He said he had told him [Lloyd George] again and again to resign and take a rest; that the coalition was not popular. I said it

was hard for demi gods to become mortals. They had all been affected the
same way, except him. He said, 'Oh, I am an accident . . .'

Later they talked about the Fascist movement in Italy. Bonar Law
asked Aubrey if he thought it would last. Aubrey, although he did not
share his mother's enthusiasm ('Fascismo is thrilling, I am full of hope'
and 'Mussolini is a wonder', she wrote), was extremely interested in the
movement. He felt unable, however, to prophesy. Bonar Law had met
Mussolini in Rome. He told Aubrey that he thought him 'very capable
but inexperienced, tenacious and cruel'.

Later Aubrey heard, from Ronald Graham, who had become ambassador in Rome, why Bonar Law thought Mussolini cruel. During lunch
with Mussolini Bonar had said, 'What do you think of Socialists?'
Mussolini had replied, 'I had sixty of them to dinner with me and then
had forty-eight shot. That's what I think of Socialists.' Ronald Graham
claimed that it was a lie, but the kind that it pleased Mussolini to tell.

In July 1923 Aubrey attended a gaudy at Balliol. He was not haunted
by ghosts of the past but wrote in his diary that he 'had as happy a time as
I have had for an age, though I was made too much the pièce de
resistance in the speeches'. Indeed in speech after speech Aubrey was
commemorated. Mr Asquith spoke of his gift of 'unanticipated information', while another dwelt on how his career at Oxford had been in
defiance of the laws of gravity and gravitation and commented that if
Newton had taken Aubrey instead of an apple, it would have upset the
whole of his theories.

The next day he spent an hour with the Master, his old tutor A. L.
Smith, who, also nearly blind, claimed that blind people were the
happiest on earth. During the course of their talk the Master gave
Aubrey some very bad, indeed fatal, advice. He urged Aubrey to have all
his teeth taken out. The Master, in accordance with a theory popular at
the time, believed that teeth and eyes were closely linked (a theory to
which Lord Grey also subscribed). He had cheerfully had all his own
removed and declared himself delighted with the result.

Soon after the gaudy Aubrey's health began to give cause for concern.
Previously it had been unusually good. In June 1922, after a visit to a
doctor, he reported to Mary that the doctor 'said I had the complexion
and the morals of a debutante. Envied me my youth and partly coloured
hair. Said I must not eat curry before breakfast . . .' In August 1923
Aubrey visited a doctor again. This time the doctor did not envy him.
Aubrey reported in his diary on 12th August, 'I stayed with Jasper and
Natalie [Ridley] and then felt very ill and went to a doctor who said I
was very ill and would surely die, but then I went to see him after two

days and he said I would surely live if I stayed in bed, which I have done.'
What the doctor did not say, however, because he failed to diagnose it,
was that Aubrey had a duodenal ulcer. And Aubrey not knowing it,
feeling ill, struggled to lead a normal life, resting more than usual, but
otherwise living in his customary whirl of foreigners and friends. That
August Pixton was crammed: the Visitors' Book shows that forty-four
people stayed between the first of August and the beginning of September.

In the second week of September, perhaps in deference to the prompt-
ings of the Master of Balliol, perhaps in answer to a twinge of toothache,
Aubrey visited a local dentist and had several teeth extracted. From this
needless extraction an infection was born which led to blood-poisoning.
Septicaemia, before the days of antibiotics, was usually fatal. The end is
soon told: bloodpoisoning; sudden agony in the night as the ulcer burst;
a dash to London; hospital, an operation; and death. He died on 23rd
September 1923, aged forty-three.

A few weeks before he died Aubrey wrote a poem. In this poem he
seemed to accept, with resignation, his blindness and the end of a life of
adventure, and to draw comfort from old memories and dreams.

> Gold-dusted memories of the Past
>   Abide like friends, but falter,
> Like morning mirages that last,
>   Yet lasting, later alter.
>
> Ah, was that mountain quite so high
>   And had its flowers that scent?
> Could winds be friendly and as shy
>   That filled night's starlit tent?
>
> And did it taste so good, that wine
>   At the dear journey's end,
> Beneath the whispering island pine,
>   Beside a singing friend?
>
> God knows the answer to these things,
>   Man is a dreamer, age and youth,
> And none forget the sound of wings,
>   No rainbow's traitor to the truth.
>
> And if these colours were not fair
>   As memory paints, still let them stand
> To be as perfect and as rare
>   As all the ghosts of that dreamland.

But was his acceptance really complete? Aubrey left one last poem, quite different in mood. It was a poem that came to him in a dream, and it is recorded in the penultimate entry of his diary, dated 4th September:

> I had a dream last night and went into Mary's room this morning to repeat it to her and make her remember it. The first lines were simply my dream, without any correction. The third I wrote when I was awake:
>
>> Ambition was amusement, but now ambition's dead,
>> So take, my pretty fellow, a little dose of lead
>> Then you and your ambition will once again be wed.

The lyricism of the conscious poem is matched by the gloom of the subconscious dream poem. Which was truer? 'God knows the answer to these things . . .'

Notes

Page
23 *An Edwardian Youth* by L. E. Jones, 1956.
35 *Ben Kendim* by Aubrey Herbert, 1924.
45 Kiazim is described under the name Riza in *Ben Kendim*. Where A.
    H's private diaries differ from his accounts in *Ben Kendim*, I have
    followed the diaries.
109 Johnny Allen was the son of the bailiff first at Teversal then at
    Pixton. He had grown up with Aubrey and although he had served
    an apprenticeship in the building trade, often acted as Aubrey's
    servant.
120 Faik Bey Konitza was the brother of Mehmed. He was the leading
    light of the Albanian intelligentsia, spoke a dozen languages and
    with Mgr Fan Noli was largely responsible for the revival of the
    Albanian written language.
129 Lord Castlerosse, later famous as a gossip columnist for the
    Beaverbrook press, was the eldest son of the 5th Earl of Kenmare
    and a brother-in-law of Tom Vesey. Aubrey wrote, 'Valentine
    amuses me v. much. His insufferable impertinence and clapper-
    like tongue make the dull days pass.'
    Lord Robert Innes Kerr was the 2nd son of the 7th Duke of
    Roxburghe.
    The Hon. George Henry Morris, Commander 1st Battalion Irish
    Guards, 2nd son of Baron Killanin. b. 16th July 1872, killed in
    action 1st September 1914.
142 Antwerp fell on 10th October 1914; Enver led the pro-German
    faction on Turkey.
179 Bekir Sami in time became Atatürk's Foreign Secretary. He and
    Aubrey met again in London in 1921 when Bekir Sami headed the
    delegation from the Angora Government to the London Confer-
    ence which failed to reach agreement on modifications to the
    Treaty of Sèvres. *The Times* reporter, expecting someone wilder
    and more exotic, wrote in disappointment: 'He might have been
    tailored in Bond Street'.
193 Mem. 26 July 1917. F.O. 371/3057 No. 148986.
219 Lady Wemyss was the wife of Aubrey's admiral, Rosie Wemyss,
    and was an ardent Turkophil and an unfortunate dabbler in poli-
    tics.
223 On this visit to the Wharf Mr Asquith told Aubrey that he had
    been asked to write a constitution for China. He invited Aubrey to
    go with him to China as his private secretary. Aubrey accepted
    but nothing came of the plan.

Index